The
CAREER
NOVELIST

The
CAREER
NOVELIST

A Literary Agent
Offers Strategies
for Success

Donald Maass

HEINEMANN
PORTSMOUTH, NH

Heinemann
A division of Reed Elsevier Inc.
361 Hanover Street
Portsmouth, NH 03801-3912
Offices and agents throughout the world

Library of Congress Cataloging-in-Publication Data
Maass, Donald.
The career novelist : a literary agent offers strategies for success /
Donald Maass.
p. cm.
ISBN 0-435-08134-9
1. Fiction--Authorship. I. Title.
PN3365. M24   1996
808.3--dc20
96-17148
CIP

Editor: Lisa A. Barnett
Production: Melissa L. Inglis
Text design: Joni Doherty
Cover design: Jenny Jensen Greenleaf

Printed in the United States of America on acid-free paper
99 98 97 96   DA   1 2 3 4 5 6 7 8 9

for Beth

CONTENTS

ACKNOWLEDGMENTS

PORTIONS OF THIS BOOK HAVE PREVIOUSLY APPEARED IN different forms in the following books and periodicals: Writer's Digest *Guide to Literary Agents*, *Mystery Scene*, *Mystery Writer's Source Book*, *Science Fiction Chronicle*, and *Writer's Digest*. I am grateful to editors Kirsten Holm, Ed Gorman, Dave H. Borcherding, Andrew I. Porter, and William Brohaugh for their encouragement and for giving me a chance to test my wings.

Thanks to my editor at Heinemann, Lisa Barnett, whose faith in this project and whose expert shepherding made it possible. Thanks also to production editor Melissa L. Inglis and publicist Heather L. Smith for their excellent work. Additional thanks to my associate at the Donald Maass Literary Agency, Jennifer Jackson, whose comments on the manuscript and proofreading were invaluable, and who held down the fort while I completed the manuscript.

Thanks also to my clients and to all the fiction writers who have so generously shared their journeys with me over the years. This book would not be possible without them.

INTRODUCTION

IT IS THE DREAM OF HUNDREDS OF THOUSANDS, PERHAPS OF millions, to write fiction full-time. This dream has a powerful allure. To do nothing but create, to spend one's working hours in the dream state of one's imagination—who wouldn't treasure that?

Making that dream a reality is the subject of this book. As a literary agent I have journeyed with many writers from the submission of their first manuscripts to the magic moment of giving notice at their day jobs, and beyond. Making the leap into full-time fiction writing can be frightening, but most who take the plunge also feel a powerful thrill. They are awed by the sense of freedom and they are humbled by the responsibility, for writing fiction full-time is not just a career choice, it is an act of faith in one's stories. It is saying, "My fiction matters."

Can the dream actually come true? Yes, it can. While there is no official count, it is beyond question that there are hundreds of full-time novelists. Thousands more derive a significant portion of their income from fiction. With roughly five thousand novels published in the U.S. every year, there is clearly a serious need for publishable novel-length material.

Of course, the first problem facing any new novelist is writing a publishable manuscript. Many have the discipline to complete one; far fewer make it over the hurdle of publication. What makes the difference? Native talent? Some have it and others do not, that is true, but in my experience talent is only one prerequisite for success. Skills like plotting, self-editing, and market sense can be learned. This book discusses not only the basics of such skills but also the fine points that make learning the novelists' craft a career-long pleasure.

Beyond writing lies the daunting business of getting published. Oh, the horror stories! You have to be at a writers' conference for only a few minutes before you hear tales of woe about rejection slips, slush piles, slow-to-answer editors, and glacially cool agents. It can be discouraging. A lot of published writers hand out the time-tested advice, "Be persistent." It's good advice as far as it goes, but it doesn't address fundamental questions that worry new writers, such as "Am I really good enough?" and "What am I doing wrong?"

This book is designed to show newcomers not only how to break in, but also how to answer for themselves such questions as "What are my chances?" or "If nobody agrees to read my material, how can I know whether it is any good?" or "Is it worth revising my manuscript, or should I move on to the next?"

For aspiring writers the farthest horizon is getting published. Once that point has been reached, it would seem that one's career should be all smooth sailing. One has, after all, passed the big test. One has been admitted, joined the club. After that, what is left but deciding what to write next?

Savvier newcomers are aware of the challenges ahead. They know that publishing is full of pitfalls. Competition is fierce and first-novel advances are low; advertising and publicity support for first novels are often scarce. It is a tough climb; nevertheless, most new writers probably believe that given time and a little luck they have a reasonable shot at making a living, maybe even at making it big.

Sadly, that is not exactly the case. The truth is that publishing in the nineties is ruthlessly focused on the bottom line. From agents' offices to retail stores, numbers rule. And what strange numbers! Once upon a time sales were all-important; today, figures like *ship-in* and *sell-through* can seal an author's fate long before the returns are tallied up.

On top of that the game is, in many ways, rigged. Only a select few authors receive the dump bins, co-op advertising, publicity tours, and other hoopla that are essential to making a big splash. The system seems horribly unfair. The brutal truth is that authors whose work does not quickly find a sizable audience can be, and often are, rushed to the exit doors.

In fact, while I have no empirical evidence to point to, I believe that fully 50 percent of the authors whose first novels have been published since 1990 have not made it beyond their second, third, or fourth book. I know this, in part, because I get calls from them every week. These novelists thought they had writing careers; perhaps they even gave up other careers only to discover that they have been mishandled, lied to, abandoned, ignored, or even worse.

Their litany of woes is by now numbingly familiar: low advances, lousy covers, editors who left, publicity people who did not care, advertising that came too late (if at all), orders unfilled, opportunities lost, books out of print before the next one appeared. Their voices are desperate, their attitude cynical. They ask for assistance, but often they are beyond help.

Sound horrible? It is, but the fact is, too, that plenty of writers *do* make it beyond their second, third, and fourth books. Hundreds *do* make a living, and scores *do* make it to the big time. It is not all luck, either. What makes the difference in these cases is that such authors have found, by accident or by design, methods to overcome the thousand and one obstacles that publishing inevitably throws in one's way.

If this book is about nothing else, it is about the practical, day-to-day solutions, methods, and techniques that I use to make my clients' careers happen. This book is the fruit of seventeen years on the job, of thousands of battles fought in the trenches. It is about marketing, contracts, hidden traps, strategies that work, ways writers go wrong—in short, everything I can think of that you might need to make your career a success.

So who am I to be handing out this advice? I am an independent New York literary agent, and have been for sixteen years. (My first year in this line of work was spent at a large and well-known "super-agency.") You will find me listed in many of the better publishing directories. You will find my offices on New York's Fifty-seventh Street, right around the corner from that short but imposing stretch of the Avenue of the Americas—Sixth Avenue to locals—that runs from Forty-second Street to Fifty-seventh Street, and that forms the central axis of North American book publishing. I am perched near the summit, and I have quite a view.

It is a view that I wish to share with you. It is not the view of a jaded professional; I am still too enthusiastic about the fiction business for that. It *is* the view of a realistic, practical, hands-on professional. It is also the view of one who has worked on three sides of this business: in the author's study, in the editor's chair, and on the agent's phone.

I started my professional life as a junior editor at Dell Publishing. I wasn't there long, for the industry decided to teach me early about life in the corporate world: one day, without warning, my job was eliminated. It being a recessionary time, I found similar jobs hard to come by. That is how I eventually wound up working at a literary agency. I was happy to have the job, and happier still to find that I liked it. Here at last was a change from office politics and endless meetings. Here was publishing at its most basic: write, sell, survive.

Here, too, were the authors whose presence and spirit I found strangely absent from the climate-controlled, high-rise world of corporate publishing. Authors are my kind of folks: independent, creative, well-read, alive. Of course, authors are human. Some can appear childish, needy, stubborn, and difficult, but on the whole they are decent people trying to do good work and trying, often, to say something important—or at least to entertain.

This has been my world ever since, though in the early days of my agency I was unable to support myself by representation alone. And so, pseudonymously, I wrote novels, fourteen that were published. Well, that is not entirely true: I did not write them only for the money. I also wrote because I loved it.

Writing fiction was, I found, the most exciting, absorbing, and fulfilling way I had ever spent my time. There is joy in a well-turned sentence. There is satisfaction in a tautly written scene. And when all the words are strung together, all the chapters in order, one may even have written a novel that says something worthwhile about the human condition.

Were my novels any good? Some were; some were not. They all, though, taught me a great deal about the novelist's craft, and, more importantly, about how it feels to write and the world view of the author. Writers, for instance, work in isolation. They go for long stretches without feedback. Is it any wonder, then, that they are furiously impatient for their editors' comments on their newly delivered manuscripts? Is it any more surprising that some of these same authors stoutly resist revision?

It is common in publishing to remark jokingly that we'd be a lot better off without authors. Authors can be highly exasperating, it is true, but if you live inside their skin for a while you can start to understand where they are coming from.

I like writers, especially novelists. They are, on the whole, interesting people as well as people interested in life. They can be compassionate toward characters nobody else could love. They have a sense of story, of the patterns that give meaning to our lives. Best of all, they have the ability to draw us into detailed, absorbing worlds built entirely of words.

And so I have devoted my working life to serving novelists. I am unusual among my colleagues in that regard. Fiction is, today, a tough business. Many agents would prefer to find some good nonfiction to sell. Placing novels is a slow, difficult, and discouraging process. It can take many books to get a career going. With nonfiction you need only one snappy idea.

Do not misunderstand: I am not altruistic. This is my living, and so my emphasis is on commercial fiction. Still, a good novel is a good novel, and when I find one that is worthy and exciting I take it on regardless. My success rate is not 100 percent, but it is strong. I sell more than seventy-five novels each year, and on top of that do scores of deals for large-print rights, limited editions, translations, movie and TV adaptations, and even, recently, for adaptation into an animated cartoon show.

I am an agent for career novelists: that is, authors who want to write fiction full-time for a living. It is to such authors that this book is directed. This book is about the little steps that add up, over time, to big results. This book is *not* for dreamers who want to get rich quick, though I have nothing against speed.

This book is also not for hobbyists, dabblers, screenwriters looking for extra money, nor, alas, for authors of illustrated children's books, who are a separate breed in a highly specialized field. To be sure, there is useful advice and information about book publishing for all writers herein, but it is to full-time novelists that I am chiefly addressing myself.

Why am I willing to share my expertise? Why am I not reserving it for my clients?

We need storytellers. In our world of dislocation, of declining institutions, it is imperative that the values that bind us together be reaffirmed. One of the primary ways we do this, I believe, is through the stories that we tell to one another.

Think about it. We tell stories all the time: on the phone to our friends; with our families at holidays; from the pulpit; in speeches; in newspapers; on TV; on-line; on the movie screen and live stage. Would we do this if it were not important, even fundamental to our mutual well-being? I do not think so.

Not all novels are equally good, of course. Some of them fade from memory almost immediately; others last. Some have a profound impact; others only momentarily delight. Some are short; others long. Whatever their shape and substance, I believe that few story forms have the power to grip an audience as firmly, as profoundly, and for as long as the form we call the novel.

Novels' power, and the imaginative level on which they engage the reader, I think account for the importance that they are accorded by scholars, critics, and readers. It is easy to excite an audience through film. The combination of script, color, moving images, sound, and music is a potent brew. But novels are pure. They are a solo art. When they succeed, it is through the imaginative power and literary skill of a single mind.

Today, so many of the stories we get are the product of a team effort. We do not need more of that. A story constructed by committee can be wonderful, I admit, but too often such stories offer us what is easy and homogenized. They are built to touch only the mass audience's lowest common denominators. Only the solo storyteller has the chance consistently to show us new ways of seeing, new paths toward understanding.

That is not to say all novels are original, or even good, but novelists are unique in their opportunity to speak with a single voice. Dance, opera, and theatre have dwindled somewhat under the twentieth-century onslaught of movies and television, but the novel, centuries old, is as vital, alive, and important as ever.

I strongly feel that novels are essential to the health of our culture. Book publishing today may, at times, seem designed to make a successful career as a novelist almost impossible. But that appearance is deceptive. There are ways through the thicket of numbers, and there are solutions to every problem that the industry has devised. Some may pine for the halcyon days of publishing long ago, but not me. I know that it is just as possible to make a living writing novels now as it ever was. You just have to know the ropes.

Solutions, strategies, knowledge, practical plans, damage control, managing success . . . in short, the path of the career novelist. That is what this book is all about.

1

CHAPTER

The Dream

WHY WRITE NOVELS?

SURPRISINGLY, MANY PEOPLE UNDERTAKE NOVEL WRITING NOT because they want to, but because they feel they ought to. That defies logic. Novels are generally difficult and time consuming to produce. The odds are against getting published.

Nonetheless, some people work at novels for years, never finishing them or feeling any joy in the writing process. Why? Such people, I believe, may have adopted the identity of "writer" as adolescents and have not yet given it up. Not surprisingly, writing comes naturally to teenagers. It helps them to make sense of their roiling emotions. Elements of the romantic myth of the writer can also fit an adolescent's self-image: writers, they think, are poor, lonely, depressed, misunderstood—and full of original insights.

There comes a time when this romantic self-image no longer serves a useful purpose. God knows, there is nothing wrong with thinking of oneself as a writer, but when people whip themselves for *not* writing, then something is very wrong.

You have probably met this type: they spend big bucks on how-to-write books, biographies of famous authors, classes, conferences, and motivational seminars. They dress the part. They acquire fountain pens and fabric-covered blank books, yet spend more time talking about writing than actually doing it. And they struggle. Listening to them you would think that novel writing is a task akin to climbing Everest or seeking nirvana.

The truth is that every writer is sometimes reluctant to write. An empty sheet in the typewriter—or, these days, a blank computer screen—is an intimidating sight. But real writers cope. They get down to work. My method is to tidy my desk, stalling until time pressure forces me past my resistance. Writers have all kinds of private rituals. The point of them is to lessen anxiety. Whatever the daily routine, I believe that writing novels should not, on the whole, be a struggle.

Do not misunderstand me: true writers' block is a real and painful condition. I know. I have had it. Writers' block will be discussed later on, but for now I would simply like to suggest that if the quest to become a career novelist leaves you feeling inadequate, frustrated, envious, or angry then *it is not worth it.*

Trust me, you do not have to do this. No one will think less of you if you are not a rich and famous novelist. If you are exasperated, burned out, getting nowhere, and cynical about this novel writing "crap," then quit. Life is tough enough.

If, however, you are still with me—and I will bet that you are—it is a good idea to look deeper into your motives for writing novels. The reasons behind your persistence have a big influence not only on your chances of success, but on the stories that you craft and the publishing decisions that you make.

Mickey Spillane declares that his reason for writing is "the urgent need for money." Generally, that rationale is expressed only by established novelists. New fiction writers rarely cite money as their primary motive. Indeed, even most established novelists are not in the game to get rich. When questioned, they will confess that all they really want financially is the chance to live comfortably, pay the bills, put the kids through college, and retire in security.

Of course, most novelists hope to get rich sooner or later, but by and large both published and unpublished novelists know that the odds of making a real killing are pretty slim.

So, what drives you? To help understand, it is useful to think back to the hierarchy of human needs posited by psychologist Abraham Maslow. (You will probably remember this from a college psychology course.) Maslow stated that human beings need, in order, food, shelter, sex, self-esteem, self-actualization. Let's skip the first three;

they are self-explanatory, I hope. The fourth, *self-esteem*, means valuing oneself and being valued by others. The fifth, *self-actualization*, is going beyond oneself: being creative, finding joy in learning and discovery, becoming altruistic, loving all humanity.

As you can see, I'm sure, we all experience a mixture of these motives. We are also a society whose basic needs are, for the most part, satisfied. There is homelessness and hunger in America, to be sure, but by and large we are well-fed, decently housed, and over-sexed. And so we seek to fill higher needs.

Hoop dreams, Oprah, "recovery," the lottery . . . there are many ways for people to obtain public recognition. For some of us—especially the bookish, unathletic, socially uneasy among us—writing novels is a natural path to this type of self-esteem. Writing lets us stay at home. It carries us away from what is unpleasant in everyday life, while at the same time instantly conferring upon us the mystical status of "novelist." Even if you have not yet published, your friends are sure to be impressed when you tell them you are working on a novel.

But that is only one side of the motivation coin. Most everyone who writes sooner or later discovers the pleasure inherent in the process. There is something indescribably wonderful about getting the words right. Finding a side to one's hero that one did not know existed is a singular joy. A funny line can make one burst out laughing. Killing a beloved character can make one cry.

There is also a deep satisfaction in the growing mastery of the craft. Like all creative endeavors, novel writing rewards practice. Many accomplished novelists sit down to write largely for the challenge of trying to write something bigger, better, more profound than before. For the dedicated novelist, there is no end of stories to tell. Some of my clients tell me that they have more ideas for novels than they can use in a lifetime.

There is more than grubby ego gratification here. In the pure, joyful time spent in the world of one's current novel, there can be discovery and surrender of oneself in service of the story. It can be a *release* from self. That is writing for its own sake.

Or maybe not entirely for its own sake . . . every once in a while I come across a novelist who writes because he or she has something special to say. I do not mean those who want to preach, or practice politics; their writing does not move me. I am talking about those novelists who are driven to explore a particular time, place, people, or style. Perhaps the most common expression of this is the writer who says, "I wrote my novel because I cannot find the kind of stories I want to read."

One also meets writers who delve into an area of personal passion. Such a writer is my client Stephanie Cowell, author of the historical novels *Nicholas Cooke* and *The Physician of London*. These novels brilliantly recreate the London of the reign of Elizabeth I. Not surprisingly, Renaissance England has been Stephanie's lifelong passion. She sings its music, studies its literature, reads about it endlessly.

Writers like Stephanie are, in the best sense, writing what they know: not the dull details of ordinary life, but the exotic, absorbing world found in some other place or time, or perhaps in the inner world of some character whose life is unlike ours.

Writing for the sake of it does not begin with the statement, "I know I can do better than that," that sneering feeling sometimes provoked by the inferior work of others. Now, I believe that the "I can do better" sentiment is perfectly valid and enormously empowering, but it is not unselfish. Writing for the sake of it is writing whether or not one will be published or paid. It is loving the activity rather than the life-style.

So, here are two pervasive reasons that people write novels: (a) *for the approval of others* and (b) *for the sake of writing itself*. Nobody does it for either reason alone. There are easier ways to get approval, and the novelist who works in isolation, never publishing, is not a true novelist but a hobbyist. Novels ultimately need readers. They are a two-way transaction.

Please take a moment to consider which motive is strongest in you. It makes a difference. What you want most out of novel writing will, sooner or later, determine the quality of your career experience.

WHO BECOMES A CAREER NOVELIST?

Are there educational profiles that lead more often than others to a novel-writing career? The easy answer to that question is no, but a more complete answer must cover the ways in which some are given if not an edge then at least a head start. As in most things in life, we are all created equal in rights but unequal in aptitude, temperament, and experience.

First the good news: there is truly no educational profile that offers an undisputed advantage in the novel-writing game. Most of the full-time novelists I represent are college graduates, and many have advanced degrees. Those accomplishments, however, are by no means universal. Several of my full-timers have earned no more than a high school diploma.

Nevertheless, one cannot help noticing that many colleges offer courses in writing. Certain graduate writing programs, such as the Iowa Writer's Workshop, are renowned. There are also reputable programs for genre writers, like the Clarion Workshop for science fiction. There is even a Raymond Chandler Fellowship for mystery writers at Oxford University, administered by the Fulbright Foundation. Are these useful opportunities?

The issue, really, is whether one can learn how to write a novel in the classroom. Analyzing Virginia Woolf's *To the Lighthouse* in a Modern British Novel course is not a bad idea. By the same token, writing assignments that explore different facets of fiction technique are certainly not a waste of time. But will either of these make you a better novelist or, indeed, a novelist at all?

Perhaps the biggest problem with novel writing courses is that their duration is generally less than the time needed to complete a whole novel. That is why most fiction courses concentrate on the short story. Even master classes in novel writing can generally cope only with a novel-in-progress. The goal in such courses is often not to complete a novel but to produce sample chapters and an outline, which is helpful but not the same.

Still, one can learn a lot in fiction classes, and I would never discourage anyone from taking them. It is worth remembering, though, that classes are taught by teachers. What and how much one will learn will strongly depend upon the ability, biases, and background of the instructor. Writing teachers are above all readers, and readers have individual tastes.

Regarding graduate writing programs, it seems to me that such programs reward word craft, evocative description, truth in character, command of theme, contemporary settings, and current styles. No doubt about it: M.F.A.'s write lovely stuff. Rarely, though, have I read a novel by an M.F.A. that had a terrific plot. M.F.A.'s do not generally make their living writing novels; mostly they teach, and perhaps there is a connection.

Most readers of this volume are probably beyond their formal education. Should you return to the classroom? Are novel writing courses worth it, or should you just take the plunge?

Experience is a great teacher, of course, but the task of novel writing is so complex that I strongly suggest that you not leap into it without some preparation and practice. If nothing else, try your hand at short stories. That will not work for everyone, of course. I, for example, have never done a short story. My first fiction was a sixty thousand–word romance novel, which was published and made me a small pot of money. However, I had a strong writing background and had also been producing reader's reports for a new line called Rendezvous Romances (later renamed Silhouette Books). I was uniquely prepared for that task.

If you do enroll in a writing class, be aware that you will learn more if your instructor is sympathetic to the type of novel that you want to write. Try to audit the class ahead of time. Phone former students. Be a good consumer. What's at stake is your confidence. Many a good writer has been hurt by a bad teacher.

Now, what about career backgrounds? Are there any occupations that can usefully prepare one for full-time novel writing? Do technical writers, screenwriters, or journalists have an edge?

Here are some of the jobs that my clients had before they went full-time: psychiatric nurse, sculptor and game designer, underground journalist, secretary, real estate developer, ad salesperson, flight attendant, civil servant, career counselor, college administrator, lawyer, copy writer, mother, and homemaker. As you can see, that is quite a variety of occupations.

The nation's best-selling authors present a similarly diverse cross section. Tom Clancy was an insurance salesman. Judith Krantz was an advertising executive. Stephen King was a high school teacher. In prior occupations you can sometimes see the roots of the fiction that followed: John Le Carré was a spy; John Grisham is a lawyer; Robin Cook is a doctor.

Others' fiction has its roots not in their *occupations* but in their *avocations*. Clive Cussler is a case in point: he was an advertising man who developed a passion for diving while in the military. Today he writes full-time, but also participates in several marine archaeological expeditions every year. Not surprisingly, mystery authors are often cops and lawyers. The science fiction field is full of scientists and engineers.

Clearly no occupation gives one a particular advantage where fiction is concerned, but it is true, I believe, that one's occupation will strongly influence not only what but how one writes.

One would think, for example, that screenwriters, playwrights, and poets would have a huge head start when it comes to fiction; after all, they have word craft and story sense. That is so, but in my experience those backgrounds do not supply a disproportionate share of our professional novelists. Why? Because such writing stresses qualities that are secondary in novels.

Take screenwriters, for instance; I am often contacted by them. Screen writing is a brutally competitive business and when the going gets tough, novel writing looks, to West Coast types, like an easy way to make money. (Needless to say, it ain't that easy.)

Novel manuscripts by screenwriters typically have several shortcomings. One is their length. Screenplays usually run 120 pages maximum, and tell stories that can comfortably fit into two hours of viewing. Premises of that sort are usually not strong enough to sustain the length of a novel.

Screenwriters also tend to underwrite their characters, which is normal for them since much of the characterization in a film is, and must be, invented by actors. Similarly, screenwriters tend to leave out exposition—the "interior monologue" that brings us inside a character's head—because in movies too much spoken exposition is deadly dull. As you can imagine, I am cautious when screenwriters send me their manuscripts.

Poets and playwrights have wonderful experience with, respectively, words and character conflicts, but those are only a few of the skills that make for successful fiction. Technical writers and journalists, too, bring a wonderful facility with words, but the same statement can also be made of lawyers, copy writers, and con men. Being good with words is not the same as being able to sustain narrative tension for four hundred pages.

Nevertheless, there is generally something about one's work that is helpful when it comes to novel craft. Teachers, secretaries, actors, social workers, and nurses all have to develop strong people skills. They are excellent observers of behavior. Engineers, corporate executives, doctors, military types, librarians, and computer programmers all understand complex systems and structures. They know how badly things can go wrong, which is a wonderful help in creating conflicts.

What is more important than any of this, though, are some qualities that anyone might have. Persistence is a big one. A first novel can take years to build; a career can take decades. Attention to detail, the willingness to revise, and the habit of breaking large tasks into smaller pieces are also useful abilities. Novelists tend to be intelligent and analytical, although the writing process itself is highly intuitive and requires going into a sort of waking dream state.

I also believe that a tolerance for loneliness is a must, as is a tolerance for risk. Getting started as a novelist means being isolated for long periods of time, as well as accepting a potential level of rejection that can be crushing.

Above all, I find that novelists are passionate storytellers. They love stories and compulsively collect them. They immerse themselves in fiction and seek out the company of other writers. They draw from many sources: myths, movies, history, current events, personal experience, family history.

Speaking of families, it is worth saying a few words about the influence of family history and personality on a novel-writing career. Just as one brings unresolved childhood conflicts to adult relationships, so it is with one's fiction career. Well-adjusted people will cope nicely with the obstacles of writing and publishing. They give themselves reality checks that assure them that their difficulties are no different from those experienced by others. They solve their publishing problems in direct and effective ways.

Neurotic types can be more driven, but will often have a tougher struggle in their careers. These folks, I find, tend to shape their adult relationships so that they will recreate their childhood traumas. The purpose is to resolve old hurts in new relationships. That rarely works. Neurotics may also feel the most comfortable in an atmosphere of turmoil and strife, and when they do not have it they sometimes create it. Neurotic novelists are the ones who are least content with their lot, most envious of others, quickest to switch agents, and most likely to demand what is unreasonable from their publishers.

From time to time I have also met authors who are actually psychopathic. These grandiose types tend to self-destruct, either through substance use, lying, bad business practices, or an inability to sustain working relationships with their publishers. They talk a good game and can be quite charming. They can also be superb at intimidating and putting down others. One may momentarily envy their power, but they do not prevail.

It is said that we marry our mothers (or fathers), and that the office is family. The germ of truth in those ideas is also apparent in publishing. Time and again I have watched starting novelists present their best side while seeking publication, only to turn childish and needy once they feel secure.

Are fiction writers necessarily more vulnerable and sensitive than the general population? Are artistic ability and business acumen mutually exclusive? To an extent it is true that entering the dream state involves opening oneself up, lowering one's defenses. But the dream state is relaxing—even refreshing. Furthermore, one leaves the dream state at the end of the day, or when dealing with one's agent or editor. Many professional novelists describe wearing two hats, their writing hat and their business hat. That is a useful paradigm.

Being creative does not automatically mean being unbusinesslike. Yet consider those novelists who were successful business people before they turned to writing. Such folks should have no trouble dealing with the real world of book publishing. Very often, though, I find that doctors, lawyers, and even powerful corporate executives suddenly act "stupid" once they become writers. They bring me manuscripts and say things like "I have no idea what I've written. I need someone to tell me where this fits in the marketplace." Also common is "I can't deal with negotiating. I need you to do it for me."

I am grateful that people seek out my business skills, of course, but frankly it is strange to hear such capable, highly intelligent people acting dumb. What is going on? The answer, I think, is threefold: (1) new novelists are genuinely in need of information and guidance; (2) these successful people may, in part, be hoping to escape stress; and (3) as in any intense personal interaction, dependency can encroach upon publishing relationships. Just as it is natural to seek mothering or fathering in marriage, so it is with publishing. We all seek to fill our unmet needs.

The trouble is, alas, that a publishing company is not a family and an agent is not exactly a psychotherapist—though, believe me, there are many days when I feel like one! A novel-writing career is a career. The novelist goes into business, and all business sooner or later involves interacting with other people, solving problems, and managing stress.

It is a good idea to think carefully about what you want out of novel writing. If escape is a primary benefit, then the business aspects of a novelist's career are sure to be a disappointment. If acclaim outweighs other motives, beware of publication. Seeing your first novel in print is a big thrill, but after that there can be a large letdown if fame, sales, rave reviews, and peer respect do not automatically follow.

The happiest beginners will be the ones who love the work for its own sake. They will have comfort—and they will need it. The journey is exciting, but also long and exacting.

GETTING STARTED: THE INFLUENCE OF ANXIETY

Oh, the happy writer who is beginning a first book! What a thrill! Sitting down at last to fulfill one's dream! How delicious is the sensation, "I am really doing it! I am writing a novel!" Endless hours in the dream state . . . this, truly, is paradise.

Needless to say, the bliss of beginning does not last forever. Sooner or later the pursuit of the dream rubs up against reality. Often that first encounter involves one's family. They worry. For one thing, the writer is spending large amounts of time away from them. That is threatening. For another thing, they can know—often better than the writer—how high is the risk of failure. They are afraid. They do not want their loved one to get hurt. Thus, the first hint of conflict appears, and with it a slight sinking sensation: writing fiction is not going to be trouble free.

Still, most families are supportive, if cautious, and the writing continues. But then, sooner or later, one's friends find out. "Oh, you're writing a novel!" they exclaim. "When will it be published?" *Published*? That question can be anxiety-provoking when one has not even finished the fourth chapter.

And so one begins to think about publishing. In fact, most novelists start to think about it long before their first manuscript is finished. Some worry about a sale before they have even begun! That is normal enough, but when writers then make premature approaches to the publishing world there is a problem.

Why? Because there is likely to be one of two unhelpful results: (1) rejection or (2) reading of one's work before it is fully ready. These may not seem like big problems, but a typical response to rejection is to adjust one's writing to meet the perceived "market need." As we shall see, that can be a dangerous mistake.

An unfinished manuscript may, perhaps, secure an expression of interest, but in the nineties that is happening less and less. More often one simply creates a negative bias in the minds of agents and editors who, had they been approached later, might have responded positively. Going back a second time may prove impossible.

But whether one begins too soon or after too much revision, it is inevitable: one must finally begin the scary task of finding a publisher. The first response to that challenge is often, "Akk! I don't know where to start! Whom should I contact? How do I go about it? I need information. Help!"

There is a paralyzing sense of ignorance. Usually that does not last long. Writers go out and get information. They talk to friends or mentors. They attend conferences and conventions. They subscribe to *Writer's Digest* and other magazines. They buy books like this one. (Thank goodness!) They uncover lists and lists of agents and publishers. While many of these are detailed and specific about what these professionals are seeking, the writer may now feel at sea. Where once there was too little information, now there is too much!

This is the point at which many writers begin to indulge in winning-the-lottery fantasies. They dream of overnight success. There is nothing wrong with that. It is a defense against anxiety. Nevertheless, there is anxiety present and it is exerting an influence.

A handful of lucky writers will indeed soar straight to the top, but the vast majority face a period of rejection. Sometimes that period can be quite long. A closet full of unpublished manuscripts may accumulate. It is common to hear stories of entire walls covered with rejection slips. All of that feeds the mythology of the suffering writer, and paradoxically makes many writers *more* determined than ever to break in.

Reinforcement for that feeling comes from writers who have already made it. "Be persistent," they advise. Other pieces of advice: *learn the language; publishing is a business, so sell yourself; get it in the mail, keep it in the mail; get an agent; you won't find an agent until you find a publisher.*

Good advice and all true, in part, but the effect of it is sometimes to diminish thinking and to enhance the determination to succeed no matter what. Is there anything wrong with that?

Determination can be a good thing, but it can also make one myopic. One can lose perspective. One can decide, "Damn it! I'll do whatever it takes to succeed!" Frustrated newcomers can begin to do silly things to get the attention of publishing pros. A friend who edits romances for a major paperback publisher told me how at one conference an overeager author followed her into the ladies room—right into an empty stall—in order to pitch her manuscript. Did it work? No way!

Typically, authors express their anxiety in more subtle ways. At my office we see it all the time in off-putting query letters, which will be discussed in a later chapter. More dangerous still is the temptation to get a foot in the door—any foot, any door! The theory behind this impulse is that "you have to start somewhere." Some publication, runs the thinking, is better than none. This is not necessarily true.

The truth is that publishing in the nineties is a ruthlessly unforgiving business. It is extremely difficult to recover from early mistakes. Signing up with the first agent who says yes, or even signing a bad contract with the wrong publisher, can be fatal. There is more discussion of these situations later in this book. For now let us focus on the feelings of anxiety.

What is this anxiety really about? It can be experienced as the desperate feeling that no one in book publishing cares a damn about you or your manuscript. One can feel it as anger over slush piles (stacks of unrequested, waiting-to-be-read manuscripts), fury over long response times, frustration with uncaring editors or agents—one can even begin to resent the success of others. What began as bliss can turn to utter misery.

I would like to suggest that these overt signs of anxiety actually mask fears of a more fundamental sort. One is the fear of failure, the terrifying possibility that one has wasted years of one's life. A second is the fear of humiliation—so many expectations to fulfill! Especially one's own!

Most fundamental of all, I believe, is the anxiety that derives from the need for validation. Above all things, writers want acceptance. They long to be judged worthy of publication. They want to be assured that they are not crazy. They need to know that all this time and effort have not been for nothing.

If the breaking-in period becomes too lengthy or too frustrating, most writers will sooner or later get desperate. Some will start to avoid the whole process, refusing to push themselves. Others will keep at it doggedly but cynically, losing all excitement and hope.

That is too bad, because that kind of burnout can lead to ill-considered career decisions. And, as I said, these days there is little room for error in the big, bad world of book publishing.

2

CHAPTER

The Reality

THE BAD NEWS ABOUT BOOK PUBLISHING

MOST WRITERS TODAY ARE AWARE THAT BOOK PUBLISHING HAS become a big business. Some can even tell you the names of the large conglomerates that own publishers such as Simon & Schuster, Penguin, and Little, Brown. (Answer: Viacom, Pearson, and Time Warner.)

Nevertheless, there is a persistent belief among writers that book publishing contains pockets of resistance to the corporate trend. Sure, the "suits" may run much of the game, but if one digs hard enough one can still unearth independent imprints and dedicated editors who will publish a book just because it is good, and damn-all if the thing never earns out.

Indeed, the thinking goes, publishing books is not a science but an art. Intuition must have some play. If every idea, every story, were subjected to a profit-and-loss estimate, would that not ultimately defeat the very purpose of publishing? Isn't it, finally, unprofitable to quantify culture instead of create it?

That is true, but it is terribly naive to believe that somewhere in the book business one can still find the profit-blind attitude associated with tweed jackets and gin and tonics at the Algonquin Hotel. If it ever really existed at all, that mentality is long gone. Editors today do care about good books, but they care even more about the bottom line. They have no choice. In the nineties, their destiny is no longer their own.

Nowadays most editorial departments must answer to high corporate masters. Although such masters run large media conglomerates, they are generally accustomed to lofty profit margins. Book publishing's traditional 2 to 4 percent return does not cut it for a cable TV giant that is used to 25 percent.

The result? Figures such as "copies shipped" and "sell-through" (see Chapter 10) are available to all editors and, believe me, they frequently check to see how their titles are performing. So do agents. There is a horse race feeling to each year's publishing season. Authors whose sales are slipping are likely to be let out to pasture. Everyone in the business deplores this state of affairs, but no one does anything about it.

Sound depressing? It is, but I believe that novelists can use the system to their advantage. To do so, however, they must first understand it.

So, first a little history: in the early part of this century, book publishing was hardcover publishing. Firms were not necessarily small, but their family origins were readily apparent. W. W. Norton, Alfred A. Knopf, Harper Brothers . . . many of the names survive today. It is tempting to think of this period as the good old days, but it was not. We know this because at the beginning of the thirties the National Association of Book Publishers commissioned an in-depth industry study.

The Cheney Report, as it was called, found that book publishing was "best-sellerized to the point of death by suffocation." It also pointed out that the industry as a whole suffered from greedy authors, too many titles, lack of list rationale, inefficient distribution, poor marketing, merger mania, a dearth of statistics, and wishful thinking. ("The industry has made a fetish of the accident," Cheney said. "It is organized not so much to sell as to wait for a bestseller.")

Later, in 1939, the paperback made its first appearance. Large numbers of books were given away to soldiers in World War II, and thereafter the paperback's importance was assured. Indeed, by the mid-fifties it was common wisdom that a paperback sale was crucial to any book's success. Still, in the fifties paperback covers were largely sensational, even lurid, and so paperbacks were considered "cheap" or "trashy."

All that changed in the seventies, the decade of the second paperback revolution. Covers improved, paper grades got better, and prices rose. The trashy image did not entirely go away, but certainly the paperback business gained a higher profile and profitability. Companies that once were shunned as low-margin supermarket suppliers now became the cores of large publishing corporations. Huge numbers of copies were sold. *The Exorcist* sold 12,400,000 copies. *The Thorn Birds* sold 10,880,000 copies.

When I entered the business in 1977, it was the heyday of original paperback publishing. The concept was not new. Back in the fifties, Gold Medal Books pioneered the idea and attracted authors like Sax Rohmer, Taylor Caldwell, and John D. MacDonald by offering them a two-thousand-dollar advance and a cent-per-copy royalty. Gothics, Harlequins, and "sci fi" were all done in original paperback editions.

Nevertheless, up to that time highly popular authors had primarily been built in hardcover. I experienced the sea change in the business when Dell, where I worked, published with great fanfare an original paperback novel called *The Promise*. (Actually, it was a novelization of a forthcoming movie, but as with *Love Story* that detail was downplayed.) The movie is now forgotten, but the author of the novel, Danielle Steel, is a best-seller. Her move into hardcover came only later.

Building an author entirely in paperback was a huge innovation, but a good one. Hardcover publication could be attempted for such authors with much less risk. Authors such as Janet Dailey, John Jakes, and John Saul were built with this strategy. In the seventies, the paperback tail was wagging the hardcover dog.

The eighties was an era obsessed with mergers and acquisitions. Hardcover houses were absorbed *en masse* by the new conglomerates (which were themselves absorbed into large multinationals). This vertically integrated type of publishing company—a *hard/soft* house, in industry slang—is today's norm. Critics complain of lost diversity and less competition, but supporters say that the industry has gained a new marketplace clout.

Other developments in the eighties had an equally important impact on book publishing. One was the rise of chain bookstores like Walden Books and B. Dalton. Located in malls, these stores not only brought books to millions of new customers but also made hardcovers affordable with generous discount policies.

For authors, though, the rise of the chains also had a downside. Since roughly 20 percent of sales were made through a handful of chain accounts, the needs of those accounts began to dominate the business. And what did the chains need? Fast-moving frontlist. Glitzy, sensational fiction. Judith Krantz and Sidney Sheldon. Backlist or mid-list, those novels deemed worthy but unlikely to achieve bestseller status? Sorry, too slow-moving.

On the paperback side, new strategies arose. One was a technique for boosting a book's exposure by flooding the so-called wholesale accounts: supermarkets, drugstores, newsstands, airports, and other outlets serviced by independent (ID) distributors. The technique worked well for historical romances, but high ID return rates ultimately proved a disaster.

Indeed, a whole genre was ruined this way: horror. Riding the coattails of the success of Stephen King, horror authors found a ready readership in the paperback racks—for a time. After a few years, a combination of overpublishing and reliance on wholesale distribution shipwrecked an entire generation of dark fantasists.

The chains introduced another element that has transformed the book business: computerized inventory tracking. Now a single buyer sitting at a computer terminal could order mystery novels for hundreds of outlets. In one way this was enormously efficient, but in another it was shortsighted. Authors came to be judged on their "numbers" alone. Nevertheless, computerized tracking is now universal in the business.

The boom of the eighties could not keep up forever, and when the Gulf War recession hit in 1991, book publishing took a dive. Companies downsized. Lists were cut. Editors were let go. Inefficient wholesale flooding stopped, and new attention was paid to traditional bookstores. Mall foot traffic declined, which sent the chains on a quest for new retail concepts. About the only good news in the early nineties was that new paper mills kept production capacity up and paper prices low.

This brings us to today. Today, book publishing is a small subsidiary of a vast, multinational media industry. Book publishing is still largely located in New York, but thanks to computers the locus of power is the superstore bookshelf. Hard/soft giants have all but wiped out independent hardcover houses. Despite that, the paperback business is in crisis. Paper and cover prices are rising, and so is consumer resistance. A net sale of a million units is now rare. ID consolidation and superstore dominance have also hurt mass-market paperbacks. The second paperback revolution is over, except in certain genres.

Today, fewer editors are editing more books. (One editor I know at St. Martin's Press is responsible for more than one hundred titles per year.) Not surprisingly, editors are changing jobs as often as ever, leaving behind "orphaned" authors. Happily, a given book's shelf life is rising, but authors have less time overall in which to prove their worth. They also have to prove themselves mostly on their own, since advertising and promotion money is as scarce as it has ever been.

On top of all that, lists are tight. Although some five thousand fiction titles are published each year, that number is down roughly 15 percent since 1991. Authors face increased competition, both from newcomers and from established authors who have been jettisoned by their publishers. Complete manuscripts are plentiful. Selling on partial and outline is increasingly difficult, unless one is already under option.

Ready for more bad news? Advances are down, too. So are royalty rates. In fact, some paperback houses are paying 2 and 4 percent to new authors. (The norm used to be 6, 8, and 10 percent.) On the back end, publishers are demanding more. Why not? It is a buyers' market. "We must have world rights" is a frequently heard demand. Publishers are also seeking all electronic rights. On that issue, publishers and agents are currently at war. (A fuller report is in Chapter 17.)

What about backlist, one's prior novels? Backlist sales are growing more important, but accumulating a backlist is hellishly hard. Rigid categorization in bookstores has also made it difficult to sell cross-genre or out-of-category novels. Worse, book companies are increasingly looking to other media for authors and content. Today's best-seller is as likely to be Tim Allen as Saul Bellow.

If all this stuff sounds gloomy, it is. But the picture is not entirely bleak.

THE GOOD NEWS ABOUT BOOK PUBLISHING

Get ready for a shock: More people than ever are reading books.

Yes, you read that correctly; readership is way up. That may seem impossible in TV-saturated America, but it is true. According to USA *Today*, reading is the favorite leisure time activity of 25.1 percent of all Americans, outweighing even sports. In 1994, Americans bought more than one billion books. (That's *billion*.) And people are going to all sorts of places to get them: chain superstores, small independents, book clubs, discount stores, price clubs, mail-order services—even the library! In Broward County on Florida's east coast, the library system in 1994 circulated 6,160,732 books, magazines, and audiovisuals to 1,431,670 cardholders. Not bad.

In terms of dollars, the numbers are even more impressive. In 1994, total industry sales were $18.8 billion. Publishing is reliably forecast to grow at a 6 to 8 percent annual rate, so by the end of the decade the book industry should annually gross $25 billion in sales. Clearly, book publishing is a lively, growing, healthy business.

Now, get ready for the best news of all: fiction outsells nonfiction. That's right! According to a study done in 1992 by the NPD Group for the Book Industry Study Group (and others) in the category of adult books, fiction accounts for 66 percent of unit sales as opposed to 9 percent for nonfiction. Of that fiction segment, 63 percent of unit sales are racked up by mass-market paperbacks. Hardcovers and trade paperbacks hold about equal proportions of remaining unit sales.

Fiction rules, no doubt about it. But what about the future? Aren't books actually headed for oblivion? Look at the children growing up amid the computer revolution. Will they buy books as adults when they learned grammar at computer terminals at school, and entertained themselves at home with Nintendo?

It may be that the future will be digital, but it will not be bookless. Consider this: the only publishing segment in the nineties that is showing consistent double-digit growth is children's books. Parents are buying books for kids, and kids are reading them. That's good news, since reading is a lifelong habit.

Looking at the industry more closely, there are some other bright spots.

For one thing, this is a great time to be a woman in the publishing business, whether one is working in the industry or as an author. Not only are publishing salaries at parity, but the glass ceiling is much higher in our business than in almost any other. Indeed, women preside over many of our biggest publishers. Their corporate masters may still be men, but publishing women even so exercise a degree of power previously unknown.

This is also the era of the woman author. Women have always appeared on best-seller lists, but never to the degree they do today. Genre fiction has likewise been transformed. No longer are women relegated to romances. Today, science fiction and fantasy authors are 50 percent female. In the mystery field, Sisters in Crime has led a revolution that has left male authors much poorer—and openly hostile. Even the western is going female. Traditional shoot-em-ups are giving way to revisionist treatments that give equal time to women and Native Americans. A new organization, Woman Writing the West, has been formed. It is small, as yet, but no doubt it will grow.

Speaking of genres, it is worth noting the predominance of the categories in current publishing and retailing. Once, sci fi, crime, and romances were small sections in most bookstores. Today they each claim as much shelf space as the fiction or literature section. Publishers and bookstores both have seen the light: genre fans are voracious readers, loyal to their category and inexpensive to reach. Writers of thrillers, mysteries, science fiction ("SF" is the preferred shorthand of insiders), fantasy, romances, and other genres enjoy new levels of respect.

They are beginning to feel their power, too. Genre writers are well organized. They meet at conventions. They have associations, sometimes several per genre. So far, in my opinion, they have not been terribly muscular in advancing their collective lot, but perhaps that will change. Indeed, I can envision a day when category writers will together demand from their publishers a level of support commensurate with their worth.

I want to be around for that. Meanwhile, genre authors enjoy unique access to their audience, and can develop—either with their publishers' help or on their own—a relationship with booksellers through signings and readings. Specialty stores help make that process even more effective.

Better still, genre authors are generally allowed longer development periods than mainstream writers. Low advances entail less risk. A good sell-through on a small ship-in (again, see Chapter 10) can be tolerated because the publisher knows that those readers will be back—maybe with friends. When a mainstream author does not explode out of the gate, disappointment can be high. That is less true with genre authors. Accepted wisdom says they must build.

Believe me, it is no accident that I represent lots of authors of SF, fantasy, and mysteries. These authors are more likely to survive their first five books, and I can often lift them up the publishing ladder quickly once they have passed that threshold.

What about price inflation? Generally, that is not a positive trend. Higher prices make readers more reluctant to buy, which, in turn, makes it harder to grow one's audience. At the same time, if an audience *has* been captured, higher prices also mean higher royalty payments. In other words, fewer writers are making it today, but those that do are making more money.

I must also mention that there are growing revenue opportunities overseas. Traditional markets like England, Germany, and Japan have hit a plateau, perhaps, but new rights sales in Korea, China, Russia, and Eastern Europe are very promising. We also face little competition from countries like Japan. The world wants American culture; America remains insular.

At home, we have a small-press segment that is growing in importance. Regional publishers and university presses are also benefiting from the unwieldy scale of New York publishing. A tiny niche for New York can be a profit center for a nimble regional. Presses like Four Walls/Eight Windows and White Wolf are even beginning to encroach on New York's genre dominance.

All in all, there is good news to be found amid the depressing situation in our downsized, competitive industry. But how can authors capitalize on it? Which strategies will work? How can they keep from being crushed under the weight of an $18.8 billion behemoth? In my experience, the first step is finding the right attitude.

THE RIGHT ATTITUDE FOR THE CAREER NOVELIST

It appears to me that much of the early disappointment felt by novelists comes from unrealistic expectations. Many imagine that publishing is—or can be—a get-rich-quick business.

It is not. There are always overnight successes, of course. One reads (enviously) of them all the time. The truth of the matter, though, is that most rich and famous authors got that way slowly. John D. MacDonald, Dean Koontz, P. D. James . . . these authors built their reputations over a number of years.

How many years? That varies, but here is my rule of thumb: generally, it takes five books to establish an author or a series. It is essential to one's survival that each book remain in print and available on the shelves as the others appear. Switching genres—or even switching publishers—is a problem. It is likely to send an author straight back to "go."

Another problem is long lapses between books. It is not that readers will not wait for the next novel by an author whose work has left a deep impression. They will. The trouble is publishers. Warehouse space is costly. Keeping backlist in stock is profitable, but only as long as reorder rates from the field maintain a certain level (generally several hundred per month).

When the rate falls below that threshold there is little reason to go back to press unless the author has a new novel on the way soon. In this situation, it is usual to see an author's backlist slip gradually out of print. The author is now in trouble. Each new book is his only book. It is hard to build an audience that way, and harder still to grow an income.

I mentioned five books . . . once past that point, is success automatic? Not necessarily. If the novelist is lucky, annual earnings may be supporting her, but in many cases all one can safely say is that things are going in the right direction. The writer is, thankfully, still in the game. Big success may not happen for a while.

How long will it take? It is not unusual for *break-out*—that sudden surge in sales that brings an author industry-wide attention—to come after ten or even twenty books. Patrick O'Brian is a case in point. So is Martin Cruz Smith. These authors served long apprenticeships. Others never make it to break-out at all.

Ideally, I would budget ten years from the time of beginning one's first manuscript to the time one is safely established as an author. Even then, I know of many authors who wrote for ten or more years before making their first sale. Does that sound like getting rich quickly to you? It doesn't to me.

Novel writing is a slow-motion business. For those who feel impatient at the slow pace of career growth in our industry, I would like to suggest a practical outlook to adopt.

First, think of writing as an end in itself. If your goal is only to be published, disappointment is likely. If you are writing mostly for the love of it, however, then as a working novelist you are already a success.

Second, think of the publishing business as a means to an end. There is a tendency among authors to talk of "markets." By this most authors mean the editors who can give them a contract. Finding those editors is the quest. Selling them a novel is the goal. But what a limited goal!

In reality, your ultimate market is your readers. They are your customers. If you serve them well they might even become your repeat customers, the ones who will finance your house, put tires on your car, buy clothes for your kids, and so on. Authors without a sense of their readers do not understand the reason for their success. These authors risk failure, too, for they know nothing of their customers' needs.

Here is another way to look at it: publishing a first novel is like opening a store. In that store, you are selling certain goods. Customers come in. They like what they find. They come back. They tell their friends. Eventually you are making a nice living.

Sound logical? I hope so. Far too many authors, though, think that their only responsibility is to write what they like. It is up to their agents to find a home for it, their editors to make sense of it, and their publishers to make it a success. Or so they think. The key group they are leaving out is readers.

Readers are consumers. Like any consumers, they are brand loyal. A brand is, by definition, something that is consistent and reliable. A brand does not spring surprises, or at any rate, not unpleasant ones. A brand is available when one wants it. One can count on a brand. Is it therefore wrong to count on one's favorite author to deliver good stories at reliable intervals? I do not think so. It is simple consumer psychology.

Take my analogy a step further: you have opened a store. Suddenly you decide to replace your merchandise. One day you are selling fruit; the next day, auto parts. Will business continue as before? Certainly not. Old customers will vanish. New customers must be won over.

Again, the principle is simple, yet a surprising number of authors believe that no harm will come if each new novel is a drastic departure. What does it matter as long as it is sold to a publisher?

In one sense it matters not at all. The nimble and talented can get by that way. What they will fail to do is to build an audience. Critical acceptance may come. They may achieve a certain cult status. Nevertheless, readership will not grow to the numbers that make success real and lasting. For that one must be mindful of one's audience, a consistent storyteller.

One more time, back to the store: suppose one suddenly closes up for an indeterminate period. Years pass. Then, just as suddenly, one reopens. Is it reasonable to expect the old customers to come pouring back through the doors? Definitely not. Customers are out of the habit. They now shop elsewhere. They must be won again.

So it is with novels. A long period without publication is like closing one's store. Customers go away—although it must be said that there is a correlation between the quality of one's writing and how long readers will wait for the next book. Joseph Heller can take twenty years between books. Lesser novelists may not receive a warm welcome after so long an interval.

Thinking of your readers as your ultimate customers can also help when publishing problems arise. Suppose, for instance, that your first novel is not selling. If your main goal is publication you will try ever more desperate tactics to get a foot in the door. If you see a sale as merely a step along the way, you might stop to take a look at your work, and possibly rewrite. Which approach do you think will be more successful?

A whole host of problems become easy to solve when one thinks of publishing only as a means. Take the problem of categorization. Some writers hate it when their novels are pigeonholed. They loathe the labels "science fiction" or "historical." They find them limiting. How can one word on the spine encompass all of their novels' qualities, all of their mass appeal?

Such writers are looking at the wrong issue. Take a look at readers. In bookstores readers head directly for their favorite section. Why not? That is where they will find what they want. Thus, the solution to the category conundrum is this: figure out in which section a novel will find the *majority* of its readers. Voilà. That is the section where it belongs.

Getting back to attitudes, I would like to make one further suggestion. Once you have oriented yourself to the real rewards and the true customers in this business, it is a good idea to formulate a career plan. This is something I do with all my clients. It can be as simple as "I want to be writing fiction full-time in five years" or as complicated as a timetable for launching lines in three categories under three different names.

It does not matter. What matters is having realistic goals and some idea of how to reach them. Every good business has a plan. If your business is writing novels, why not draw one up?

Later in this book there are three "strategy sessions" designed to help starting, midcareer, and break-out-ready novelists identify their choices and the issues facing them. If you like, use these to draw up your plan or to measure your progress.

3

CHAPTER

Pitching Errors

FIRST IMPRESSIONS

YOU CANNOT PUT IT OFF FOREVER: SOONER OR LATER YOU WILL
have to bring your novel out into society. It is a daunting prospect.
Invitations are scarce. Once you arrive the parties can prove to be
very crowded. Will anyone care to meet your young protégé? In large
part that depends upon you. Your introduction will make all the difference. If pleasing, the suitors will flock around. If not, your little
one may never be asked to dance.

Enough metaphor. You see my point: the way in which you intro-
duce your novel is crucially important. Whether you first approach
authors for blurbs, or agents for representation, or publishers for
publication, the process begins with a pitch.

Not long ago I was a guest speaker at the Pacific Northwest
Writers Conference (PNWC), an annual gathering that brings together agents, editors, established authors, and new writers who are at
various stages of breaking in. The pros numbered, perhaps, two
score. The newcomers numbered in the hundreds. You can imagine
what happened. Like fearful settlers anticipating attack from a
bloodthirsty tribe of Apaches, the agents and editors quickly band-
ed together.

Happily, no circle of wagons was needed. The conference orga-
nizers had told the new writers not to ambush the pros, but to shoot
their arrows only during scheduled, fifteen-minute appointments.

And that was how I came to spend an entire weekend in a roomy, blue-curtained cubicle listening to pitches.

That may not be everyone's idea of a good time, but for me it was fascinating. In addition to hearing a number of good story ideas, I was also able to spend three days studying new writers' pitches—and their pitching errors.

Some pitches worked better than others. Why? Before answering that question, let me address the skeptics. Some writers think that the pitch does not matter very much. They feel that the only purpose of a pitch is to get people to read their stuff. If no one bites, well, that just means that their pitch needs to be louder, faster, or funnier, right?

A pitch does more than just grab attention. It says a lot about you, too. It may say that you are serious, or it may hint that you are a hothead. Given the avalanche of material that thunders into Manhattan every day, is it not worth refining your pitch so that it gives the right impression?

In case you are still skeptical, let me say a bit more about that avalanche. How big is the slush pile, each company's stack of unrequested manuscripts? At the Donald Maass Literary Agency we receive, on average, about five thousand queries a year. Now, out of those five thousand queries only one or two per day persuade us to request a partial manuscript. That means that as few as one in nineteen are chosen for this limited appraisal.

A more enthusiastic response from us is a request for a complete manuscript. We read about forty per year, only a handful of those having been requested following our reading of a partial. The odds of getting to this point? About one in one hundred and twenty-five.

Now, I will admit that it is not the pitch alone that catches my eye. Recommendations from editors, clients, and other professional writers carry weight. Publications credits are also a strong selling point. Those who cannot offer such enticements, however, must use persuasion alone to catch my attention.

I hope I have made my point: when the odds are longer than calling the flip of a coin, it is best not to leave much to chance.

Learn to pitch.

Indeed, established authors will tell you that the need to pitch does not end once you find an agent or sign a contract. The need to pitch arises throughout one's career. It may be a radio interview, or a talk with your editor about your next book, or a query letter to a potential new agent. Perhaps you cannot foresee it now, but some day the pop quiz will be sprung. Better to learn the art of pitching now than to cram the night before the test.

FAMILIAR PITCHES AND WHAT THEY TELL ME

Certain pitches recur in face-to-face meetings, on the phone, and in query letters. The following are some of the most common:

"My novel is very timely. You have to move fast!" Writing a novel is risky. Sending it out is riskier still. As we have seen, the odds of success are quite long. Given that, one cannot really blame aspiring authors for claiming that their novels are hot.

Is there really such a thing as a novel that is as hot as today's headlines? Not really. While it is true that so-called "instant" nonfiction books can be written, produced, and shipped in a matter of weeks, this is never done for novels (save for the occasional movie tie-in). From the date of delivery to a publisher, virtually all novels take a year or more to reach the stores.

One year! Can you remember what was on the front pages exactly one year ago? Most people cannot. That is the reason that the *My-book-is-hot!* pitch fails. Even if your story does reflect a current news trend, by the time the book hits the stores that trend will be ice cold.

Authors who employ this pitch may, unconsciously, want to relieve their rejection anxiety. Putting pressure on an agent or publisher, they imagine, will shorten the agonizing wait for a response. Unfortunately, all this approach really accomplishes is to lengthen the odds against a positive reply.

"I know my novel is dynamite. Impartial test readers have told me so!" Advance readings may serve to reassure you of the salability of your novel, but do they persuade me of it, too?

Just the opposite. One reason is simple psychology: like most people, I do not want my mind made up for me. I want to form my own opinion.

But hold on. These are impartial readers with no close connection to the author. If they enjoyed the novel, is that not proof positive that the book is worthy? Possibly, but probably not. In my experience, test readers are not reliable forecasters.

Even if novels are somewhat flawed, test readers may be impressed by the sheer accomplishment of setting down so many words. They may also want to avoid hurting the authors' feelings, even if they do not know them and will never meet them. Trashing a published book is one thing; criticizing an unpublished work is another. Authors of works-in-progress are vulnerable. I think that even impartial readers sense that and demur.

On top of that, most test readers are not publishing professionals. Even the pros can be wrong, God knows, but it is also true that working in the business gives one some awareness of market trends. Test readers may lack that. The serial-killer novel that terrifies your neighbors may be, to me, old hat.

Perhaps the main reason that I discount testimonials from test readers is that they have so often disappointed me. I have been stung many times, I confess, and I have grown wary.

Having said all that, I will also admit that there is one time when outside testimonials carry weight: that is when they come from authors, editors, or agents whose opinion I respect and trust. When a client whose writing I adore tells me he has discovered an author whose writing *he* adores, I am sold.

"This book is my baby. I want an agent who loves it as much as I do." That sounds reasonable enough, does it not? Given the many pitfalls facing a novel prior to its publication, it is undoubtedly prudent to sign up only with an editor or agent whose enthusiasm for one's work is genuine, right?

Right. This is advice I give all the time. I even did so at the Pacific Northwest Writers Conference: "Look for enthusiasm for your work. It is your best insurance against mistakes." I stand by that advice, too. But let us look more closely at this new writer. Is he simply being prudent? Maybe.

In my experience, though, writers who say things like "This book is my baby" can be a wee bit irrational. Their emotional attachment to their work can cling beyond a useful point. That is not always true, but there is a certain correlation.

Sometimes such authors are simply in mourning. A sense of loss accompanies the completion of a novel. It is the end of a happy time: months or years in the dream state. This type of emotional attachment is not a big problem. It fades with time.

Another reason for the *book-as-baby* pitch may be a simple fear of humiliation. By making the submission a highly personal matter the writer is asking an agent or editor to be generous. The underlying message is, "I am fragile. Do not hurt my feelings!"

A more serious concern is that this pitch may mask an unwillingness to give up control. I am wary of authors who demand enthusiasm not out of rational self-interest but because they want to run the show. They will never be happy in the book business.

Ironically, such authors often appear eager to hear criticism. "My writing could improve," they will say, yet with the next breath they ask how quickly their manuscripts will be read or how soon they can get an advance. These sorts of authors will, at best, be pests. At worst they will make lifelong enemies and sabotage every step of the publication process.

Most worrisome of all is the new author who says, "This book is my baby" and means it literally. This unrealistic author probably wants book professionals to grant her the same uncritical love and acceptance she gets from family members.

Needless to say, disappointment is in store for this writer. Requests for revision will make her defensive. Each career setback will seem to her a personal affront. Over time she will grow frustrated and bitter. She may be a problem author in the making, so can you blame me for shunning her pitch?

"Never before has there been a novel like mine. It breaks new ground!" This may sound like a good way to stand out, but although innovation is good it can also be a potential drawback. There is little that is harder to sell than books that are ahead of their time.

Let's look a little more closely at the psychology behind this pitch. Is this author merely an activist on his own behalf, or is he a raving egotist? Hoping for appreciation is one thing; to insist on it is another. No one wants to work with an author who becomes excited, even furious, over every bad review or imagined slight.

"My novel combines the terror of Stephen King, the suspense of Tom Clancy, the glitz of Judith Krantz, and the romance of Danielle Steel! It will dazzle mystery fans and history buffs alike!"

Any idea what sort of novel this might be? I certainly do not know. This author has overcompared. No novel could be all that is claimed; or, if it is, I suspect it will prove something of a mess.

Underlying this pitch is not an excess of ego, but an excess of humility. This author has decided that you cannot fight city hall. If publishers want commercial product, he is damn well going to give it to them. The problem is that his pitch is confusing.

Ironically, the author using this pitch may be following some oft-given advice: *Compare your novel to others like it.* Good advice, but it is also a good idea to keep such comparisons simple, otherwise your prospects may wonder why you are trying so hard.

"Believe me, I am your dream client! No one will work harder for you than me!" I will say this, this author has at least grasped a fundamental of my business: I need not only good writing, but diligent authors who can produce novels on a regular basis.

If overeagerness was the only fault here, I would overlook it. Almost without fail, however, this type of author also offers me a menu of options. He has two, three, four—possibly more—novels in his drawer waiting to be dusted off, rewritten, polished to a high sheen. And he has tons of ideas. All he needs is my input and expertise to turn these projects into sure-fire winners. Together we'll soar to the top!

What is worrisome about this situation? It should be obvious: not only has this go-getter failed to sell his fiction in the past, he now hopes I will rescue his many mediocre projects. Not a cheerful prospect! Mind you, I like to work hard. And giving editorial advice to my clients is part of my job.

This author, though, is suggesting a fire-everything-and-see-what-hits approach. Some agents may like that, but in my experience a focused strategy works better for most writers—sharp-shooting, if you will.

What is really going on underneath this pitch? Possibly this author is only expressing his hope of becoming a full-time novelist; however, he may also be revealing a tendency to let others do his thinking for him. That is dangerous. Part of my job is to give career advice, true, but in the end only the author himself knows which career moves will work best for him.

Perhaps this pitch also hints at a lack of self-confidence, a lack of perspective, or even a bit of laziness. If so, that is too bad. Confidence, vision, and persistence are crucial qualities for players in the fiction game.

"Mr. Maass, *this is your lucky day!*" Unless you are uncommonly bold or insensitive I will bet that you do not march up to total strangers and announce, "Howdy! Here's why you are dying to be my friend. . . ."

A pushy manner is off-putting. Amazingly, it is also the most common tone in query letters. I'm not kidding! You'd be astonished how often I receive letters that sound something like this:

> Dear Mr. Maass:
>
> This is your lucky day! I have carefully analyzed the best-selling techniques of authors such as Stephen King, Jeffrey Archer, and John Grisham. Thus, I can guarantee that my terrifying apocalyptic thriller, GENE POOL-UTION, is a page turner that no reader will be able to put down.
>
> Ripped right out of today's headlines, this novel cannot miss. Believe me, you will long remember the day when you rushed to the phone to request my manuscript, Mr. Maass . . .

You get the picture. So, if the hard-sell is no fun at parties or in query letters, why do authors fall back on it? Insecurity is one big reason, I believe. Another is the advice that authors too often find in writers' magazines: "You've got to sell yourself! You must show that you understand the market! Get their attention and don't let it go!"

Do not get me wrong: I like authors who understand what they are selling. Setting that out for me briefly and knowledgeably is not pushy. It is a plus. But that is far different than the hard-sell.

Treat your prospect like a sane and sensitive publishing professional and, believe me, you will be way ahead of the game.

PITCHES THAT WORK

By now you are probably thinking that there is nothing you could possibly say in a pitch that would excite me. Maybe silence would work! Well, no. Silence from a writer is not helpful.

At one time or another, all of my clients were unknown to me. Many were previously published, true, but many were not. Something they said or wrote convinced me to read their work. There *are* pitches that persuade. What makes a pitch successful?

Before going into that, let us examine the best means for making contact. I am bemused when people ask how to contact agents. How do you contact anyone? Probably in person, on the phone, by fax, by letter, or through e-mail. Any of those avenues will work. About the only method I would not recommend is carrier pigeon. Most agents are not set up for that.

But which method is best? Arrange a meeting? Would-be clients frequently offer to travel to New York to meet me. I appreciate their willingness, but, really, what is there to discuss until I have read their writing? Save the airfare for later.

Phone calls have an immediacy that other methods do not, but not every author has a terrific phone manner. Still, this method is appealing because the results are quick. Provided you get through to your prospect, you will know in minutes whether or not you can send your submission. So what is wrong with that?

Nothing, really, except that the impression made in a phone call can easily fade in the course of a busy day. A better way to make your message last is to write. Your letter will probably be filed—and referred to again. Besides, when you write you can be sure you are saying exactly what you want to say.

Directory listings usually tell you the preferred method of contact for a given publisher or agent. Most often it is a query letter sent with SASE (a self-addressed and stamped envelope) in which the agent may send his reply. The SASE is courteous. Return postage on my five thousand queries each year would cost me $1,600; more if sample pages or entire manuscripts had to be returned. For the same reason a fax is also somewhat discourteous, as it arrives without an SASE.

E-mail, many feel, is the superior, low-cost way to communicate. The only problem with e-mail is that electronic messages are so easy to send *en masse*. E-mail queries frequently feel like junk mail: anonymous and unappealing. They will improve, I expect, but for the time being I do not invite them, nor do most agents.

Now, to specifics: how to compose your letter. A relaxed but businesslike approach is probably best. Lots of advice is printed on achieving winning effects, but I find that the most memorable queries are simple and straightforward. They tell me the following:

1. What the writer wants
2. What is being offered
3. Information helpful in selling the work
4. Something (but not much) about the writer

One of the most effective query letters I ever received began simply, "I am looking for an agent." Sound obvious? Dull? Perhaps, but it is supremely businesslike and that is a plus.

The tough part is making your manuscript sound appealing in just a few lines. That is difficult; therefore many authors do not limit themselves to a few lines. They spend many paragraphs—sometimes many pages—describing their novels. I receive query letters of this type often. Without preamble, such letters usually launch into long summaries. Afraid I will not listen, these authors insist upon shouting.

I had a similar experience during some of my appointments at the PNWC. Nervous writers rushed to cram their entire plot into fifteen minutes. Usually I had to stop them and get the answers to the only questions I really needed answered:

1. Where is your story set?
2. Who is your hero or heroine?
3. What is the main problem they must overcome?
4. Where do you think this novel fits in the marketplace?

When one reads twenty query letters every working day one comes to appreciate brevity. Encapsulating one's intentions can also be a useful exercise for an author. Many novelists have told me that they gained new insight into their stories when they were forced to write summaries; some were inspired to revise.

I admit that summarizing is not easy; even so, it is a skill that can be learned. It is not impossible. After all, we summarize plays, TV shows, and books for our friends all the time. Doing so for the purpose of a query letter is not much different.

A Model Query Letter

COMMENTS

1. Proper letter format shows that the writer is serious and businesslike.

2. Introductory paragraph makes a connection (albeit remote) between agent and writer and states the writer's purpose.

3. Although a bit cute, this summary is short and to the point. Note that the writer has included only the three key components to her story:
1. Setting
2. Protagonist
3. Problem

4. Writer limits biographical details to those that are relevant to the story, enhance her writing stature, and provide information useful in marketing.

5. Closing offers two options for submission. SASE is enclosed.

Conclusion: Though there are already CPA mystery series on the market, this letter scores.

Edwina Writer
101 Main Street
Anywhere, US 00000

1. Donald Maass
Donald Maass Literary Agency
157 W 57th St, Suite 1003
New York, NY 10019

January 1, 1997

Dear Mr. Maass:

2. Your name was given to me by Dean Koontz. He suggested you as a possible agent for my first mystery novel, DEATH BY DEPRECIATION.

3. DEATH BY DEPRECIATION is set in the corporate halls of the Big Eight accounting firms. My protagonist, Jill Tracy, is a sexy CPA who can make a balance sheet get up and dance. She also has a problem: Her biggest client, a clothing designer, is cooking the books. The IRS is closing in on him. So is the mob. He owes money to both. When he turns up dead in Jill's shower she must number-crunch like crazy to save her bottom line.

4. I am both a CPA and a writer. My short stories have appeared in *Ellery Queen's Mystery Magazine* and CPA *Journal*. The enthusiastic response of my fellow CPA's to my stories has encouraged me to try a novel.

5. Would you care to read the manuscript, or a portion and outline? I enclose an SASE for your reply. Thank you. I look forward to hearing from you.

Sincerely,
Edwina Writer

enc.

The key to a good summary is distilling the essence of your story. What would you tell me about your plot if you had only one minute in which to pitch? There is your focus. Build your pitch around that core. If you are still having trouble getting a handle on it, go back to the first three questions I listed above:

1. Where is your story set?
2. Who is your hero or heroine?
3. What is the main problem they must overcome?

The shortest possible answers to those questions are probably enough to hook your reader. Indeed, they are the essentials of any story: setting, sympathetic protagonist, compelling problem. Everyone loves to read a story, including the person reading your query letter. So give her one, even if it is in miniature. The rest is embellishment.

Now, what about the market for your novel? Does it fall into a category? Is there anything special about you or about it that might help in selling it either to a publisher or to the public?

If you have a background or expertise that is relevant to your story, that is useful to know. If you have been published before that is a selling point, too. Have you already been on the best-seller list? Please do not fail to mention that!

More difficult is deciding what not to say. It is enjoyable to learn that a query writer is a lung surgeon, or a breeder of bassett hounds, or has been writing since the age of eleven, but, really, how relevant is any of that? It does give a human face to the writer, but only one or two such details are needed.

Queries that are limited to one page are especially nice. If there really is more to discuss, fine, but for a simple query, the purpose of which is solely to describe the work, one page is probably enough. Too little information is not good, either, but believe me most folks err in the other direction.

Do you still hate the idea of pitching? Does it seem distasteful to be so crass and commercial in offering your novel?

If you feel that way, I do not blame you. However, consider this: few consumer products get off the ground without effective advertising. Thirty seconds of TV is not the same as brushing your teeth with Pepsodent. Watching a movie trailer is not the same thing as viewing the movie itself. But without the advertising, how else would you know about these products?

Like it or not, the pitch is a fact of life. Learn the art. You will thank yourself over the years if you do.

4

CHAPTER

Choosing an Agent

CHOICE? THERE'S A CHOICE?

HOW MANY HUNDREDS OF HOURS DID YOU SPEND WRITING your last novel? How many thousands of hours have you spent on your writing career? Work it out; the sum is probably quite high. In fact, if you write fiction even part-time then you have certainly made a huge investment of hours—hours that you might have spent with your family, or earning extra money in a less demanding pursuit.

If you are a full-time novelist your investment is probably far greater. It is measured in tens of thousands of hours, perhaps hundreds of thousands. Some novelists swear their careers have cost them blood. It astonishes me that having invested so dearly most novelists then spend so little time choosing an agent.

"Now hold on," you say, "I spent ages searching for an agent. I sweated. I agonized. Do not tell me that I ducked that process!"

Perhaps not. For many writers, though, the agony is mostly that of waiting for replies. What about the rest of it? A true search involves not only finding names and checking reputations, but making a full comparison based on a broad range of factors that foretell whether the author/agent relationship will be successful.

Not many authors go to great lengths. Believe it or not, the majority spend about as much time choosing an agent as they would choosing a coat.

For new writers, that is understandable. They have already experienced a lot of rejection. They do not want more. Their dearest wish is to find an agent who will say yes, and as soon as they do the search is over. Who can blame them? New writers feel, with some justification, that they are not choosing but being chosen.

You would think midcareer writers would be more savvy. They have been published. The pressure is off. What they should be after is a *better* agent.

Amazingly, though, writers in this position often give themselves no more choice than beginners. Again, the reasons are not difficult to understand. If midcareer writers are thinking of a switch, it is probably because things are not going well. They feel neglected. Perhaps their last book did not get sufficient publicity. Maybe they see lesser talents getting more advance money.

Midcareer writers in this situation are looking for a boost. Consequently, they may automatically narrow their choices to one: the agent who appears to have the most "clout." Again, who can blame them?

Especially when the agent in question has a star client, the midcareer writer, feeling insecure, will often convince himself that the star's success will rub off on him, too. Why? Because they write similar books? Because they have similar styles? No, because they will share an agent. Seen objectively such reasoning is flawed, but writers in crisis are not necessarily rational.

Well-established writers do not often search for a new agent. They have long since learned their needs and have usually settled down with the agent that best suits them. Anything wrong with that?

Perhaps not, but the comfortable old marriage of author and agent can have its drawbacks. We tend to believe that well-established authors are successful, if not rich, but many are not. With their big books behind them, their careers have begun to slide. Their advances are declining. Their reviews are mixed. No doubt you can think of several authors in this unhappy situation.

While the fault is sometimes the author's, it is sometimes the agent's, especially if that agent does not stay abreast of industry changes. Career management is an evolving art. Strategies that worked ten years ago—or even two—may not work today. An agent who is not on top of things may drag his clients down.

Given that, why do some well-established writers stay in place? Perhaps because they are comfortable doing business in an old-fashioned way. The old rules, they may feel, were easy to understand. The new world of publishing, on the other hand, can be cold and corporate. To these writers an old-fashioned agent may feel like an ally in a hostile world. They want to hold change at bay.

That is a shame, because when you think about it such writers may be holding back their careers, perhaps even their creative development. If so we may be missing out on some great stories.

So, you ask, how does one actually give oneself a choice? Is it really possible? And what criteria should one use in evaluating agents?

CHECK THE MENU

The first point to grasp is that agents come in many different varieties. I am not talking about the obvious difference that everyone knows about: New York vs. out of town; big shops vs. small independents; specialists vs. generalists; 10 percent commissions vs. 15 percent commissions. These are important points, of course, and I will soon discuss them at some length.

However, there are other factors that separate agents, factors that may seem incidental at first, but that over time have a major impact on one's career. These include background, business style, editorial skill, accessibility, total results for all clients, and others.

To illustrate these factors, I have created a roster of fictitious agents. These amalgams are inspired by my colleagues, but none is a *roman-à-clef*-style portrait of any particular agent.

The King Maker. Formerly an entertainment lawyer, this agent is one of the biggest names in the business. His client roster reads like the *New York Times* Best-seller List. A sharp dresser, he can be seen most lunchtimes at the Grill Room at the Four Seasons, publishing's number-one power scene. However, his clients speak with him far less often than publishers do. It is said that he takes calls only from clients whose books are hot. Unknown to them, all but his top-grossing clients are actually handled by subordinates. The results are mixed. As for editorial help, his clients receive none; that, he feels, is the editor's job.

The Celebrity Agent. This agent earned her nickname not because of the many movie stars whose autobiographies she has sold, but because of the appearance of her picture so often in the trade magazines. Seen at all the right publishing parties, she is the industry's gossip queen. She has made some huge deals, too. No wonder: at her mega-agency, status depends solely on the dollar value of an agent's last deal. While she does represent some successful fiction writers, they tend to be young and trendy. Her biggest best-sellers have been authors of glitzy nonfiction books. Editorially, she is strictly hands off. If a novelist needs help, she will quickly fix him up with an expensive "book doctor" (editor/rewriter).

The Rights Broker. Once the subsidiary rights director of a small publisher, this agent is addicted to deals. She is especially good at selling subsidiary rights. Nothing gets her blood going like an audiocassette offer. Her phone is glued to her ear, and her clients love that. Some, though, wish that she was a little more helpful editorially. Career planning? She does not indulge. Her motto: "Who knows? One day you're hot, the next you're not."

The Discounter. A talented self-promoter, this agent's name is well known. His list of clients is long; his sales volume is enormous. Some publishers privately complain about his business practices, but most cannot seem to stop doing business with him. Why should they? His prices are the lowest in town. Most clients believe that the Discounter personally handles their work, but he, too, has a legion of helpers who handle the majority of tasks. He boasts of his clout, but what his clients really get is safety in numbers.

The Trend Guru. This agent's motto is "Give the editors what they want." She gathers tips over lunch, then immediately phones her clients, who churn out quickie proposals. Because she is ahead of every trend, she has obtained some six-figure advances for writers whose previous advances were far lower. This usually happens only once; after that, her clients flounder and fade.

The Career Builder. This former editor has few star clients, but does represent a solid list of midcareer novelists. His specialty is suspense, and few understand that genre as well as he. A hands-on agent, his clients get plenty of editorial advice and it is never coercive. The book is the author's, he feels. His client's average income is in five figures—not bad. Most are happy, except when they write out of genre. The Career Builder has a spotty record with mainstream novels. His sub-rights record is weak, too. What he most loves to do is edit.

The Start-Up. A new agent, this former real estate saleswoman knows how to hustle. Though her clients' average income is low, she makes "deals, deals, deals." Her proudest moment was selling lunchbox rights to *The Valley Girls' Book of Lists.* Because she has more clients than she can handle, she is constantly frazzled and apologetic. Her commission is high, too: 15 percent plus all expenses. Most editors in the business consider her "up and coming."

The Part-Timer. This former English professor lives in the Midwest. Looking for a part-time career to keep himself busy in retirement, he decided to become an agent. His list is small; less than a dozen clients. Needless to say, he is easy to get on the phone. One of his clients is successful; the rest have not sold. He travels to New York twice a year to meet editors and see Broadway shows. The rest of the year he mails manuscripts with a "selling" cover letter.

The Mail Drop. This former actor has been an agent for three decades. Indiscriminate in picking clients, he is famous among editors for the low quality of his submissions. Even more amazing, he fails to market 40 percent of the material his clients send him. (When asked, he tells them he is "testing the market.") Even so, there is one area in which his record is superior: the sale of movie rights. His name often appears in Paul Nathan's column "Rights" in *Publishers Weekly.* He travels annually to the Cannes Film Festival.

I could go on, but you get the picture. When you sign on with an agent you are not getting a fixed commodity. You are not even guaranteed a minimum standard of performance. Remember, the literary agency business is unlicensed and unregulated. Agents' training varies.

When you get an agent, what you are getting is a person with strong points and weak points. Those strengths and weaknesses will drastically affect the course of your writing career—and I am not talking only about income. They will affect the books you write (or do not), how well you write them, and how smoothly (or not) your career goes.

An agent is more than his or her reputation. Your research should start, not end, with his or her client list. Get all the facts. Weigh all the factors that make a difference to a writer's career over the long haul. Most important of all, give yourself a choice. After all, there is a lot riding on your decision.

THE BIG ISSUES

In approaching agents in the real world, which issues are critical? What kinds of questions should you ask? How do you know if a given agent is a good match? How can you give yourself a true choice?

The big issues, the ones most authors feel are of top importance, are the following:

Specialists vs. Generalists. It is a rare author indeed whose ambitions are limited to one type of book. Most genre novelists have a mainstream novel percolating inside. Others want to write screenplays. Still others want lots of sub-rights action.

Those are healthy signs. Authors with many goals and needs are actively engaged in their careers, not just passively waiting. However, finding an agent whose areas of expertise exactly match one's interests and needs may be difficult. Should one, then, seek out a generalist—an agent with experience in all areas?

For the truly versatile author, a generalist can make sense. Here, though, you must be honest with yourself: do you regularly write *and sell* in a variety of markets? If so, a well-rounded agent with wide contacts will be useful to you. And if not?

Most novelists sell primarily one type of book—science fiction, say—and only sometimes make excursions into other areas. If this is you, you may be better off finding an agent who has a strong track record in your primary field. That is obvious, you would think, but you would be surprised. When genre authors call me up, many open the conversation asking, "Do you also handle mainstream?" I do. That reassures them—but not necessarily me.

Do not get me wrong: I like authors who stretch themselves creatively, but the first and fundamental job is to look after one's bread-and-butter business. A mystery novelist whose first stated goal is to get out of the mystery field makes me wonder. What does this need to escape signify? Is he just daydreaming? Is he temporarily burned out, or does he have chronic career problems?

If agents' specialties are not obvious from their client lists, ask each of your prospects what he or she has sold in recent years. Listen carefully to the answers. Your candidates may sound enthusiastic about your work, but their record may reveal that other types of books hold a stronger appeal for them. If so, don't be surprised if later you feel like a second-class client.

Suppose you sign up with, say, a top-notch romance specialist, but then one day you have an idea for a biography. Should you worry? Switch agents? Probably not, unless your change of direction is permanent. A reputable specialist always keeps one eye on the rest of the market. If so, she will know what is selling where and what other agents are getting for books like yours.

Finally, if you should come across a superspecialist—an agent who handles a large list of technothriller writers, for instance—think twice before signing up, even if technothrillers are your thing. While such an agent might be right for you, sometimes the competition among an agent's own clients can cause mistrust. That you definitely do not need.

Big Shops vs. Small Independents. You are a human being, not a number. Naturally, then, you expect a high level of personal service from your agent, something small independent agencies can surely provide.

But don't large agencies have more clout? And how about subrights? Large agencies have marketing breadth, true, but aren't independent agents less likely to let small deals slip through the cracks?

Without a doubt, mistakes happen in big bureaucracies, but being big does not necessarily mean that an agency will be inefficient. Plenty of small agents have sloppy sub-rights records, too.

A more telling complaint one hears about the mega-agencies is that their various departments—literary, film, TV, talent, or whatever—are run like fiefdoms. Agents in one area, the lament goes, lavish attention on their own projects and neglect—even disdain—projects brought to them by agents in other departments. So much for the benefits of an agency with broad-based exposure!

Another beef one hears about some big agencies is that they only want to package "in-house." That is, if a hot novel comes along, its movie rights may be offered only to directors and stars that are also agency clients. Efficient? Self-serving? You decide.

The most common complaint about large agencies is that clients feel lost in the sauce. The reason for this may not be size alone; plenty of small agencies neglect their clients, too. Rather, the reason may have something to do with corporate culture. Both big and small agencies are in business to make as much money as possible, but at big agencies the emphasis can tend to be on deals, not clients; on individual books, not whole careers.

Indeed, it is said that at certain Big Shops the agents get monthly reports stating how much income they have brought in. Needless to say, this puts the emphasis on the deal of the day, the bigger the better. Frontlist fiction and hot topical nonfiction will thrive; first novels and genre novels will not. Agents who want juicy year-end bonuses will naturally focus on big deals. Wouldn't you?

Does it sound like I am a tiny bit biased in favor of independent agents? I suppose that I am, being one myself. In defense of big agencies, I must admit that for certain kinds of novelists—ones who value large deals above all else—a Big Shop can be a fine place to be. Not that small agents cannot do big deals, as well. I have done a few in my time. But there is more to a long-term career than just doing deals. What are some of those factors?

One of them is career planning. A good agent will, from time to time, take stock of your progress, discuss your future books with you, set goals, devise strategy—in short, help plan your career and get you where you want to go. If this matters to you, you may want to think small. Independent agents have the ability to wait for strategies to unfold and for young writers to mature.

Okay, okay . . . some independent agents are disorganized. Others have limited experience. A smattering just do not know *what* they are doing. Small is not necessarily beautiful. But the most common reason for bad agenting is a client load that is too demanding, and that can happen at a literary agency of any size.

What is the optimum number of clients per agent? In my experience, fifty to sixty is about the most one agent can comfortably handle. However, not all agents have the same work capacity, and not all clients need the same level of service. There is no hard rule. Even so, if I were agent hunting I would wonder about agents with fewer than, say, twenty clients. I would also be concerned about an agent carrying more than, say, seventy-five. Would either really be able to give me the attention I need?

One more point: if there were even the slightest doubt about who at the agency would actually handle my work, I would look elsewhere.

New York vs. Out of Town. Once upon a time, this was an easy call. New York agents might have been good or bad, went the rule, but out-of-town agents were the pits. Not so anymore. There are agents with outstanding reputations working in Boston, Washington, Chicago, Minneapolis, and Seattle, among other places.

There are plenty in New York, too. The point is that geographic location is no longer the most important item on an agent's résumé. Far more important is how a particular agent got started.

If you are agent shopping, ask about your prospects' backgrounds. While many reputable agents belong to the AAR (Association of Authors' Representatives), the business itself is unlicensed and unregulated by any government agency. Anyone can call himself or herself a literary agent, so it pays to know exactly with whom you are dealing.

If your prospective agent has a posh New York address, but was a hairdresser until a year ago . . . well, good luck. If, on the other hand, you are a romance writer and you find an agent who formerly edited for Silhouette, but who now lives in Kansas City . . . well, I would take that agent's experience seriously, regardless of address.

10 Percent Commissions vs. 15 Percent Commissions. No doubt about it, new authors do not seem to give a damn what commission an agent charges them. All they want is the validation and security of representation.

Old-time pros, of course, are a different matter. They bristle at the idea of paying 15 percent. To them, 10 percent is traditional and fair; 15 percent is just a lousy rip-off.

Who is right? I will bet that you can guess my position on this point: the question should not be "How much?" but rather, "Which is the right agent for me?" Much better the right agent at 15 percent than the wrong one at 10.

Having said that, I should point out to new writers and old pros alike those commission levels that are generally considered excessive. They are (a) 15 percent plus *all* expenses; (b) 25 percent on overseas sales; and (c) anything more than 10 percent on overseas sales that are made not by the agent but by the publisher.

As for reading fees, do not pay them. Reputable agents do not charge them, not even nominal fees to cover handling. In fact, the Canon of Ethics of the AAR allowed reading fees only with extensive advance disclosure to the author, and then only until the end of 1995. Now, reading fees are banned altogether.

Certain nonmember agents will continue to charge such fees, I am sure. Should you pay them? I do not recommend it for mere consideration, though critiques are sometimes offered for your money. Are these worth it? Ask to see a sample critique ahead of time. Also find out who will actually read your manuscript and how long it will take to get the report.

Even then, there are choices other than literary agents if you want to pay for manuscript analysis. There are plenty of free-lance editors and "book doctors" from whom to choose. Their services may prove more expensive than agents' critiques, but in the long run those services may also prove more beneficial. For names, look in the industry reference book LMP (*Literary Market Place*) in the section called Editorial Services. Or contact the Editorial Freelancers Association. Be sure you are paying for quality advice.

A last word on commissions: unfortunately, I must report that I recently have heard rumors of agents who have escalated to a 20 percent commission on ordinary domestic sales. I have no names, but that is the talk. A sign of the times, perhaps? Maybe the "buyers' market" of the nineties is working in favor not only of publishers, but of agents now, too. If so, let the writer beware. . . .

Market-timers vs. Fundamentalists. In the stock market, a "market-timer" is a trader who moves with the trends. Market-timers pay little attention to the merits of individual stocks, and lots of attention to various indicators that forecast the market's overall direction.

"Fundamentalists," in contrast, ignore the ups and downs of the market and stalwartly buy and sell stocks based on their "fundamental" merits, such as the company's outlook, earnings, or cash value.

Literary agents have similar characteristics. Some believe in meeting the market's needs. They closely track the movement of editors from publisher to publisher, monitor genre trends, glean tips over lunch, and work (sometimes at lightning speed) to get their clients' proposals on an editor's desk at the right moment to make a sale. These are the market-timers, the ultrahustlers among agents.

Fundamentalist literary agents are not concerned with jumping onto bandwagons. Their clients follow their own stars, writing the stories that they must write, even though that can sometimes mean being out of fashion. Fundamentalists believe in their clients' destinies. They are patient. They devise strategies and stick with their clients through thick and thin.

Obviously, this dichotomy is a bit exaggerated. Most agents balance market-timing with fundamental, long-term planning. Even so, a given agent is likely to lean one way more than another, and it is worth finding out about an agent's proclivity before signing on.

How do you know what mix you need in an agent? Here are some questions to ask yourself: Do I need to know what's "hot"? Do I comb through the market reports in trade magazines, and study lists of recent sales? Do I need work-for-hire contracts to round out my income? If your answer to any of these questions is yes, then you probably need an agent with a healthy dose of the market-timer in him.

Now ask yourself, Do I ignore trends and write books that I have no choice but to write? Do I see my market more as readers than as editors? Am I loyal to my publisher, even though bigger advances might be had elsewhere? If your answers to any of these questions is yes, then your agent should probably be a die-hard fundamentalist.

If you are agent shopping you may need to be crafty in order to discover what sorts of agents you are talking to. Agents, being salespeople, are very good at finding out what you want to hear and telling it to you. Here are some useful questions: "What is your position on writing for packagers?" "What is hot right now?" "How many books a year do you think I should write?"

The tone of the answers will tell you a lot about your prospects. Trust your instincts. It pays to make the right match.

Brokers vs. Editors. A top science fiction author once told me, "I don't like agents who edit. My agent's job is to sell."

That sentiment is often expressed by older pros. They remember book publishing the way it used to be. Today, though, things have changed. The nineties is a time of downsized staffs, overburdened editors, best-sellers who may receive little editing, if any at all.

Long gone are the days of Maxwell Perkins, the legendary Scribner's editor who shaped the books and directed the careers of such twentieth-century giants as Ernest Hemingway, F. Scott Fitzgerald, and Thomas Wolfe. Editors today spend most of their time in meetings, on the phone with agents, at lunch, and preparing for triannual sales conferences.

Perhaps I exaggerate, but not much. Most editors complain that they have little time for doing what they love best: editing. Reading is rarely done in the office. Like most line editing, it is done after hours and on weekends at home. Is it any wonder that tie-ins, packaged books, and nonbook products have become so big?

On top of that, editors tend to change jobs. That means that authors' most long-standing publishing relationships are likely to be with their agents. That has also forced agents into a new editorial role.

You may not want an agent who helps shape your writing, but chances are that at some point in your career you will need one. That will be especially true when you are making a switch of publishers.

How can you tell if a prospective agent is also a good editor, or at least the right editor for you? The answer to that question lies in what agents will have to say about your writing. If you need a market-timer, search for an agent who offers advice on tailoring your writing to current market conditions. If you need a fundamentalist, find an agent who does not dictate what to write, but rather points out weaknesses in your work and suggests logical ways to achieve the effects you desire.

Either way, watch out for bad editorial advice. If it is too vague ("Study the market") or too dictatorial ("Sex is back in—make it hot") your career may be headed for a crash. In my experience, the best editorial advice empowers you to write what you write best.

Isn't that your aim?

5

CHAPTER

More on Choosing an Agent

THE SEARCH AND HOW IT FEELS

IF YOU ARE A NEW AUTHOR, THE FIRST THING TO REALIZE AS you search for the right agent is that you probably feel anxious. Oh, there may be good moments—moments when you feel confident that your work is at least as good as anything out there.

Then there are the bad moments when you remember what you've heard about the odds, slush piles, agents. Maybe you have heard that it is easier to get a contract than to get an agent. Or that without an agent no decent publisher will read your work.

The truth, here, is that you have a choice of agents. You may not feel like that, but you do. Understanding it, believing it, is your first challenge. To help you, here are three common feelings that block the empowerment I am talking about:

Okay, just one more rewrite and it will be perfect. A reluctance to let one's novel go is a common experience. The problem is that it is so easy to rationalize rewrites: most novels probably *could* use another rewrite . . . and another . . . and another. . . .

Where does it end? That can be difficult to decide, but end it must—sometime. Now a whole bunch of fears arise. Chief among these may be the horrible feeling that you have missed something, that there is one more change that must be made—a change that will mean glorious acceptance instead of humiliating rejection.

Authors with manuscripts on submission are forever sending me replacement pages, chapters, and even whole new manuscripts.

Panicky notes accompany these rewrites. The notes implore me to "DISREGARD THE EARLIER VERSION!" How much different are the rewritten pages? Usually not much. After a while the process seems a bit silly. It is symptomatic of low empowerment.

The answer is to cultivate objectivity about your writing, even though at the end of a year or two (or more) of writing objectivity is the last thing you may feel. But try. Step back. Put the manuscript aside for a while. Read it again with a fresh eye. When you are sure you feel good about it—and about yourself—the novel is done. It is finally time to submit it for consideration.

Oh, what does it matter? No one's going to want it anyway. You are no fool. You know the score. If you are extremely lucky you might land a decent agent but the odds are against it, right?

If this describes you, you are also having a common experience. Offering your work in the marketplace is risky. The chances of getting hurt—even humiliated—are high. The easiest way to lessen the pain of rejection is to plan for it in advance.

The problem with this defense mechanism is that it leads authors to feel that the process is out of their hands. Why discriminate? Why push? Why feel anything but shock and joy when some randomly chosen agent finally says yes. No reason. And so begins many a woeful publishing tale.

I don't know where to begin. "Help! There's too much information! All these lists! How do I know which agency would be best?"

There's no panic worse than that of beginning a scary task. One way to cope is to put it off. Another is to rush. Witness: quite often when I respond positively to a query letter, I get back a hurried note saying the manuscript is not quite ready.

Really? Then why was it offered for consideration? The reason, of course, is that new writers—heck, all writers—are anxious for validation. They cannot wait to find out if they will make the grade. Is there anything wrong with that? Yes, if the novel that I finally read is less than completely ready. Remember, the odds *are* long. Why test those odds with unfinished work?

Similarly, throwing up one's hands at the array of choices among potential agents is not helpful. It is like throwing up one's hands because there are too many car models to choose from.

You have to start somewhere. Where? Well, deciding on your criteria is probably a good place to begin. What do you want in an agent? If you are not sure, reread the previous chapter. In it I discuss six large issues that distinguish agencies from each other. Where do you stand on those issues?

WHEN TO LOOK

A moment ago I was discussing the decision as to when a novel is finished. Another question of timing is when to approach agents.

First ask, "Do I need to look at all?" That is, as a new author do you really need an agent? Opinions differ. Most professional authors have agents, but it is often said that first-timers will not get a noticeably better deal if they are represented.

That is true to a point. With few exceptions advances for first novels are low. An agent may get you a few thousand dollars more up front, yes, but why pay a commission when royalties eventually close the gap anyway? What's the difference?

The difference shows in a couple of ways. First, because many major publishers will not read unagented manuscripts, an agent can open doors. Even more important, a savvy agent who knows individual editors' tastes and publishing houses' relative strengths can be an effective matchmaker, pairing your work with the company best able to make that work a success.

There are also contracts to consider. Advance levels, royalty rates, copyright, options, and control of subsidiary rights are all vital issues in which a new author can benefit from an agent's expertise. Take, for instance, the right to publish your novel in German. The unagented author typically cedes control to his publisher, who typically keeps 50 percent of the proceeds from licensing this right. On a first novel deal, most agents like to retain control. The cost to the author thus drops to 20 or 25 percent. More money for you.

Maybe right now money is not your first priority. What about reaching more readers? Well, that will not happen overseas if your novel is not sold overseas. Large publishing companies have departments responsible for just that, but are they efficient? Not necessarily, especially if your novel is one in a catalogue of hundreds. To an agent small sales can matter more.

Okay, let's assume you're convinced. When should you approach agents? Before you start to write? After you've sold a few stories? When you've finished your first novel? When you've got a publisher interested in it, perhaps even an offer on the table?

Working backwards through those options, it should be obvious that approaching agents with an offer in hand is going to produce powerful results. Agents are drawn to commissions like bees to honey. If this is your situation, expect to hear some highly flattering buzz about your writing.

But how deep is that enthusiasm? To find out you will have to listen hard and cut through much self-serving PR. It is wise to begin this scenario with a strong idea of what you want in an agent.

Most authors do not wait so long. Of the five thousand query letters I receive each year, most come from writers who have finished a novel. But must you necessarily have completed a manuscript to make contact?

The truth is that it is difficult to the point of impossible to sell a first novel that is not finished. (These days it can even be difficult to move an *established* author from one house to another with only a partial manuscript to show.) Hence, for me there is little point in reading an unfinished manuscript by a first-time novelist. Authors with a sales history—particularly a good one—are a different matter.

Short story sales are useful credits to have. Sales to national magazines never fail to catch my eye. In and of themselves such credits don't guarantee a brilliant novel. Nor does their absence necessarily mean anything bad. But they do suggest that an author is on the road to being a full-time professional. Sell some short stories if you can. It helps.

Last word: the time *not* to contact an agent is before you have written any fiction at all. Unless you are a big-name celebrity. (If you are, call. We'll talk.)

WHERE TO LOOK

This is the easy part. There are excellent general source books around, and plenty of source books for mystery writers and other genre authors. Check the reference section of your local bookstore.

Still, even in-depth agency profiles can leave you feeling lost. What happens if your top choices turn you down? What if (happy day!) several agencies want you? On what basis will you choose? Is it possible to know—really *know*—what you are getting into?

In order to distinguish one agency from another, you must first give yourself permission to gather information. It is true that agents, especially the top ones, are busy folks. They guard their time. Breaking through that barrier can be tough.

Oddly enough, some authors actually enjoy being seduced by the aura of power and secrecy that surrounds agents. These authors do not want to know how agents do their work. They are romantics. They would rather believe in magic.

Still, as an author you are a consumer. And the service you will be buying is quite expensive. You have a right to information, but if you want it you may have to look beyond source books. One good way to start is to join a writers' organization. Its officers and members may be helpful. So may its national and regional newsletters. Agents' names, clients, and recent sales often turn up in their pages. So do interviews with agents.

To develop a more refined feel for agents' styles and effectiveness, talk to their clients. Here, both writers' organizations and writers' conferences can be helpful. Head for the bar. That's where writers most often hang out, and where you will hear the most candid talk about agents. (Be discerning, though. Frank talk is one thing; gossip is another.)

Going on-line is another option. Network around. Your goal is to learn not merely who handles whom or which agents are looking for what. You need a sense of agents as people. It is often said that the author/agent relationship is like a marriage. How true! It not only involves trust and respect, but also involves getting to know your partner painfully well.

Recognize that you will probably work with your agent for a long time. You owe it to yourself to choose one you like and enjoy, one who lets you feel free. Freedom is the foundation of creative growth.

PROTOCOL QUESTIONS

There are many common worries. *Should you send an outline with your query*? Common sense: if a listing suggests it, yes. If not, then it depends on whether you can write an effective synopsis. If you cannot, stick with a tantalizing capsule description in your letter. *Should you go ahead and send the manuscript*? Common sense: it takes much longer to read a book than a letter. Do you really want your novel to languish on a slush pile, miles behind the manuscripts that were requested?

Is it okay to write/submit to more than one agent at a time? Yes, but it is also polite to let your prospects know what you are doing. Besides, if they know the heat is on they may get back to you more quickly. *What if an agent demands to have my novel exclusively*? Well, it is up to you. Are you significantly more interested in that agent than in others? What if that agent says yes? Will you really keep looking?

WHAT TO ASK AGENTS

I hope you enjoy your agent search. For me it is a fascinating dance. Eventually, though, all authors hope to hear the following: "I've read your novel and I love it. I want to represent you." The usual response is delirious joy. Nothing wrong with that, but do take a moment to ask some important questions.

The most urgent question is not, "How much do you charge?" but "What do you think of my novel?" The answer to that one will tell you volumes about the experience you are about to have.

The first thing you want from the answer is enthusiasm. For agents, handling new novelists often means taking a loss. Commissions do not usually cover the overhead involved in the first few books. It is a rough road. It can take years to swing that first sale. Even after that, problems may abound.

What sustains an agent through that? I will tell you: passion. By that I mean an irrational faith in a writer's future or at least the conviction that their writing is worthy, even brilliant. You must have that. Without it you are already sunk.

The second thing you need from the answer is a sense of your prospective agent's editorial vocabulary and approach. *Editorial*? Yes. As I said earlier, your agent is going to serve as your first and most long-standing editor. But what is good editorial advice? That depends. If you are a facile, outline-handy, trend-watching sort of author then you probably want an agent to tell you how to tailor your fiction to what's hot, what's selling. If, however, you are a slow, style-conscious, trend-ignoring type of author then you probably want an agent who nurtures your own unique voice.

Above all else, you want an agent who understands your type of fiction.

That leads to the second most important question: *How much of my type of writing do you handle?* A lot? Exactly how would the agent describe your work?

And that leads to another crucial question: *What plans do you have for marketing my work?* The answer had better be detailed and logical. Today there are many more strategies to choose from than in years past. Once, the best possible hardcover deal was always the top objective; not so anymore. Hard/soft deals with large commercial houses are far smarter for many novels. Certain others are best served by original paperback publication. What type of novel is yours? And why? Ask.

Okay, now you may ask, "*How much do you charge?*" Fifteen percent on domestic revenues has become standard. A trickier issue is whether expenses are charged on top of that, and if so which? Certainly outside legal, public relations, and accounting advice need not be covered by commissions. But policies vary widely on things like photocopying, messengers, phone charges, overseas postage, and such. If charged, must you front some money or will the agent foot it? Do you get advance clearance?

Next vital question: *Are you a member of the* AAR (*Association of Authors' Representatives*)? While membership does not guarantee you will get brilliant representation, it does mean that your prospect has met certain minimum performance standards and has signed a Code of Ethics that addresses the handling of funds, the availability of information, confidentiality, expenses, conflicts of interest, reading fees, and other issues of real importance to your writing career.

Keep going: *How many people work at your company? How many are agents? Who will actually handle my work? How are overseas sales and movie/TV sales accomplished? Will you consult with me before closing every deal?*

Will you ever sign agreements (especially subsidiary-rights agreements) on my behalf?

Still more: *Are you incorporated? When you receive money for me, how quickly will you pay out my share? Will you issue a 1099 tax form at the end of the year? What happens if you die or are incapacitated? How will I receive moneys due to me?*

Aren't you glad you are asking these questions now? There's one more big issue to consider, so big that it deserves a section of its own.

THE AGENCY AGREEMENT

I use the simplest and most trusting form of contract with my clients: a handshake. I do this because unless there is a high level of mutual respect involved I do not feel that we have a useful working relationship. Also, if my clients are unhappy I feel they should be free to leave at any time.

Not everyone is comfortable with that, however. Most agencies have written agreements with their clients. Review yours before you sign it. What follows is a discussion of some of the most common provisions you will come across:

Commissions. Naturally commission rates are set out for domestic sales, movie/TV sales, overseas sales, special sales. Expenses to be charged and clearance procedures should also be spelled out.

Works covered. Will your agent handle everything you write, down to essays you dash off for your industry trade journal? Or will only specific work be handled? You may want representation only on a per-project basis. If so, establish that in writing.

Duration. Most agency agreements lock you in for a certain length of time. Two years is typical. After that, the agreement is renewed by mutual consent. A highly important aspect of duration is what happens to unsold rights after termination. Does your agent retain control? If so, for how long? Believe me, when agents and authors split, no issue causes more grief than this one. Work out something equitable in advance.

For contracts still in force upon termination (that is, for novels still in print and earning), the agent generally continues to receive funds and his commission as long as earnings continue. Another situation that few agency agreements cover is this one: your agent submits a project to a publisher, but while it is still under consideration you and your agent split. Now an offer appears, but who negotiates the deal and collects the commission, your old agent or your new agent? That's a tricky one, huh?

Generally, ad hoc arrangements are made in these cases. Perhaps the new agent approves the deal, but does not get a commission. Or perhaps the new agent does the deal and splits the commission with the old agent. Whatever the arrangement, be sure you feel comfortable with the way the deal will be handled.

WORKING WITH YOUR AGENT

Phew! You made it! Now you and your agent are off and running. What now? How much feedback can you expect? How often should you call?

If you have chosen well, you are probably paired with an agent whose experience, temperament, and business style are well suited to your needs. But even author/agent relationships have a honeymoon; after that comes the bumpy breaking-in period.

The important thing here is to identify accurately what you need and communicate it clearly to your agent. That is not always easy. It can be tough to separate, say, a need for reporting on submissions from feelings of anxiety if a novel is not selling. Here you must know yourself and your agent. Be patient.

One thing that helps, I find, is a career plan. You know that old job-interview ploy, "Where do you want to be in five years?" That is a good question for you and your agent to ask. What are your career goals? How will you get there? What specific steps are needed?

A career plan is especially important if you intend to or already write more than one type of novel. It is not unusual for mystery authors, in particular, to write more than one series. Is that best done under a pseudonym? Should you stick with your first publisher for both series, or put the new eggs in another basket? Work this stuff out with your agent.

I also find that a career plan gives both my clients and me a way to measure progress. In fact, recently I have begun making up advance *marketing* plans for individual projects. Together with new clients I choose potential publishers. We then follow our progress through the list, adjusting as circumstances change. A sense of participation is healthy.

About calling . . . no one likes to be a pest, but at the same time waiting for news can be depressing. How often should you call? I advise my clients to phone any time they feel a need for information. Some call every few days. A few call twice a year.

As you go forward, you will probably come to rely more and more on your agent for advice and counsel. Some of this is mere "handholding" while waiting for offers, contracts, checks. However, some of the comments you hear may change the way you write. Some may even change the entire direction of your career.

Given clear goals, hard work, good communication, and a bit of luck, the author/agent relationship is usually happy and mutually profitable. Sometimes, though, it does not work out so well. I hate to drop clients. On occasion they leave, and that hurts, too.

Let us examine the first scenario: being dropped by your agent, or, more usefully, how *not* to be dropped by your agent.

KEEPING YOUR AGENT

Oddly enough, I think that the key here lies not so much in your relationship with your agent as in your relationship to your writing. Marriages can go stale. So can friendships. So can your engagement with your own fiction, if you do not strive to keep it fresh.

I am talking about growth. Getting better. Taking joy in your strengthening command of technique. The occasional creative plateau will not hold you back, but laziness and/or ego will. There is nothing sadder than an author who thinks that he or she knows it all. Such authors do not usually last.

One curse upon creative vigor is anxiety. It can derive from early success, which is daunting to maintain, or from financial pressure, common among authors who have gone full-time too soon. Whatever the cause, if the result is writers' block then it can be years before the author's career gets back on track. In such cases I am usually slow to cast a client adrift. I first ask myself if I am part of the problem.

Speaking of creative problems, there is another that often besets genre writers: weariness with a series. Arthur Conan Doyle got sick of Sherlock Holmes, so why shouldn't you get sick of *your* series? It will probably happen at some point. When it does you will probably feel pressure to keep everything status quo. And why not? If you have come to this point then the series is undoubtedly successful. So what should you do?

The solutions are as varied as the writers who devise them. Some authors start a second series. Others develop other types of fiction. Still others drink (which I do *not* suggest). Whatever your solution, stay fresh. If it makes sense, your agent will support your diversification and help you strike a balance between your bread-and-butter writing and your developmental work.

Stay alive, grow, and more likely than not your agent will happily keep you. But what if you do not want to keep your agent? Some thoughts follow.

MOVING ON

How do you know when it is time to leave your agent? Boy, that is a tough one. Having taken over many authors from other agencies, I can tell you that the level of problems authors experience varies. Some problems are slight, but of long standing. Others are so sudden and big that they boggle the mind.

One factor that remains constant, though, is that leaving your agent sheds light on your own shortcomings as well as your agent's. Smart authors use this opportunity to examine themselves and their writing.

But back to the first question: how do you know? Breakdown of communication is one warning sign. Do your calls go unreturned? Is there no follow-through on routine requests? If so, examine the situation. Are you being unreasonable? Are there differences or disagreements causing bad feelings?

Lack of progress is another worry, but again it is wise to study the situation before making any moves. Say that your advances have hit a plateau; is this your agent's fault or yours? Maybe your writing has hit a plateau. If your sales are not growing either and your publisher is not at fault, well . . . perhaps it is time to take an objective look at your storytelling.

Certainly there are problems for which only your agent is to blame. Blown deals. Lost manuscripts. Misunderstandings with your publisher. That kind of thing is just bad business. Even here, though, I advise caution. Are there mitigating circumstances? Did your agent's spouse recently die? Is she facing surgery?

Once you do decide to move on, try to maintain a businesslike demeanor. You will thank yourself later. Dignity is a precious possession.

And when you hook up with your new agent? Well, you begin a new honeymoon. And soon thereafter, the bumpy part. But if you have taken my advice you will have learned a lot about yourself during the divorce. And that self-knowledge should serve you well as you stride toward new levels of success.

THE ULTIMATE TRANSACTION

I hope that all this talk of agents has left you feeling empowered. There is, however, one relationship that is more important to an author's career than any other: his relationship with his readers.

When you publish your first novel you invite readers into your imaginary world. If you have painted it well, they will probably return. Repeat customers are the foundation under your career. Give them good value, reopen your store on a regular schedule, and they will make you successful beyond your dreams.

Remember, too, that your fans are unique to you, a discrete subset of all readers, to borrow a phrase from mathematics. They want *your* characters. *Your* settings. *Your* style. Ultimately, your readers will know your writing better than anyone else.

Think about it. Your query letter gets you, perhaps, one minute of an agent's attention. The cover on your book gets, maybe, a few seconds from a buyer for a bookstore chain. But once that book is sold to a customer, taken home and opened . . . ah! You have hours upon hours in which to lure that reader into your story, then take her on a ride she will never forget.

Given that, where should you put the lion's share of your time and energy? The answer to that question is easy: into your writing.

6

CHAPTER

The Marketing Game:
How I Sell Novels

EMPTYING THE CLOSET

SOON AFTER I SIGN UP A NEW CLIENT, A CURIOUS RITUAL usually begins: the Emptying of the Closet. Every unsold manuscript, old outline, out-of-print book, and list of capsule ideas is sent to me for appraisal, usually within a week or two.

A letter generally accompanies these mothballed manuscripts. "Can you do anything with this?" the letters plaintively ask. What my new clients really want to know, I suspect, is this, "Can I make any easy money off this old material?" I appreciate my clients' confidence in my ability to sell, but sadly the answer to their hidden question is almost always no.

I used to hate the Emptying of the Closet. It meant weeks of extra work, not only reading mediocre manuscripts but also, in some cases, explaining to my clients what their prior agents were too lazy or uncaring to explain: why this or that piece did not sell, or why marketing it now would be a mistake.

Today I have reformed my attitude. I use the Emptying of the Closet as an opportunity to learn more about my clients' writing. Mothballed manuscripts inevitably show me their weak points and bad habits. When I point these out my clients are usually sheepish. "Yeah, you are right," they say. "I sensed that myself."

Emptying the Closet is useful in another way. It keeps authors in the habit of measuring their manuscripts against a high standard. It can also help them to formulate their career goals and decide upon the various steps to take to reach those goals.

Here is a career-planning principle in which I firmly believe: if an author has three manuscripts to sell, one is going to be a more logical step toward that author's goal than the other two.

Where does your current manuscript fit into your career plan? Is it a break-in novel? Is it the continuation of a series? Is it just for the money? Is it a radical departure from your previous work? Does it feel to you like a logical next step?

Some authors protest that it is pointless, even dangerous, to plan a novel. Novels happen. Each one is a calling. Such writers work organically, molding and shaping their stories as they go. For them, a career plan may be impossible. Indeed, for them to attempt any novel that does not flow unchecked from a wellspring deep inside can be a waste of time, or worse.

If you are such an author, your best plan may be no plan at all. If so, be patient with your agent. It can be tough to keep a career moving forward when every new novel is a surprise. Also recognize that when new novels are departures, some readers will fall by the wayside. While some readers love authors for their prose alone, most love authors for their stories.

If you are a genre author, or a writer of commercial mainstream novels, or simply an author who wants to write fiction full-time for a living, then you will probably have an easier time choosing what to write next and forming a career plan.

In doing so, I suggest not planning too far ahead. A couple of novels down the road is far enough to look. As you mature and your craft improves, you will find that your story interests will change, too. A story that you burn to tell today may seem to you simple, even sophomoric, in a few years.

Keep your readers in mind. What makes them unique? What draws them to *your* fiction over hundreds of alternatives? Is your current novel going to satisfy them? If you are stretching your talents will they go along for the ride?

I am not suggesting that you should slavishly write the same book over and over. That is grim servitude, and probably will not please your readers for very long, either. I am suggesting, however, that every writer has an audience that is utterly his own. Tending to that readership, growing it, is primary.

So, back to the closet: what are your options? Which projects still need work, and which are ready to go? Of those ready for market, which one is the most logical one to sell next?

That is the one to shop around.

MATCHMAKER, MATCHMAKER

One of my primary tasks as an agent is to select the editors to whom I will send my clients' work. I consult with my clients, of course, but most leave those decisions up to me. And so I rank potential editors, not according to whether they are hot (or not), but in order of suitability for a given novel and author.

Here are some of the factors that I weigh: Is an editor young and hungry, or experienced and selective? Is she better at editing or at marketing? For which publishing house does he work? What are the politics at his company? Can she obtain for this novel all that it needs in order to be a success? Most of all, is this novel to the editor's taste? Will he adore it?

Many authors and agents feel it is best to start at the top, to sell a novel only to the senior-most employee who can buy it, usually the editor-in-chief or editorial director. It is not a bad practice, but it has drawbacks. Powerful editors often have a stable of authors they have developed over the years, their favorites. They are also offered plenty of new manuscripts.

In spite of the stiff competition, there are times when only a big-name editor will do. That is especially true when I am looking to place a big-name author. Such an author may need marketing muscle more than editing *per se*. For her, the editor who can obtain advertising and the other extras is probably best.

At the other end of the scale are the young and hungry editors, the ones who are still searching for the novels that will make their reputations. Obviously, they are more eager to buy. They may also be more willing to work with authors whose writing is, shall we say, developing. Given that, it might appear that young editors would be the top choices for first novelists.

But that is not necessarily true. Working with young editors can have drawbacks, too. Young editors may find their lists playing second fiddle to those of editors with more clout and savvy. Being sometimes in a hurry, young editors can also tend to change jobs more often than their older colleagues. While that is good for them, it is often bad for the authors whom they leave behind. This abandonment is so common in the industry that there is even a term for it: being "orphaned."

Given these pluses and minuses, I try to balance reality with my clients' needs and arrive at a selection of potential editors that offers my clients the greatest opportunities and the least risk.

After that, there is the question of what the client will most need once the contract is signed: sensitive editing or marketing savvy and support? Some editors work brilliantly with text. Shaping a novel through revision suggestions, then refining it with adroit line editing is truly an art. Some say that art is dying, but I have seen powerful evidence to the contrary.

Other editors are better at in-house politics, writing jacket copy, obtaining cover art, schmoozing with salespeople, and so on. An author whose work is "clean"—that is, which needs little editing— is a candidate for an editor with this kind of business head. Then again, all authors need a strong advocate on the inside. As always, I try to strike a balance, weighing the author's relative needs against the prospective editor's relative strengths.

Beyond the author/editor match there is the question of publishing companies. They are big or small (and, these days, rarely in-between). They may be oriented to hardcovers or paperbacks or to both. Most companies are comfortable with some sorts of fiction but not others. And no publisher is perfect.

Once a list of likely editors is chosen, I look over the publishers for whom they work. Here experience and staying abreast of industry changes are important. For instance, many authors whose work is high in literary integrity will ask for submission to Alfred A. Knopf. That is natural enough, given Knopf's legacy. However, over the last ten years Knopf has evolved. While still a house associated with quality, and on whose list one can find authors such as Ann Beattie, Albert Camus, Kazuo Ishiguro (*Remains of the Day*), and Elie Wiesel, Knopf's list is also chock-a-block with such popular writers as Anne

Rice, Carl Hiaasen, Dean Koontz, Richard North Patterson, and Andrew Vachss—fine storytellers all, but not authors one normally associates with rarified themes and literary prose. Knopf's list today has a decidedly commercial tang.

There is also the matter of whether a publisher is oriented primarily to paperbacks or hardcover. Without exception, today's largest houses publish both. But their roots do show. You can see it in the types of novels they choose and the styles in which they market them. Pocket Books goes for a mass-market sort of novel. Viking-Penguin is a bit more *up-market*, that is, oriented to novels that might need good reviews to work.

Sometimes it can be difficult to tell just what sort of publisher you are dealing with. Big houses today can seem almost schizophrenic. On the one hand, they may tell me that they want something new, novels that break the mold. When I give them such novels they often turn around and tell me that they have no idea how to market this excellent but unusual material.

Make up your mind already!

In the end, the choices are finite, and sooner or later I arrive at a selection of editors and publishers that seem workable for a given author and his current novel. But before beginning my submissions, there are yet more factors for me to ponder.

Company politics is one. Did Publisher A's parent company recently make a major acquisition? If so, a high corporate debt load might mean advertising and staff cuts down the road.

Editors go in and out of favor with their bosses, too. In addition, their lists fill up. A great time to submit to an editor (as every agent well knows) is when that editor is newly arrived at her job. Two years down the road, however, that same editor will probably have enough novels "in inventory"—that is, soon to be delivered or waiting to be published—that even the next *Gone with the Wind* may not get an offer.

Is it possible for unagented authors to obtain this sort of intelligence about editors and publishers? Certainly. They need only do what I do: study trade magazines, network with industry professionals over lunch, and get on the phone and dig.

Does that sound difficult to do from Indianapolis? If so, there is an easier way to get a handle on what is going on in book publishing: walk into a bookstore and take a look around.

Which companies are doing a good job getting their books out? Which companies are producing books with the format, look, and price that you want for your book? Check the spines, then call the company, and ask for the name of the editor who edited the book whose quality is most in line with what you need—not what you want in your dreams, but what you need in reality. That editor is step one in your marketing plan.

The final factor I consider before sending a manuscript to a particular editor is taste. Is this the kind of story, and the quality of prose, that turns my prospect on? Does the novel fit his or her own career plan? Sometimes I must disregard what an editor tells me he wants. Editors like to imagine themselves bold innovators, and sometimes they are, but just as often they acquire the fiction that makes them comfortable.

In many ways, that is a good thing. Passion is as important to the editor/author equation as it is to the agent/author one. Many problems lie ahead. Authors need editors who will stick by them, and who acquire novels that they love.

SINGLE SUBMISSIONS, MULTIPLE SUBMISSIONS, AUCTIONS

Nothing gets inexperienced authors more excited than the idea of an auction. Heck, many hardened old pros get excited, too.

Imagine it: a group of publishers who are otherwise slow and cautious scrambling to buy your book. Frenzied bidding! Offers in the stratosphere! Advertising guarantees tossed on the table like poker chips! And at day's end, success: a high six-figure advance. Your agent says, "No sweat. I knew we'd get it."

The losers? These unlucky publishers sadly call each other and do postmortems on the bidding.

Ah, bliss! Ah, fantasy! Can it happen for you? Well, maybe, but believe me it is a rare novel that can achieve success at auction. Indeed, few are really suited for it. Auctions are not a magic bullet. They do not always hit the mark. They are actually a calculated risk that can cruelly and easily backfire.

What makes a book a candidate for auction? A variety of factors. First, the novel in question must be one that more than one publisher wants—badly, if possible. Competitive bidding is fueled not only by a book's commerciality, but by the ego, greed, and drive of the humans involved.

In publishers, this primitive need to acquire is inspired by the sure thing: the novel that is guaranteed to make money. Fine writing? Not enough. Great story? Uh-huh. Author with a track record? Now you are getting warm. Author who is already a best-seller? Ah, *now* you are talking about a hot auction!

I am sure you see the point. The more a novel looks like a sure thing, the greater the chances that it will inspire acquisitive lust. Certain factors can enhance that look, for example, a movie sale, a major prize, advance blurbs, or a ready-made audience.

Talking of advance blurbs, a recent case of auction fever illustrates the importance of appearance in these situations. In 1991, a novel called *Just Killing Time* was brought to auction by agent Peter Lampack. With it came glowing endorsements from Clive Cussler, Joseph Wambaugh, and John Le Carré. Simon & Schuster won the bidding with an offer of $920,000.

When the news reached Wambaugh and Le Carré, they were not amused. Both denied that they had read or endorsed the book. (Cussler, also a client of Peter Lampack's, stood by his recommendation.) Simon & Schuster dropped the book. Most observers saw this as a cautionary tale, but later on *Just Killing Time* was picked up by another publisher for roughly $450,000. Moral: blurbs can more than double the price of an otherwise risky book.

Good timing is another factor that can drive up prices, although what makes timing good is sometimes not obvious. For example, our last recession was in 1990–91, yet some of the highest prices of the nineties so far were paid during those years, $12.3 million to Ken Follett for two books, $20 million to Jeffrey Archer for three. Illogical? Not really. These publishers, although thirsty for sales, also saw an approaching recovery.

Movie sales can help escalate auction prices, too. That was a big factor in Dell's $3.15 million acquisition of Nicholas Evans's *The Horse Whisperer* in 1994. Movie rights had already sold to Hollywood

Pictures, a Disney division, for $3 million. Would the book advance have soared so high if it were not certain that Disney would be helping the book's sales by pumping money into promotion of their film? You tell me.

The mechanics of auctions are actually fairly simple. Generally, a *floor bid* is first set. This is a minimum advance that one publisher guarantees to pay. In exchange for getting the ball rolling, that publisher usually obtains a *topping privilege*, that is, the option to better the highest bid by 10 percent (or perhaps by 5 percent at high levels).

Finally, a *closing date* is set and on that day publishers are called according to preset rules. Bidding proceeds in rounds. The winner is the highest bidder. That is terrific—if money is all you want. But what if it is not?

Suppose you want the option to choose your publisher? If so, you will need to select another marketing route over the auction. A multiple submission is the next strategy down the scale. While not as hot as an auction, a multiple submission can still put some heat under a novel. It is competitive, but less so.

In a multiple submission the manuscript is sent to several publishers at once. There is no floor bid. In some cases there is no closing date. There is pressure upon the publisher since competitors are involved, but generally the pressure is less.

The lower temperature of this situation is intentional. Publishers are less likely to be scared off. The effort involved in putting together an auction position is reduced. The personal stakes are lower. Whereas an auction forces publishers into (or out of) the game, a multiple submission coaxes them in.

Unfortunately, the multiple's less formal structure can also make it harder to manage. With fewer rules, publishers are freer to try strategies such as the *preemptive bid*, a high offer that, if accepted, means the agent and author involved will not entertain other offers. The preemptive bid can be an exciting result, but it can also leave the seller with enemies.

Most of the time I employ the multiple submission for properties for which I want some combination of fast action and choice. Since marketing can be painfully slow, it might seem that multiple submissions are a panacea, the best of all worlds.

Not always. Because some degree of pressure is present, the multiple can still chase away publishers who have only a borderline interest in a novel. For that reason, multiples are often not the best choice for debut novels or novels that do not fit neatly into a publishing "slot." For them the traditional one-at-a-time submission is often most successful.

Many authors think that single submissions are a fool's errand, being wastefully slow. I disagree. Slow they can be, I admit, but they can also be useful to foster a sense of discovery on an editor's part. In fact, for that very reason I sometimes play down a book in my pitch, saying things like, "This is an interesting one. I would value your opinion."

The editor is now free to discover the book on his own. The hard-sell raises expectations and makes disappointment more likely—especially if my pitch has been less than entirely candid.

New authors and genre authors are generally safest submitting singly. Are there times when their work can be auctioned? Yes. When an author is ready for break-out, or when a first novel is unusually commercial, a well-managed and well-timed auction can bring a high price. In addition to Nicholas Evans's $3.15 million for *The Horse Whisperer*, here are the prices paid for some other early-career novels in recent years:

- $800,000 for *Mallory's Oracle* (a first novel) by Carol O'Connell
- $500,000 for *The Juror* (a second novel) by George Dawes Green
- $2 million for *The Day After Tomorrow* (a first novel) by Allan R. Folsom

If these figures fill you with envy or shame, relax. Not only are these novels one-in-a-thousand exceptions, supernova advances are far from the only way to begin a successful career. In fact, if you study the careers of big-name authors you will find that a great many built slowly over time: John Jakes, Dean Koontz, John D. MacDonald, Martin Cruz Smith . . . the list is long.

Remember that the name of the game is not obtaining contracts, but gathering a following among readers. That can be accomplished at a walking pace far more easily than it can be done at the speed of light.

PROPOSALS, PARTIALS, COMPLETE MANUSCRIPTS

Let us get right down to it: if you are a first-time novelist it will be all but impossible for you to sell anything but a finished manuscript. There are exceptions (I was one), but do you really want to gamble on being an exception?

Finish your novel.

All done? Okay, let us survey the ins and outs of the different forms in which a novel can be submitted. Completed manuscripts have one advantage: there is no guesswork for an editor. What you see is what you get. Also, a finished novel has behind it the power of a whole story. All the emotions are in place. The twists and turns are there. Reading a whole novel is like trekking across Nepal; you fully experience the journey.

A fear that many authors have when submitting complete manuscripts is that the editor in question will not actually read the whole book. It is a well-grounded worry. The fact is that at many major houses your novel will first be read by an outside, free-lance reader who will send it back to the editor with a one-page report.

If this report is positive, great. If negative, the book quickly comes back, usually without getting a second look from anyone in-house. What a horrifying thought! It is the reality of the business, though, so the best idea is to get used to it. Besides, you are confident about your novel, right? You feel certain it will strike a chord with most readers, do you not?

Another worry about complete manuscripts is that the response time will be inordinately long. Once again, this is a well-grounded fear. Partials generally (though not always) get a faster look. But that is not to say that complete novels will languish. Let me tell you, I am sometimes amazed at how quickly a four-hundred-page manuscript can come flying back to my office!

Here is the story on partials. They work best when the novel they represent is an *option book* (your next work that you may be contractually obligated to offer your publisher) or when we are in an expansive era in our industry. When good fiction is in short supply, a partial can tantalize publishers with its promise of delights to come. Indeed, I have lived through certain years when partials routinely won bigger advances than finished novels.

The nineties is not one of those periods. In book publishing, the nineties is a buyers' market. Publishers have a "prove it to me" attitude. They also want to shorten the time between laying out money for a book and getting revenues from bookstores; thus, they purchase complete, ready-to-go manuscripts. In addition, there are simply a lot more whole manuscripts making the rounds these days. Editors can pick and choose.

For all of those reasons partials are somewhat less salable than they used to be. The one exception, as I mentioned, is the option book. Here partials are customary, except among those admirable authors who resist deadline pressure or who do not want to expose their fiction before they are certain that it is fully ready.

Sometimes you will hear the word *proposal* being used in the business. What exactly is that? In the fiction game, pros tend to use *proposal* interchangeably with *partial*, which itself generally means "several sample chapters with an outline."

Technically, the word *proposal* is more applicable to nonfiction projects. It means a document that describes a work to be written later. With fiction there is little point in describing a book to come; better just to write it, or at least some of it. A fiction proposal is chapters and an outline.

About that word *outline* . . . little causes new authors and some established authors more anxiety than the idea of summarizing their story. How unfair! How limiting! Their feelings are justified, but outlines are a fact of life in the fiction game.

Outlines for as-yet-unwritten stories can also be useful, once one gets over the fear that they will somehow sap the juice out of the writing process. Outlines are simply maps to character development and plot. You can stare at them and ignore the trip, if you wish, or you can savor the scenery secure in the knowledge that you know where you are going. It is up to you.

Lots of authors find that outlines set them free. Even those who hate them sometimes have to write them, so for all concerned I have included a sidebar on the art of writing outlines.

The Art of Writing Outlines

Over the years I have written some forty outlines for published novels, and have read thousands more. Here are some tricks I have learned.

First, remember that before you sell your story to the public you must sell it to an editor. In other words, your outline should be as smooth, professional, and polished as your final manuscript.

Next, in publishing terms *outline* really means *synopsis*. Forget roman numerals and all that stuff. Organize yourself in that format, if it helps, but for presentation tell a story.

Indeed, the best outlines are more than plot summaries. They are novels in miniature. They use a variety of fiction techniques—action, description, exposition, even bits of dialogue to highlight dramatic moments—to give the reader the illusion that she has read an entire novel.

Length? Five pages is too short, unless the intended reader is familiar with your work. Fifty pages is probably too long. If that much detail is necessary, why not write the entire book? Besides, the point is to get the story across quickly. This is an *outline*.

Another tip: try using present tense and third person regardless of the tense and person of your novel. Not only is this traditional in the business, that combination lends a certain punch and immediacy to an outline.

Some authors swear they get better results when outlines are single-spaced rather than double-spaced. The theory is that when an editor sees a double-spaced page, he looks for things to change. A single-spaced outline, on the other hand, is said to discourage editing.

Take your pick. If you do single-space, though, try leaving one line of space between paragraphs or sections. That may help your outline to read faster.

Finally, explain everything. Do not assume that your reader will supply missing logic or will mentally fix a weak motivation. She will not. You are the author. Show that you are in command.

Once you have written an outline, are you locked into it? Are you forbidden to make changes, or even to make small improvisations?

Of course not. No editor expects a finished book to conform 100 percent to an outline. An exception is if you are making major changes in the very nature of the story. If so, it is probably a good idea to run those changes past your editor. No one wants to order steak for dinner, but then be served sushi instead.

7

CHAPTER

Strategy Session I: Breaking In

HOW TO USE THIS STRATEGY SESSION

The purpose of this chapter is to help you plan the practical steps you will take to get your novels into print. We will also examine the first important issues facing you as you make your opening moves in your gambit for a full-time fiction career.

This chapter is interactive. You will have choices. I cannot, should not, presume to give advice that will apply to all writers in all cases. No two novels are exactly alike, and no two fiction careers will unfold in exactly the same way.

You must decide what is right for you. Nevertheless, there are certain fundamental choices that confront all beginning novelists. By making you aware of them now, I hope to help you make your opening moves as strong as possible. You may also, I hope, avoid some early pitfalls by being prepared.

At the end of this chapter you will find a checklist that summarizes all the choices I am discussing here. When you are done filling it out you will have a plan for the early part of your career. Having a plan does not guarantee success, but I firmly believe it will raise the odds against failure.

Here we go.

WHAT TO SELL

If you have only one completed novel, then your initial choice may be simple: your first submissions will be of your first novel.

But hold on: consider whether your first manuscript is really the one with which to launch your career. Of course you want the validation of finding an agent, or selling to a publisher, but although this manuscript may accomplish those things for you, will it also put you on the map in the wider world of bookstores and readers?

Think hard. Be honest with yourself. Is this novel really as good as it can be? Is it better than the novels with which yours will compete on the shelves? By that I do not mean, "Is this novel publishable?" Probably it is. Nor do I mean, "Is this novel better than 90 percent of the crap that's out there?" It may well be.

What I mean is this: when you compare your novel to those of the leading authors in your section of the stores, do you sincerely feel that your fiction can compete? It is not enough just to sell. Obtaining a contract is not the end of the game. When you publish, the game is just beginning. After that comes the play-by-play struggle for an audience. Your publisher may give you some help, but the brutal fact is that most first novels are sent out with very little support, if any at all.

Do you feel that your novel is so compelling that it can sell itself? Will it spread by word of mouth? Will it win over fans? If so, it may be the one with which to begin. If not, you may want to revise it or to put it aside in favor of another project.

Some pros and writing teachers will be up in arms over that last suggestion. How can authors judge their own work? Shouldn't agents and publishers be the judges? Haven't there been plenty of cases in which a wise and discerning editor recognized the potential in a flawed manuscript and nurtured it?

I cannot deny that you may find supporters out there in book publishing. I am suggesting, though, that at the start of the game some moves are strong and others are weak. If you feel your first manuscript is weak, consider moving on to another project. Your writing will improve. You may also find that a future manuscript has a better chance of capturing a wide readership.

If you have more than one manuscript in the proverbial closet, take inventory. Which novel is likely to be the most popular? Which one might be the beginning of a bread-and-butter business that will draw readers back time after time?

That is the one with which to begin. The others? Should you let them sit? Perhaps not, but realize that the buckshot approach—fire everything and see what hits—is not a plan, it is gambling. It may seem that the odds of selling will go up as the number of circulating manuscripts rises, but in my experience that is not true. Three weak or problematic novels do not add up to one irresistable manuscript.

Play from strength. Market those manuscripts that you feel will make successful books: books with a real, live following.

IDENTIFYING YOUR AUDIENCE

Most authors do not think much about their readers when they write. They write for themselves. There is nothing wrong with that, but sooner or later comes the moment when those authors have to face the marketplace and sell—but to whom? Here is a new choice.

Many authors duck this issue, saying, "That is what I have (or want) an agent for. I do not want to be concerned with the market. I want to write. After all, that is what I do best."

Adopt that attitude if you want to, but you will do so at your peril. Businesspeople who do not understand who their customers are—or, more importantly, what they want—are not going to be in business for very long. It is the same in the fiction game.

Another often-heard remark from authors is "I cannot think about readers. I write what I write. I compose stories that please me, and I assume they will please others."

I cannot argue. That is as good a reason as any to write. But we are no longer talking about writing. Now we are concerned with getting printed and bound books into the hands of bookstore customers with cash to spend and credit cards to run up. We are talking retail, and the many steps that precede a sale at a bookstore cash register.

Among those steps are approaching a likely publisher, editing, packaging, advertising and promotion, solicitation, ordering, printing, shipping and distribution, and shelving in a bookstore. At every step along the way the people involved need to know what sort of reader is likely to buy a given book.

Of course, you can leave that decision to the publishing professionals, but in my experience no one understands readers better than writers. Writers are the best-read folks I know. They devour current fiction, and have strong opinions about what is good and bad. Frankly, writers are our best marketing experts; they just do not think of themselves that way.

So, get your hands dirty. Make some decisions about where you belong in the marketplace. Do not be afraid that identifying your audience or drawing comparisons will limit you, or keep you from getting that out-of-the-blue million-dollar advance. That thinking is for amateurs. You are a professional. You want to get your books out into stores in the way that will most efficiently allow your readers, your fans, to find them.

To begin, try to place your novel in one of these broad categories:

- romance
- mystery/suspense
- science fiction/fantasy
- horror
- frontier/western
- gay/lesbian
- other

Is it a tough choice? Those categories correspond to the crude divisions you will find in most bookstores, where the choices *are* limited.

You may have noticed that I have not yet included the terms *fiction* or *mainstream*. Although often used in the book business, those words do not usually help inexperienced writers identify their audience. The word *mainstream*, in particular, conjures visions of wide popularity and wonderful sales. Authors often believe that if a novel can only be categorized "mainstream" then it will automatically ship to stores in large quantities and sell to customers in big numbers.

That belief is naive. So-called mainstream novels can sell in tiny numbers. That is even more true of a category called *literary fiction*, which is meant to denote novels of superior quality and a certain nebulous group of subjects such as small towns, real people, or hard lives. Authors with such labels face a double struggle in building their audience. For one thing, they cannot tap into the popularity of an existing genre. They must build from the ground up, creating a category where none existed before—their own.

It can be a tough job.

So where do you belong on the publishing map? To decide, identify that section of bookstores where you are likely to find *most* of your appreciative readers. There. You have narrowed it down.

Now look more closely. Within any given category, there are likely to be many subcategories. Mysteries are not just mysteries, they are cozies (those inspired by British country house crime novels), private-investigator novels, police procedurals, humorous, regional, or whatever. Where does your novel fit within your category? Or, more to the point, which author's work does your own material most resemble?

Authors hate to be compared to others. It seems so unfair, and it is. But once again we are not talking about literary value judgments; we are talking about efficient distribution. An apt comparison is useful in making that happen.

Here is an exercise: go to a well-stocked general bookstore and cruise the section that you have already selected as your base of operations. Study the novels. Now, which author's work is closest to what you are writing? Do not cheat. Do not indulge your fantasies. Try to find the one writer whose work most closely resembles yours in setting, time period, story type, cast of characters, prose style, and so on.

If you have done that exercise faithfully, you will have identified your competition. Believe me, if you do not do it for yourself now, people up and down the publishing ladder will do it for you later.

You now have the means to give publishing folks an accurate report of your location on the category map. Further, you have the chance to draw important distinctions between your work and that of the competition. Make yourself look good. (Why not?) Tell people what makes your work different, if not superior.

In thinking about these issues you are probably also identifying those qualities that your readers value. Fans of literary fiction enjoy, for example, evocative description. Romance readers, in contrast, want ardor and care little about beautifully turned prose. (Let's be honest. Why else would so many poorly written romances still sell?)

When asked for comparisons, some authors substitute a list of their influences. That can be interesting, but is less helpful in getting a handle on marketing hooks. If, for instance, an author tells me that he emulates Dickens, Tolkien, and Proust . . . well, what am I to think? Perhaps he has written a Victorian fairy saga that will find its biggest audience in France?

I think you understand me. Identifying your audience will give you an edge both as you pitch your project inside the publishing community and as you search for your readers outside of it.

WHOM TO APPROACH FIRST: AGENTS OR PUBLISHERS?

If you already have an agent, skip this section. If not, you face a conundrum. Since many major publishers will not accept unagented submissions (or rarely buy from their slush pile), it seems necessary for you to have an agent. However, agents—the good ones, anyway—can be hard to get. In fact, it is frequently said that the surest method to get an agent is to first find a publisher.

Does this sound like Catch 22? It does to me. Sad to say, I do not have a perfect answer to this conundrum. My feeling is that authors are best off working with agents from the beginning of the novel-marketing process. I have to admit, though, that because of the volume of writers who petition me it is difficult for unpublished authors to get my attention.

What is one to do? Ultimately, it is up to you. I would try agents first, and if that does not work try publishers. I would especially target publishers if I were a genre author. Genre editors are sometimes more open to unrepresented submissions than their mainstream—that word again—counterparts. If a publisher has expressed interest in a novel, that is a strong incentive for me to take a look.

An offer from a publisher is even more persuasive. But the scenario I am suggesting is tricky. While most publishers will not mind if an agent steps in to handle a deal, some will not like it. All you can do is be firm and businesslike.

You have a right to representation. If you do use an offer from a publisher to open doors with agents, just be sure not to say yes to any contract terms, as tempting as that may be. You want an agent to take a look at the offer and respond to it appropriately.

SINGLE TITLES VS. SERIES

What should you write and sell, a stand-alone book or a series? The advantage of a series is obvious. If successful, readers will come back for more. Yet with a stand-alone novel you have flexibility. If your first novel is unsuccessful, you may be able to cut your losses and move on. Which is the right choice for you?

If you are a mystery writer or a fantasy author, the best plan will suggest itself by the very nature of the stories you write. Historical novelists and romance writers can prosper with sagas, too. As for others, in most cases novels will stand alone. If desired, there is usually a way to devise a sequel.

What about the situation in which one has completed the first book in a series, but it has not yet sold? Should you be working on the second in the series, or should you work on something else?

That can be a tough question to answer. To do so, you may find it helpful to put on your business hat again. Once the first of your trilogy, series, cycle, or saga is under contract, you are in business. Investing more time and effort in that enterprise is obviously a good idea. New contracts are likely. Until that first sale, though, are you really in business for yourself?

In reality I find that most authors do not have much trouble deciding what to work on next. For those prolific types who find themselves with an embarrassment of choices, I would like to suggest returning to a principle I discussed in the previous chapter. Among your options, one novel is going to be a more logical next step to achieving your career goals than the others.

So, what is your most logical next step? The answer, I hope, will be obvious to you.

ONE-BOOK DEALS VS. MULTIPLE-BOOK CONTRACTS

Most first-time authors would love to be presented with this choice. Amazingly, it happens more often than you might think.

Multiple-book contracts make sense for publishers. The initial outlay can be low; also, if the first novel is a success the advance levels on subsequent books will not be subject to inflation. The terms are locked in. The publisher has room to breathe, and a period in which to enjoy a profit margin.

Should you take a multiple-book deal if it is offered? That depends. For authors in certain categories it can make sense. For instance, if you have written or are planning a fantasy trilogy there is little reason to be cagey. You will almost certainly want all three volumes to be published by one house.

The same reasoning probably holds true for mystery writers beginning a series. There is every reason to keep the books together; indeed, it is nice to get a long-range commitment on so speculative a venture. The worry is that if the first book proves highly popular the author will then be unable to take advantage of it. With the terms locked in there will be little possibility of demanding a better deal.

For that reason it is probably a good idea not to commit too many books at once. Three is a good limit. With three you get all the advantages of a multiple deal without delaying too long the pleasure of obtaining better terms if your books are a hit.

One sneaky contract point to watch out for in multiple-book deals is something called *joint accounting*. This allows your publisher to lump the advances for all the books into one sum, which must be completely *earned out*—that is, royalty earnings due to you must add up to that figure—before additional royalties will be paid. It can be highly frustrating to wait for royalties that are due to you simply because all of the books in the contract have not yet been published.

I rarely agree to joint accounting, particularly at low advance levels. The rationale for this hold-back feature is that it mitigates the risk the publisher is taking with a new author. But at what financial level does risk begin? If you ask me, it does not begin at the level where most first-novel advances typically start. Four-figure advances, even tripled, are not much of a risk.

One situation in which a multiple-book deal is probably a bad idea is when the novel in question is a hot, stand-alone, commercial novel. If there is a real possibility of gigantic success, it can be far better to swing the next deal once the results on the first book are in. I follow this principle even when the success I anticipate is at a lower level.

Advances can be important tools. Best not to let them rust from lack of use.

HARDCOVER VS. PAPERBACK

Which is the best format for you, hardcover or original paperback?

Certain strategies are obvious. If you have written a mainstream novel that is *not* a surefire blockbuster, then you will probably depend on good reviews to make your novel fly. In that case, hardcover publication is your only really safe choice. It can be difficult to get original paperbacks reviewed.

If, on the other hand, you are a category romance writer, or an author of science fiction or fantasy novels, then original paperback publication is a safe bet. Readers of such novels are used to discovering new authors in paperback; indeed, they will probably recoil at the price of a hardcover novel.

Come to think of it, a lot of consumers are resisting high-priced hardcovers these days. At thirty dollars a shot, who can blame them? For that kind of money, most people want to be sure they will get a high-quality book—and one that they are certain to enjoy.

Thus, there is a loose sort of rule that one can apply to the hardcover-vs.-paperback question. If the book under discussion is intended for consumers who demand high-quality writing, hardcover can work; indeed, it can be essential to creating the cachet that transforms a novel from a book into an event.

If, in contrast, the consumer for whom a novel is intended is either price-sensitive or is primarily reading a novel for reasons other than that novel's literary quality, then original paperback publication can be a useful choice.

There are quite a few exceptions to that rule of thumb. Take Star Wars novels; as popular as they may be, you would not imagine that consumers would pay hardcover prices for them. Yet such is the demand that Star Wars hardcovers always hit the top of the bestseller lists. Some people cannot get enough, I guess.

One format that has proven increasingly useful to novelists over the last ten years is the trade paperback. Once the domain of nonfiction, trade paperbacks have become, probably for reasons of price, the format of choice in many categories. Literary fiction has always done well in this format, especially with young upscale buyers (hence the term *yuppie-backs*).

The surprise is that many types of commercial and genre fiction are also beginning to sell well in trade paperback. With cover prices up sharply, and unlikely to come down anytime soon, it is probable that trade paper will grow increasingly important as a format for creating excitement over new authors.

So, which is the logical route for you? In answering this question, you will need to know your audience and be objective about the quality of your writing. If you have written a light, cozy mystery novel that is similar to others on the market, you may want to choose original paper as your format. Consumers may resist paying hardcover prices for your novel, and reviewers may be unkind because your story type is familiar. Why tempt fate?

On the other hand, perhaps you are an established author who is ready for a break-out. If you have been publishing in paperback, the time may be ripe for an aggressive move into hardcover. Consult your agent.

One final thought: today most large publishers do both hardcover and softcover novels. I would not let that alone dictate my choice of publishers, but there is one advantage to having both editions done by a hard/soft house. Paperback royalties, which used to be split fifty-fifty with hardcover-only houses, are paid through 100 percent to the author under the terms of a hard/soft contract.

Sounds like a good deal to me.

WHEN TO GO FULL-TIME

It is a rare novelist who does not dream about writing fiction full-time. Fantasies of a book-lined study, smoking jackets, a well-worn Remington typewriter, and afternoons spent in contemplative leisure may not exactly match your desires, but I will bet that you harbor your own version of the dream life.

So powerful is the allure of the writing life that many authors rush into it, particularly those with the means to do so. I am astonished at how often doctors quit hospitals, CEOs cash in stock options, and middle managers take early retirement in order to pursue the illusion of a stress-free life as a writer.

For folks with the means, this self-indulgence is not harmful; that is, not until the money runs out. For most others, though, going full-time too soon is a mistake that may have drastic consequences. Regular financial crunches, frustration, and scraping the barrel between advances can be a soul-destroying.

Perhaps the worst consequence of turning full-time too soon is the cynicism that creeps into the outlook of writers who undergo repeated financial crises. While joy may not vanish from the creative process, the business half can become an unendurable misery. That, I think, is a shame.

Cynicism about the business is avoidable if you plan to go full-time only when royalties are finally able to support you. Notice that I use the word *royalties*, not *advances* or *earnings*. There is a reason for that. It bears discussion.

Many authors make the jump to full-time status during the first year in which it seems that their gross revenues will support them. They wishfully imagine that their advances and first sub-rights sales will continue at their current levels or better. Perhaps their advances will grow steadily; perhaps the stock market will always go up, too. It may, but historically we know that the stock market at times gets ahead of itself and goes down or maybe even crashes, causing panic.

So it can be with advances. The reason is that advances are, underneath it all, an estimate of eventual royalties. Advances may outstrip royalty earnings for a time, but not forever. If an author's advances have been unrealistically generous, eventually that author will face a day of reckoning. In the nineties that day tends to come sooner rather than later.

When the reckoning comes, the result can be a rude and painful shock. Authors who imagined that they were secure suddenly find themselves demoted or even fired without the possibility of collecting unemployment insurance. It is panic time. There are bills to be paid, the mortgage is due, the kids need braces. Suddenly family finances are stretched beyond the breaking point.

Desperation sets in. The closet is emptied again. A sale—any sale—is urgently required, not only for the money but to bolster the shaken self-image of the full-time author. A lot is at stake, and going back to one's previous job is unthinkable. Writers in this situation may fall into the work-for-hire trap (see Chapter 15). They may unwisely change agents. They will certainly feel hurt, abandoned, disillusioned, or worse.

If I sound like the Ghost of Christmas Future, it is for a reason; I have seen this happen to too many authors. Avoid their mistakes. Think carefully about when to make the big move.

My recommendation is this: when royalty earnings—remember, I mean royalties from actual book sales to actual customers—equal your annual minimum income requirement for *two years* running, then it is safe to think about going full-time. Leave out movie sales, book-club advances, translation sales, and audiocassette advances. Consider those one-time, unreliable income. Over time, sub-rights revenues will grow more regular, but that is not necessarily the case early in one's career.

Here is another consideration: *the five-book threshold*. That is, once you have five books published and on bookstore shelves, all in print, all reordering, then it is probably safe to assume that you have found an audience and everything is going well.

I am sure that the common sense of this yardstick is obvious. Since it can take up to a year for the final performance of one's first novel to be tabulated, most authors arrive at that point with their second novels already out (or in the pipeline), with possibly a third novel under contract. Three books do not make a career. Three books are the minimum necessary for a publisher to determine if an author is a success.

Five books, though . . . that is another matter. If one reaches the five-book threshold, it is probably because things are going well. Shipments of new novels are heading up; reorders of old novels are holding steady. This author is probably in business.

When counting to five, go back to square one when you change publishers or genres. Why? When switching genres, you are probably starting over in a new section of the bookstores. Former fans will not necessarily follow you all that distance.

When you switch publishers, it is likely that your previous novels will go out of print and vanish from shelves. Not only is your royalty income then damaged, your ability to grow an audience is also impaired. The problem may not be as acute for authors whose work

Breaking In Checklist

1. The next novel I will market is:

2. This novel is:
   - ☐ a stand-alone
   - ☐ part of a series

3. It is in the form of:
   - ☐ a partial
   - ☐ a complete manuscript

4. The category this novel belongs in is:
   - ☐ romance
   - ☐ mystery/suspense
   - ☐ science fiction/fantasy
   - ☐ horror
   - ☐ frontier/western
   - ☐ gay/lesbian
   - ☐ mainstream
   - ☐ literary fiction

5. My closest competitors are these authors:

6. I will first approach:
   - ☐ agents
   - ☐ publishers

7. I would like to shoot for:
   - ☐ a one-book contract
   - ☐ a multiple-book deal

8. The best format for my novel is:
   - ☐ hardcover
   - ☐ original paperback
   - ☐ trade paperback

9. The logical next novel for me to work on is:

10. I am planning to go full-time when:
    - ☐ my royalties have exceeded my income goals for two years
    - ☐ I have passed the five-book threshold
    - ☐ other:

is reprinted in paperback, particularly if there is a separate paperback house keeping the backlist available. Hardcovers go out of print anyway. Continuity is the key.

Now, I am not a fool: I do not imagine that anyone is actually going to follow my advice about when to go full-time. The decision tends to be emotional. It is tied up with ego, self-image, stress at work, long-time dreams, envy of others, and other factors.

If you are considering turning full-time, however, I hope you will think carefully about your timing. The number-one mistake I have seen authors make over the years is going full-time too soon.

8
CHAPTER

A Tour of the Genres

GET YOUR TICKETS HERE

FOR AUTHORS WHO ARE UNCLEAR ABOUT WHERE THEIR FICTION belongs on the publishing map, it may be useful to get an eagle-eye view of the landscape. Authors who are sure of their category position might like to measure their genre knowledge.

Welcome to your walking tour. The genres are everchanging, and for that reason I will not attempt to point out every current microtrend. Rather, I will be offering a long-term perspective, a historian's approach. We will be looking at megatrends.

No doubt you already have your own perspective on your category of choice, and your own ideas about where your genre should be today. That is good. Authors without opinions, who merely chase microtrends, are unlikely to make a strong mark in their field. Indeed, most subcategories began because a single author invented a new kind of story, or at least a new twist on an old formula. Being an innovator can be lonely at first, but authors with strong convictions and original ideas can eventually find themselves sailing at the head of a fleet of imitators.

Readers want up-to-date-feeling novels, stories to which they can relate. At the same time, however, the fundamental elements of many genre stories have not changed much over the years.

ROMANCE ROUND-UP

Once upon a time, the romance business was simple. There were three types of stories, several of which are still around today:

1. Regency romance is a genre that harks back to the genteel novel-of-manners *Pride and Prejudice* by Jane Austen. The field was (and still is) dominated by a twentieth-century author, the late Georgette Heyer. Accomplished as her many imitators may be, they are still runners-up. Today the Regency category survives, though in a severely weakened condition.

2. Gothic novels, and their cousins romantic suspense novels, were once another stable category. Harking back to the dark, threatening heroes created by the Brontë sisters, they presented a story in which a vulnerable heroine falls under the spell of a man who, at first, appears to be a threat (usually on several levels). A surprise revelation at the climax inevitably leads to a happy ending. Sadly, the ending for gothics and romantic suspense novels as a category is not as pleasant. Despite recent attempts to revive them, both are virtually dead.

3. Finally, there were Harlequins, short contemporary tales of love found, or lost and found. Canadian-based Harlequin had this field virtually to itself, and is still a major player.

That was then.

Today, the romance field is a booming business (nearly $1 billion a year), ruthlessly fought over by every major commercial publisher. In their quests for market share the houses have tried and succeeded with a variety of strategies. One of the most significant trends has been the explosion of imprints.

As of this writing, here are some of the imprints tempting readers on bookstore shelves: Denise Little Presents, Desire, Dreamspun, Fanfare, Heartfire, Homespun, Intrigue, Love Spell, Lovegrams, Loveswept, Monogram, Shadows, Special Editions, To Love Again, Topaz, Treasure, and Wildflower.

Some of these imprints cover a variety of story types, others are narrowly focused on a particular subcategory. And what subcategories! Current romance novel types include American, Native

American, western, historical, contemporary, time travel, reincarnation, futuristic, fantasy, paranormal, and vampire.

Vampire? How can one possibly keep track of all the different romance incarnations? Amazingly, romance readers and retailers do, and have strong opinions about what works and what does not. Writers also need to stay abreast of the trends. However, trend-chasing is not a surefire path to success.

Many editors in the field say that they do not publish different types of romance simply to fill subcategory slots. They maintain that for them quality of writing is the most important factor. While "quality" is not a word one always associates with romance writing, the underlying point is well taken. Readers are brand-loyal, meaning they repeat with favorite authors because those authors consistently deliver satisfying stories.

The moral, then, is that it pays handsomely to give readers what they want: romantic tension and plenty of it. Having said that, let us look at some of the field's megatrends.

Romances long ago lost their virginity. Indeed, that was a key innovation of the great historical romance writers of the seventies: Rosemary Rogers, Kathleen Woodiwiss, Johanna Lindsey, and others. Sex—sometimes with serial partners—reflected reality in that liberated decade. That rape was a key means of seduction in Woodiwiss-style "bodice-rippers" is hard to explain, but nevertheless, sex is now a fixture in romance novels.

In fact, in the nineties romances have moved a step beyond premarital sex: they are pregnant. Or at least their heroines can be, and their men are actually happy about it. Bizarre plot devices may be needed to maintain conflict with this premise, but the point is that once again romances reflect both the realities (the Baby Boom echo) and the desires (men who care enough to do prenatal class) of contemporary women.

Today's more unusual twists on the romance formula may also reflect cultural changes. Take the Native American historicals: the fantasy of capture and seduction is eternal, but the Native American lover is an innovation. Has multicultural awareness made Native Americans sexy? Obviously so, since it is likely that twenty years ago this formula would not have worked.

Reincarnation romances like *Whispers in Time* by Becky Lee Weyrich or paranormal romances like *Emily's Ghost* by Antoinette Stockenberg may reflect a contemporary concern with the mystical, a concern showing up in other publishing sectors, too.

What about that other primary function of romances, providing a means of escape? The mental getaway is as much a part of romances today as it ever was, but current novels offer fresh itineraries. Consider time-travel romances like *Outlander* by Diana Gabaldon, fantasy romances like *The Prince and the Barbarian* by Betina Krahn, or futuristic romances by Kathleen Morgan. Unusual they may be, but they are escapes nevertheless.

One thing that has not changed in the nineties is the sales power of romances, or the outlets in which they are purchased by readers. According to the Book Industry Study Group, romances account for 48.6 percent of all mass-market sales. Think about that: roughly one of every two paperbacks sold is a romance!

You would think that romances would be a booming business for independent bookstores, but in fact only a tiny 4.2 percent of romances are sold through independents. Even chains have only 15.7 percent of the market. Most romances are sold through outlets serviced by so-called IDs, that is, distributors who mostly slot magazines into places like supermarkets, drugstores, and variety stores. Unlike bookstores, in ID-serviced outlets it is the IDs themselves that decide which books will go in the racks.

Obviously, the process of making a name as a romance writer is very different from the process in other categories. While it is true that independents and chain stores count more heavily in bestseller tabulations, the high proportion of sales made through ID accounts probably indicates that story content and cover art are the most important elements in establishing an audience.

Can romance authors break out into wider mass-market success? They can and regularly do. Even authors of short contemporaries (confusingly called *category romances* in industry slang) can move up to best-sellerdom. Janet Dailey and Nora Roberts are two big names that started out in the category racks.

To sum up, it is important for romance authors to be aware of imprint requirements; marketing manuscripts can be difficult otherwise. Still, slavish imitation may not lead to big success. For that, an author must be a market leader, an innovator.

And how does one do that? By finding a new romance formula that reflects contemporary social conditions or taps into modern women's fantasies, while at the same time giving priority to the three romance elements that are eternal: (1) man, (2) woman, (3) happy ending.

SCIENCE FICTION/FANTASY: INVASION OF THE MEDIA TIE-INS

Like the romance field in the last decade, science fiction (SF) and fantasy have undergone major category fragmentation. Some distinct story types to be found on the shelves nowadays include "hard" SF, military SF, space opera, cyberpunk, high fantasy, dark fantasy, urban fantasy (called *elfpunk* by some), alternate history, and something termed *steampunk*.

Despite the proliferation of narrow subcategories (or in part because of it), SF and fantasy are big businesses. Together with horror, these categories account for roughly 11 percent of all paperback sales. That is a pretty big slice of a pretty big pie.

SF/fantasy is almost the opposite of romances with regard to the outlets in which it sells. While supermarkets, drugstores, newsstands, and variety stores sell half of all romance novels, they sell a mere 20 percent of all science fiction, according to studies by Gallup. A whopping 71 percent of SF/fantasy is sold in bookstores, and specialty stores have a noticeable share of that.

On top of that, the SF/fantasy field is highly organized and has powerful lines of communication open among writers, stores, and readers. Magazines like *Locus* and *Science Fiction Chronicle* devote themselves exclusively to trade news and reviews. And that is to say nothing of news segments on the Sci Fi Channel, columns and letters in magazines like *Isaac Asimov's Science Fiction Magazine*, and the hundreds of lively "fanzines" published by fans around the world. Conventions abound; indeed, fans and pros mingle at them almost every weekend. Pros and publishers alike covet sales-boosting Hugo Awards, which are awarded by fans.

Then there is the World Wide Web. Not surprisingly, the computer-literate authors of this field have embraced the Internet. The volume of their e-mail is staggering. The members-only Science Fiction Writers of America (SFWA) special interest area on GEnie is a roiling hotbed of information exchange, discussion, debate, rant, and lawsuit-inducing "flame wars." Novices enter this electronic agora at their own risk. For readers, many authors offer their own Web pages.

The good side of all this organization is that individual authors can connect with fans and potential fans far more easily in the SF/fantasy area than in nearly any other. Convention appearances, bookstore signings, and other sorts of self-promotion are easy to arrange. Web sites cost little to establish (as publishers, too, have discovered). The field also has the healthiest short story market anywhere on the literary scene.

With such strong sales and all that support, SF/fantasy should be the darling of publishing, but amazingly it is not. SF/fantasy editors tell me that when pitching new projects at editorial meetings they are still, at times, stared at as if they are mutant alien freaks. It is certainly true that SF/fantasy authors are not, as a group, allocated advertising and promotion budgets commensurate with their revenues.

In the wider world, SF/fantasy "don't get no respect," either. Major newspapers and magazines that regularly review, say, mystery novels completely ignore SF/fantasy. Academics sneer at it, despite its roots in the work of Mary Shelley and H. G. Wells, and the existence of a devoted organization called IAFA (International Association for the Fantastic in the Arts).

Media coverage of the field is also condescending. At the biggest annual convention, Worldcon, outside reporters can usually be counted on to write about costumed fans in tones of snide amusement. To be sure, these wounds are partially self-inflicted. For some reason, fans and pros alike enjoy their outcast image. Everything from fandom's special music, *filking*, to its special attitude and argot, *smoffing*, seems designed to exclude outsiders and foster among insiders a cozy sense of otherness.

Professional SF/fantasy writers can also be prone to elitism. In SFWA, in-fighting is common. Currently, the group is debating a proposal that would make membership requirements more exclusive. What is going on? Why do these pros seem to relish fighting each other more than fighting publishers?

I do not know, but they had better wake up because opportunities for new single-author, brand-name positions are being diminished by one of the most striking developments in publishing today: the invasion of the media and game tie-in products.

Today a significant portion of SF/fantasy lists is devoted to books connected to SF/fantasy movies, TV shows, role-playing games, comic-book characters, and computer games. It is not hard to see why. Media-related properties bring an instant audience. Their cost of marketing is relatively low, making them attractive even where absolute unit sales may be no better than those of individual authors. It is an alarming trend.

What is most amazing is that authors are lining up to write these tie-ins. Never mind that many of them are work-for-hire rip-offs with low royalties attached. Those few series that have made their writers serious money, even at low royalty rates, are tempting others—especially hungry newcomers.

To be fair, some writers want to write Star Trek and X-Files novels because they love the shows. Many authors also legitimately need the money. However, too many authors allow themselves to be seduced for more insidious reasons: the ego boost, easy validation, automatic status, less creative work to do.

The truth is that while certain work-for-hire assignments can pay handsomely—indeed, I have a few clients who earn six-figure incomes from such work—most of them do not repay authors more than their own fiction would. Authors who do work-for-hire for ego satisfaction alone are selling their own stores and opening franchises for the large media giants. Ultimately, they are making others rich at their own expense.

If I sound a little strident on this subject, it is for a good reason. Publishing is one of the few entertainment sectors in which a lone individual can turn himself or herself into a brand name. By embracing tie-ins, book publishers are giving away that birthright. They are trading the power of authorship for easy profits. As a business we are coming to depend on other media for our product, and that is terribly shortsighted.

Fortunately, there is hope that this may be a temporary trend. Not all media properties are well suited to novelization. Many tie-ins have bombed. In addition, to sustain book sales over time there must be a level of fan devotion to the movie, show, game, or whatever that is quite extraordinary. Publishers may be growing more discerning about what they license.

I hope so, anyway. Now let us examine some genre megatrends.

There is something of a dichotomy between science fiction and fantasy. Science fiction began, in its Golden Age, as a literature of rationality, optimism, and wonder. While some novels of the fifties and sixties forecast a dark and gloomy dystopian future, even these were concerned with change, science, and what was to come. SF looks forward, presupposing progress.

Fantasy, in contrast, is a literature of escape, retreat, and return to myth and mysticism. It is an expression of our discontent with the technological world and the future we are heading toward. Critics decry fantasy literature's turn from rationality, and are alarmed by its embrace of authoritarian social systems.

It is odd, to be sure, that our scientists, inventors, engineers, and programmers seem to be the group of readers most willing to be swept into magical worlds whose ethos is so unlike ours. Still, humans need comfort and order. Part of us is not rational. We want to believe in magic. We long for dreams to come true. Call it cowardly or pre-Oedipal, but fantasy literature undeniably taps into a primary facet of human nature.

What does that mean for writers? It strikes me that during economic booms, when we feel good about ourselves, we are more willing to look forward, to think. During times of recession, when we feel discouraged about the future, we long to escape.

That is simplistic, I know, but I have noticed upsurges in fantasy sales during periods of anxiety, and the nineties certainly qualifies as one of those. Indeed, fantasy has been on a roll since the Gulf War recession of 1990–91. And not just any sort of fantasy: most folks want only the most traditional and escapist "high" or "epic" fantasy, the type that finds its roots in the work of J. R. R. Tolkien. While there is an audience for urban fantasy, in which magic bursts into our present-day world, it is not nearly as popular as the traditional stuff.

Will there be a return to science fiction, a new Golden Age? I expect that there will someday. Human beings, and especially

Americans, are by nature optimistic. In addition, we hunger to know the future. Of all genres only SF can give us a look ahead. But do not expect a major swing toward SF until this decade's employment picture improves and consumer confidence returns. Until then a majority of readers will escape into the familiar comfort of fantasy.

HORROR: DEAD OR JUST RESTING?

In the eighties, the corpse of horror fiction rose from the grave and seemed to take over book publishing. Driven by the success of authors like Stephen King, Anne Rice, Dean Koontz, Peter Straub, and Clive Barker, it seemed invincible, a supergenre.

Horror had everything going for it, not least of which were literary roots that stretched back nearly two hundred years to novels like Ann Radcliffe's *The Mysteries of Udolpho* (1794) and Matthew Gregory Lewis's *The Monk* (1796). Later work by Mary Shelley, Edgar Allan Poe, Ambrose Bierce, H. P. Lovecraft, and others only added to this dark literature's pedigree.

The genre seemed healthy, too. A writers' organization, the Horror Writers of America, was formed and began giving out its Stoker Awards. Semiprofessional magazines and small press publishers thrived. Best of all, book sales boomed. It seemed that any black cover with a skeleton on it would sell like crazy.

In the end, many authors complained that it was the very tendency of publishers to overdo a good thing that slew the monster. In the early nineties, horror crashed. Sales plunged. Lists were slashed. Many publishers raced away as if fleeing a graveyard. Apologists claimed that publishers had simply oversupplied the stuff, putting inferior product into print just to fill slots. No wonder readers were disenchanted. It was a cyclical downturn, they said. Normal. The genre would soon bounce back.

Well, we are still waiting. What happened? Was horror never a true genre? Was horror in the eighties merely a best-seller-driven fad? To answer that question, let us dissect the corpse.

Horror in the eighties was really two bodies of work: the serious and the popular. The popular stuff was paperback horror that sold primarily to teenagers, who would sometimes buy novels primarily because the covers were cool-looking, as with Rick Hautala's otherwise-worthwhile *Night Stone*, which had the industry's first holo-gram on it.

At the same time, an older category of reader with a more dis-cerning taste for the horrific was seeking out new work, and finding it in the semiprozines (non-commercial magazines aimed at serious fans) and in book lines like Dell's Abyss. An even smaller, strong-stomached audience also began to appreciate a group of writers that brought to horror a new realism, plus a cutting-edge extremism and a fascination with violence. This bloody fiction has earned the nickname "splatterpunk."

Those readers and writers are still around, but they are struggling with little support from publishers, who burned themselves selling to a fickle readership. The core audience keeps the faith, but their numbers are small and their prospects somewhat dim. If a revival comes, it may well be because a new wave of best-sellers excites fresh interest from publishers and readers.

Indeed, throughout the twentieth-century the field has primarily been best-seller-driven. In the period between the world wars, a boom in oriental and occult terror was led by the British authors Sax Rohmer (creator of Dr. Fu-Manchu) and Dennis Wheatley. In the post-war atomic era, Shirley Jackson led a movement toward realis-tic horror with strong psychological elements, a movement that included Robert Bloch's seminal novel *Psycho* and the fiction of Richard Matheson. William Peter Blatty's 1971 novel *The Exorcist* spawned a host of imitations that lingered for a decade.

Examining the sales patterns of horror in the eighties, one finds that much of the horror that was popular then was also poured from the molds of a few best-sellers. Stephen King, for example, led a boom in small-town horror. John Saul and V. C. Andrews started a category that insiders called "spooky kid novels." The sympathetic vampires of Chelsea Quinn Yarbro and Anne Rice were also the beginning of a long-term trend.

Speaking of that, vampire fiction is the one remnant that contin-ues to thrive today as a genuine subcategory. Readers cannot seem to get enough of it. Anne Rice may be the queen, but others can still break through. Kim Newman's *Anno Dracula* and Roderick Anscombe's *The Secret Diaries of Laszlo, Count Dracula* (a nonsupernatural treatment by a doctor who has worked with the criminally insane) are both successful recent entries. The vampire craze will probably intensify with the approach of the hundredth anniversary of Bram Stoker's *Dracula* in 1997.

For new authors seeking to enter the horror arena, it is wise to expect an icy reception. Still, strong sales for a few young authors like Poppy Z. Brite, Kathy Koja, and Alan Rodgers are encouraging.

However, publishers will not soon be rolling out the bandwagons again. That is too bad. The graveyard is a lonely place to be.

WESTERNS: NEW FACES ON THE FRONTIER

Not too long ago, the traditional western shoot-em-up was gunned down in the publishing business back east, and was declared dead.

Although certain long-running series like Lone Star, Gunsmith, and Longarm have continued, the last few years have been a tough time for series in the traditional mold. It is the sunset of a proud heritage that gave us novels by Luke Short, Les Savage, Jr., Max Brand, and the grandmaster of them all, Louis L'Amour. It also closed a writing school that had nurtured such authors as John Jakes, Marvin H. Albert, and Elmore Leonard.

Now, though, a new day is dawning for the western. Fresh blood and original approaches have brought new life to this genre. For one thing, the historical periods covered under the umbrella term "western" have expanded. The mountain man era, the French and Indian War years, the Civil War period, and the declining days of the territories are all being examined in new American works of fiction.

Revisionist approaches to the role of Native Americans, African Americans, Hispanics, and women have also enlivened the western scene. Don Coldsmith's twenty-book Spanish Bit Saga is one such innovation. Elizabeth Fackler's *Blood Kin* recently gave us an eye-opening look at women in the West.

The cover look of westerns is also changing. Instead of action scenes with blazing sixguns, one is today more likely to find on a western cover a daguerreotype photo, a Frederic Remington or Charles Russell-style painting or a saga-look collage.

Even that grizzled old authors' organization Western Writers of America has some new company: Women Writing the West. The times they are a'changin', and authors who hope to prosper writing American historical fiction would be wise to change with them.

What unites all the new western forms is a concern with a realistic depiction of the times. Goodbye to black hats and stereotypical sheriffs: today's western is built of accurate detail, true events, and characters whose experience is taken from history.

To be truthful, that same accuracy was the secret of Louis L'Amour's success.

MYSTERY MEGATRENDS

No fiction category has been more successful in western culture than the mystery. In 1986 a Gallup survey found that 62 percent of all adults had read a mystery book. The percentage was even higher among the college educated (74 percent), and among women (69 percent).

Popular belief holds that mysteries sell mostly to an older segment of the population. That is not true. While 54 percent of people aged 50 and older had read a mystery, according to the Gallup survey, that figure rose to 65 percent for the 35–49 age bracket, to 68 percent for adults 25–34 years old, and to a truly astonishing 70 percent for people in the 18–24 age group. Mysteries are reaching a wider cross section of the population all the time.

What accounts for the broad popularity of mysteries? Certainly the form has had plenty of time to refine itself. Many trace the mystery to Edgar Allan Poe's three Dupin stories of the 1840s; in fact, the form may go as far back as William Godwin's *Caleb Williams* in 1794. Regardless of its birthdate, the mystery form has clearly been blessed with a family of great storytellers: Wilkie Collins, Arthur Conan Doyle, G. K. Chesterton, Agatha Christie, Dorothy L. Sayers, Margery Allingham, Ngaio Marsh, Josephine Tey, Ellery Queen, Dashiell Hammett, Raymond Chandler, Ross Macdonald, John D. MacDonald . . . the closer we draw to our own decade, the longer the list grows.

On top of that, the two best-selling American authors of the twentieth century (measured according to cumulative lifetime sales) were mystery writers, Mickey Spillane and Erle Stanley Gardner. With powerhouse sales like theirs at the top of the field, it is perhaps no wonder that mysteries have attracted so many readers.

I believe, though, that there is more to the popularity of mysteries than just great writing. I think that mysteries invoke a common human fear—the fear of the darkness dwelling inside of us— more readily than any other form of fiction.

Mysteries are set in real places and involve ordinary people. To read a mystery is to experience vicariously the sudden violence that can descend upon any of us, anywhere, at any time. Suspense, horror, and science fiction novels can do the same thing, but their plot lines are more exotic, farther removed from our own experience. Mysteries insert violence into the everyday, and then assure us that it can be brought under control. That is a fear—and a hope—to which I think anyone can relate.

Today the mystery field has taken as its domain just about every time, place, and people that one can imagine. From the world of wilderness tours to inner-city lesbian bars, there are mystery novels for all tastes, backgrounds, and interests. Mysteries are also taking us as far back in time as ancient Egypt. Sometimes I wonder if there is any milieu still unused.

In addition to the great variety of content, there is also a broad range of plots and styles in use, everything from pseudo-documentary realism to the cozy English country house puzzle.

If there is one overriding trend in the mystery biz, however, it is the ascendance of women: authors, editors, agents, bookstore owners, police officers, PI's, amateurs—you name it. Men are still in the game, to be sure, but women have won control of the field.

In part this reflects a reality: the readership is mostly female. It is also a correction of a long-time dearth of mysteries by and about women. Nancy Pickard once remarked in *Publishers Weekly* that women who grew up reading Nancy Drew had to jump to Miss Marple as adults. While that was never entirely true (witness P. D. James's Cordelia Gray and Dorothy Gilman's Mrs. Pollifax), the balance for years weighed in favor of male detectives.

Much of the credit for this reversal of status belongs to an organization called Sisters in Crime. Formed in 1985, this group of writers, editors, readers, and booksellers has been extremely active in advancing the cause of women in the field. Its newsletter, biannual lists of members' books, speakers' bureau, specialty bookstore lists, guide to self-promotion, booths at ABA (the annual convention of the American Booksellers Association), ads in *Publishers Weekly*, and so on, have empowered women and left some old-time male authors privately fuming. (They needn't: men can join Sisters in Crime, too.)

It would be a mistake, however, to think that simply being a woman author or writing a woman PI will make it easier to get published. That is not so. Competition has taken care of that. Standing out in today's glutted market takes something more.

Strong regional settings seemed a surefire idea for a couple of minutes, but that moment has passed. Some feel that African American authors are shoo-ins these days, but while the work of Walter Mosley, Blanche Neely, Eleanor Taylor Bland, and Hugh Holton, to name a few, is a welcome correction of a long-standing lack, ethnicity is not an automatic ticket to ride.

Nor does employing a gay detective guarantee publication, despite the success of Joseph Hansen's books. Lesbian protagonists are not a sure thing, either, Sandra Scoppetone's success notwithstanding. Being cozy, comical, culinary, or historical is also not surefire, though each of these approaches has had its year in the sun and retains its subcategory leaders.

So what does work? Ask editors today, and they will tell you they are looking for a "unique voice," by which they seem to mean something fresh and original. But even that may not be enough. Recently I have been marketing the most original mystery manuscript I have ever read. Editors agree with me about it, yet time after time they have turned it down with the remark, "I don't know how to sell this"—meaning it is *too* original!

It makes you want to cry. In spite of all this, my best advice to new authors is to ignore trends and market tips and write the mysteries that they want to read but are finding nowhere on the shelves. Just be sure that those novels have compelling hooks, great prose, captivating characters, vivid settings, and, on top of all that, utterly superb mystery plots!

Oh yes, and be sure that your mystery novel is the start of a series.

Once in the door and on the way, making one's mark does not get much easier. Often it can take five books just to establish an audience for a series and win over bookstores. New authors also get very little in the way of advertising and promotional help from their publishers. It is a tough road.

Fortunately, mystery authors who are willing to push themselves rather than wait for their publishers to do it will find that many stores are wonderfully receptive to such efforts. In the U.S. there are at least sixty highly active independent bookstores specializing in mystery fiction. (Some forty of them have even formed the IMBA, the Independent Mystery Bookstore Association.) The relationship that these stores have with their customers is very special. Favorite authors are "hand sold" to readers, and newsletters and signings are regular features for them.

Indeed, independent bookstores have a higher share of total sales in this category than in any other. Marketing to them with postcards, flyers, bookmarks, and such is one route to try. More useful are in-store signings; since these bring in customers most stores like them. Of course, the distances involved can be prohibitive for many authors, but dedicated authors are beginning to band together to share costs for group signing tours.

For authors of limited means there are other options. Convention appearances are one. While not as plentiful as in the science fiction field, there are several big mystery conventions every year (BoucherCon, Malice Domestic, and Left Coast Crime being three of the biggest). In addition, there are perhaps a dozen regionals.

The Internet is another option. The electronic bulletin board DorothyL is one of the principal meeting places for fans and authors. There are scores of printed newsletters, too, an additional opportunity. Some authors have also made a small splash by writing for the field's many magazines and semiprozines. *Mystery Scene*, for one, welcomes articles from authors.

Awards should not be discounted, either. Smart authors make sure that their publishers submit their novels for the Edgar, the Shamus, and the Nero Wolfe. (Other awards like the Dilys, the Macavity, the Anthony, and the Agatha are awarded by popular vote.)

Review mailings and publicity can also be handled on the cheap, though it is important to know how to do it properly. (For tips, see Chapter 11.)

Fortunately for cash-strapped authors, mysteries do offer one no-cost way of attracting attention: their titles. There are three basic approaches: cute/comical (e.g., William DeAndrea's TV-industry mystery *Killed in the Ratings*); series-connecting (e.g., Sue Grafton's *A is for Alibi*); and finally, those that intrigue simply because they are mysterious. Some examples:

- *The Concrete Blonde* by Michael Connelly
- *Bootlegger's Daughter* by Margaret Maron
- *The Face of a Stranger* by Anne Perry
- *The Curious Eat Themselves* by John Straley

Whatever one's approach to building a mystery career, authors in this field can be sure of one thing: the mystery category is one of publishing's everlasting and most dynamic sectors. It may be different in ten years, or even in ten months, but it will still be around and going strong.

SUSPENSE: GOODBYE SPIES, HELLO AMERICA

Who would have thought that we would miss the Cold War? That, strangely, is the situation in the world of suspense novels. Since the fall of the Berlin Wall and the collapse of the Communist government in the former Soviet Union, the public no longer feels threatened by traditional evildoers.

The search is on for new categories of global-scale villains, but the hunt is not going terribly well. Persian Gulf dictatorships, South American drug cartels, Japanese business cabals, computer criminals, atomic terrorists, environmental blackmailers . . . all these have been auditioned in recent thrillers, but none of them have caught on as a durable new source of conspiracy. Perhaps readers do not feel personally threatened by them.

So, is it Nazis to the rescue? These reliable suspense villains can still be revived, although as World War II recedes into the past it grows increasingly difficult to turn them into a credible present-day threat. Even a recent best-seller by Allan R. Folsom, *The Day After Tomorrow*, could not make neo-Nazis seem dangerous. Only by bringing Hitler's frozen head into the picture (supposedly to be attached to a healthy new body) was the author able to conjure a conspiracy with a true terror quotient.

Perhaps global suspense will revive; indeed, there are promising signs. U.S. good guys have teamed with overseas counterparts to useful effect in *Gorky Park* by Martin Cruz Smith and other novels. Foreign spies might also find a following here. A recent thriller by American author Steve Hartov, *The Heat of Ramadan*, gave us a compelling Israeli intelligence agent and an equally fascinating Arab assassin who is hunting him.

World War III novels and technothrillers also kept the action going overseas for a while, but those categories are fading. For the most part, American readers are today finding their villains at home. The one arena in which they frequently pop up is the courtroom. No doubt about it, the formula of the moment is the legal thriller. Every lawyer is writing one.

There have always been courtroom novels—consider Erle Stanley Gardner's Perry Mason mysteries—but it was really Scott Turow's *Presumed Innocent* that kicked off the current wave of courtroom suspense in 1987. John Grisham is another big wheel in this area; Richard North Patterson is, also. Is there room at the top for more best-sellers? Perhaps, but the competition is fierce and the market leaders are already in place. New authors will have a hard time making their mark in this crowded subcategory. Sorry.

If it is any consolation, our changing world will always supply new sources of mass terror. The trick is to identify those that produce a gut-level response in the public, and then to make those threats utterly credible. It is not easy to do.

For example, take viruses. In this age of AIDS, the Ebola virus has triggered a widespread panic response. This is good for thriller writers. So far, however, no novelist has been successful at making the virus threat feel real, except perhaps Michael Crichton in *The Andromeda Strain*. Indeed, the most successful virus book has been a nonfiction title, *The Hot Zone*.

Credibility is the problem, too, with several perennial types of villainy one sees in slush-pile novels: small-town corruption, computer hacking, and corporate conspiracy. These are indeed real-life terrors, but few manuscripts really make those threats palpable. Hooks that demonstrate the threat's consequence for ordinary people are often lacking. Personification of the evil conspiracy is oftentimes weak.

Authors who wish to scare the bejeezus out of large numbers of readers will have to master the techniques of making abstract terrors concrete. After that comes the even more difficult business of keeping suspense alive on every page of a novel.

One thing is for sure: despite the difficulties, the payoff for finding a successful new formula will keep authors busy writing suspense novels for many years to come. I look forward to finding out what will terrorize us next.

SHARKS, SERIAL KILLERS, AND OTHER ENDANGERED SPECIES

Every once in a while a trend seems to emerge out of nowhere. For a brief time it captures the attention of the book business, gets written up in *Publishers Weekly* and the *New York Times*, then fades away. Is there any reliable way to predict trends?

Sad to say, trends cannot be forecast; they can only be identified once underway, and by that time it is usually too late. Authors and publishers who are foolish enough to try to capitalize on them at a late stage are starting the race well behind the leaders.

Take serial-killer novels: the massive success of Thomas Harris's *The Silence of the Lambs* set off a wave of novels on the same subject. *Sliver* by Ira Levin, *Mercy* by David L. Lindsey, *Shadow Prey* by John Sandford, and several thrillers by Jonathan Kellerman were a few of those that sold well in the wake of Hannibal Lecter.

And then it was over . . . well, not quite over: serial killer-novels are still being published by the dozens each year, but few of them are selling as well as those published at the height of the boom in 1990–91. To attract attention, new serial killer novels are offering increasingly shocking methods of murder. All for little benefit. The bandwagon has rolled on by.

Here are some other recent trends that are candidates for the history books:

Sequels to Classic Novels. This trend was kicked off by the retail success of Alexandra Ripley's *Scarlett*, a sequel to Margaret Mitchell's

Gone with the Wind. Others following on the heels of that best-seller were Susan Hill's *Mrs. de Winter*, a sequel to Daphne Du Maurier's timeless *Rebecca*, and two separate sequels to Jane Austen's *Pride and Prejudice*. Since then dozens of sequels have been done, few with any big success.

Generation X Novels. These began, appropriately enough, with a novel called *Generation X* by Douglas Coupland, author also of *Shampoo Planet*. If the Gen-X novels bear a faint resemblance to such eighties stories of dissolute youth as *Bright Lights, Big City* and *Less Than Zero* or to the even older rebel classic *Catcher in the Rye*, it should not be surprising. Every generation feels itself alienated from the generation gone before, and thinks it is the first to feel that way. Authors who can capture that fleeting moment of tragic ennui, empty rage, and passionless longing will, with luck, be able to catch the once-a-decade wave—maybe.

Transgressive Fiction. The fiction of sexual frontiers and extreme life-styles is often associated with authors like the Marquis de Sade, William Burroughs, Charles Bukowski, and Henry Miller, but their work is somewhat tame compared to the harrowing stuff of Jeff Noon, Dennis Cooper, Kathy Acker, Will Self, Jack Womack, and Steve Weiner. Bret Easton Ellis's *American Psycho* is often touted as the top of the category, but for a more authentic walk on the wild side try Noon's *Vurt*, Cooper's *Try*, or Weiner's *Museum of Love*, a novel deemed so dangerous that, in spite of its good reviews, no publisher was willing to do a paperback reprint of the Overlook Press edition. With content so upsetting, it is hard to see how this trend can sustain itself for long.

Pseudomysticism. This trend is led by the best-seller *The Celestine Prophecy*, but is perhaps better represented by Marlo Morgan's *Mutant Message Down Under* and Frederick Lenz's *Surfing the Himalayas*. Spiritual quest and discovery of the wisdom of the ancients (or the healing powers of primitive cultures) are the subjects of this fiction. Reflective of our *fin de siècle* times, this trend will probably last only a few more years.

Perhaps you have spotted some trends, too. If you have, congratulations. You have observed a rare species on its way to extinction.

CHRISTIAN FICTION

From as long ago as the appearance of Bunyan's *The Pilgrim's Progress* and Dante's *The Divine Comedy*, we have been fascinated with humankind's struggle for faith and quest for spiritual truth.

The fiction of spirituality and faith has a strong legacy in our own century, most notably in the work of the Oxford literary club called the Inklings, whose members included C. S. Lewis, Charles Williams, and J. R. R. Tolkien. Their use of fantasy to portray the spiritual journey is mirrored in the work of such contemporary authors as Stephen Lawhead (*The Endless Knot*) and Calvin Miller (*Guardians of the Singreale*).

Another twentieth-century strand of Christian fiction is the historical novel. Henryk Sienkiewicz's *Quo Vadis*, Taylor Caldwell's *I, Judas*, and Lloyd Douglas's *The Robe* are but a few of the popular works in this rich tradition. Contemporary examples of this approach abound: the Shiloh Legacy series by Bodie Thoene, the Emerald Ballad series of B. J. Hoff, Donna Fletcher's *Glastonbury*, and Robert Wise's *The Fall of Jerusalem*.

Familiar genre forms have also been combined with Christian concerns. Christian mysteries, thrillers, and westerns can all be found. Christian romances have moved far beyond the inspirational tone of Grace Livingston Hill and Catherine Marshall's *Christy*. Today, authors like Janette Oke (*Heart of the Wilderness*, *Too Long a Stranger*) are bringing the tone of Christian romances more into line with current tastes.

Joseph Girzone's *Joshua* novels and the enormously popular Christian thrillers of Frank Peretti have also helped to shatter the outdated images of sentimental moralism and insipid writing that have limited Christian fiction. That is not to say that Christian fiction has gone mainstream. In spite of efforts by publishers to characterize this work as "spiritual fiction" rather than as "inspirational fiction," it is still mainly shelved in religion sections in bookstores (where happily it thrives).

Given the appeal of the faith journey for outstanding writers such as Dorothy Sayers, Madeleine L'Engle, and Mormon author Orson Scott Card, there is no doubt that the category will continue to grow. For now publishers Crossway, Bethany House, Thomas

Nelson, Macmillan, and Harper San Francisco have the field mostly to themselves, but that will probably change over time, too.

One thing that will not change is readers' fascination with faith, grace, spirituality, conversion, and the struggle to come to terms with Christian values. As subjects for fiction, those will doubtless be with us for several millenia more.

MAINSTREAM: YOUR OWN GENRE

As I suggested in Strategy Session I, the term *mainstream* is somewhat misleading. There is, *per se*, no such thing as a mainstream novel. Customers browsing in bookstores do not think to themselves, "Gee, I feel like a good mainstream reading experience." Rather, they seek out favorite authors, or at least stories of a type that they want to read.

For that reason, I maintain that so-called mainstream authors are not tapping into a preexisting readership, but must grow, one reader at a time, their individual audiences. They must make their own genres.

Doing this is as easy—and as difficult—as writing a novel that is distinctive from all others, yet that captures the common experience of many. A few unique voices that I admire are Irwin Shaw, Pat Conroy, John Updike, Anne Tyler, Jonathan Carroll . . . I could list dozens. I am sure that you could, too.

To be sure, some authors are chameleons. They can leap between periods, change styles, and borrow from the genres with ease. Joyce Carol Oates is one example. These authors are admirable, but somehow their *oeuvres* do not satisfy me as deeply as those of authors who stick to a single vision, a personal outlook. F. Scott Fitzgerald, Erskine Caldwell, even P. G. Wodehouse . . . I am drawn to them by the unity of their work.

That is not to say that authors should imitate themselves. That would be creative suicide. I do think, though, that there is something to be said for sustaining one's focus on a particular corner of the world, exploring one's given outlook and gifts.

One of the century's best-sellers, underappreciated today, was Nevil Shute. A British aeronautical engineer, his fiction was always informed by his flying and military experience, leading him to tales

as diverse as his religious allegory *Round the Bend* and his great apoc-
alyptic novel *On the Beach*. He did not try to be a novelist he was not.
He was true to himself. That he was also so popular was not, I suspect, an acccident.

Being truthful, recording and reflecting upon the world as one
sees it: that, to me, is the ultimate privilege of the novelist. Perhaps
it is also a responsibility. We readers, I think, are in turn obligated
to judge according to a high standard. Whether an author is a mainstream voice or a genre storyteller, it is our task to demand that
authors give us their best. If we settle for what is easy and common,
what is only passingly entertaining, we are surrendering control of
our dreams.

Ultimately, we may also be diminishing our freedom.

9

CHAPTER

Crossover Novels

PUSHING THE ENVELOPE

MANY COMMERCIAL NOVELISTS, ESPECIALLY WRITERS OF genre fiction, feel that they are stuck in a ghetto. The snobs at the top of the publishing ladder, they have noticed, seem to hate commercial fiction. They rigidly categorize, rake in genre profits, then squander all of their advertising budgets on flash-in-the-pan literary writers and a handful of proven best-sellers.

How is a hard-working commercial novelist supposed to get ahead? One route that many authors are traveling, both for creative and practical reasons, is that of writing crossover novels; that is, novels that borrow devices from several genres.

On paper it seems like a good idea. Let us say that you write a noir tale about a detective who is hired by Satan to trace a man who has sold his soul. Let us also say the detective lost his memory in World War II—and gradually comes to realize that the missing man is someone important to him.

Sounds hot, yes? Not only will this please the mystery audience, it may also be appealing to horror and occult fans, not to mention people who simply like a good suspense tale. Surely this is a way out of the ghetto. How can you lose, in fact, since your audience has just doubled (or more) in size—right?

Unfortunately, while that sounds good in theory, it is not so in fact. Crossover novels can be wonderful; indeed, it would be impossible to tell some stories without going the crossover route. But crossovers are also risky. Authors who undertake them are gambling with their careers. Is the gamble worth it?

To help answer that question, let us take a look at the tricky dynamics of crossover publishing.

THE PROBLEM WITH CROSSOVERS

The first thing to realize is that publishers do not believe that combining genre elements—setting a mystery in a fantasy realm, say—will automatically capture two markets. Rather, they suspect that the only audience such a novel will win is the small overlap in the readerships between those two categories.

In other words, it is not a question of one plus one; it is a matter of losing most of two whole groups of readers with a novel that does not entirely satisfy either. Does this seem like faulty reasoning? Does it even seem, perhaps, a bit shortsighted?

Lots of readers cross genre lines, do they not? I do, and I will bet that you do, too. And so do your friends. In fact, is it not true that most readers dip into a variety of categories? It may seem that way, but the truth is otherwise. Most readers are category-loyal. Publishers' beliefs are based on hard experience.

So what about Dean Koontz? Michael Crichton? Cathy Cash-Spellman? Stephen King? Phyllis Whitney? Ira Levin? Robert R. McCammon? Lori Herter? (I have named just a few.) Crossing genre boundaries does not seem to have hurt *them*. Surely publishers are wrong?

I wish I could say that they are, but the evidence is to the contrary. As for best-selling authors who have written crossovers, one has to take a detailed look at their careers: how many of them *established* themselves via crossovers? Very few. A close look at their sales would probably show, too, that their crossovers did little to advance them—and may even have hurt.

There are exceptions, of course. Dean Koontz is one author who has fought to keep limiting category designations off his novels. His success is obvious, but it has been a long and tough battle, as he will quickly tell you.

Certainly editors approach crossover projects with caution. One

I called while preparing this chapter told me about a big-name author whose insistence on writing crossover books effectively wrecked her career. Stretch genre limits, but do not try to straddle two categories, this editor cautioned.

What about the argument that readers cross genre lines so authors might as well, too? Let us face facts: authors and their friends are not a relatively large, or even a very accurate, sample of the general reading public. Most people buy what they like and only what they like. Crossovers go against the flow.

Do not get me wrong: average readers are not intractable; they are just not eager for something new. To get them to sample something different one has to trick them, or "sell" them, if you prefer.

Another editor I talked to does that with covers that lead readers to expect that the novel they are buying is of a sort that they already like. Sometimes it works, sometimes it does not—as he knows from the mail he gets accusing him of deceptive packaging.

SOLUTIONS

So, if publishers are conservative about crossovers, what is one to do? Not write them? That is not practical. A good story is a good story, and some just have to be written that way. Besides, advances in genre fiction come when the envelope is stretched. It is healthy to test boundaries. It is even necessary.

Perhaps the problem lies with the whole idea of categorizing? Sure, spine labels and dedicated sections in stores lead readers to books they want, but they also route them away from books that they might enjoy. Should we do away with spine labels?

Alas, that is just not going to happen. Our whole retail structure is built around categories. This method gets as much support from publishers as it does from stores. For one thing, breaking a large list into smaller imprints makes it easier to get stores to order broadly from that list. For another, inside the stores themselves categories are the most efficient way to get mysteries, say, into the hands of mystery fans.

Spine designation also makes the bookstore's job easier. Without them, overworked sales assistants would have to make their own decisions about shelving. True, most bookstore clerks are smart and capable, but they cannot possibly read every book that comes in. I do not think most authors would want shelving decisions made for them on the fly, either. Disasters happen as it is. We need spine labels; just ask any author who has ever found his novel shelved in the nonfiction section.

Okay, why then cannot crossovers simply be labeled "fiction"? Would that not put the novel before the broadest possible audience anyway? Possibly, but remember that if you have built an audience writing, say, romances, you will want to bring those readers with you into your new section of the bookstore.

Will they follow? Maybe, maybe not. Some readers are adventurous browsers, but most are timid and comfortable creatures of habit. "Fiction" on the spine is not the be-all solution. It may not even be a good solution. The greatest number of potential readers for a crossover novel may not be browsing the fiction section; indeed, they may be somewhere unexpected.

Consider P. N. Elrod, author of a very popular series called *The Vampire Files*. These are vampire detective novels set in gangsterland Chicago and written in a snazzy, hardboiled style. In the first book, *Bloodlist*, reporter Jack Fleming wakes up on a beach one night to discover that he has been shot through the heart—but the point is, you see, he wakes up. He has become a vampire. He goes on to solve his own murder.

Now, in which section of the bookstore would you put *Bloodlist*? Mystery? Horror? Since the overlap between those readerships is not great, it seems that *The Vampire Files*, rather than straddling genres, should probably fall into a crack and die.

But that is not what happened. Elrod's publisher, Berkley, published the books in the Ace imprint as fantasy. Lo and behold, the novels found an enthusiastic readership. Six in the series are out, and four related novels are also in print. As you see, the right label for a crossover novel is not always obvious. And what if you are aiming high?

For many authors, hardcover publication and mainstream status sound like the magic answer to all of their problems. In mainstream, they feel, they will soar above the crowd. Genre will become irrelevant. Are they right? As I suggested in the last chapter, every mainstream author makes her own genre, and that can be harder than tapping into an existing category.

On top of that, for a crossover to make it big it must have certain mass-market appeal. Take Ira Levin's *The Boys from Brazil*, for instance: this is a thriller with a plausible science fiction premise at its core. Even so, its science fiction content is marginal, a mere device. Levin wrote a thriller that is accessible to everyone.

Michael Crichton did the same thing in *Jurassic Park*. Again, the science fiction in this novel is secondary. (In fact, it is not even original; several earlier novels such as Harry Adam Knight's *Carnosaur* use the same premise.) What makes *Jurassic Park* so popular is that it is a story that millions of people can relate to. It is not laden with genre conventions and devices. It is flat-out, uncomplicated, good storytelling.

Look at any crossover novel that makes it really big and I think you will see the same thing: genre trappings and ideas are kept to a minimum. The focus is instead on a taut, well-structured story. Genre fans may sneer when best-selling authors ignore genre rules, but millions can still relate; witness Anne Rice.

One more point about solutions: covers. They are key to reaching a paperback audience, and they become even more important in crossover publishing. In most cases decisions in this area are up to the publisher. Some authors may feel disappointed if their covers do not fully reflect the many dimensions of their story, but they need not fret. Trying to signal too much on a cover is a mistake. The message a cover sends must be easy to understand, otherwise customers will pass it by.

PITCHING THE CROSSOVER

All right, now that you know a bit more about the ins and outs of crossover publishing, what next? How should you manage your project?

In the writing stage, most authors should probably just do what works. Write the most effective story you know how to write. Do not worry about marketing. You will have plenty of time for that later.

Okay, now it is later. The book is done. Your next task is to sell it, unless it is already under contract. Here you and your agent need to plan carefully. Your story combines genre elements, but what is its *primary* audience? In which section of the bookstore will it probably find *most* of its likely readers?

That is your target market. Do not worry about the other markets. Trying to reach customers in several categories at once makes it likely only that you will reach none at all. Marketing is about what is possible. The objective is to get the greatest number of customers in *one* category to buy the novel. That, at least, will produce some degree of measurable success.

In approaching agents and editors, you might try presenting your novel as something they understand how to sell. Avoid overloading your pitch. For example, this pitch seems off-putting:

> "My novel uses one of the most popular science fiction devices ever: time travel! Using a time-travel method that is actually possible—as my novel shows—our heroine journeys to the eighteenth century and meets her twentieth-century husband in a prior incarnation. Can she love him then as totally as she loves him now? Romance fans will adore this story, and science fiction readers will find it fascinating too."

What is odd about this pitch is that it promises to deliver more audience than any crossover could possibly manage. Romance fans resist science fiction gimmicks, and SF fans hate large doses of florid romance writing. This pitch is a no-win.

Now try this:

> "My novel is a romance. The heroine is a widow so lost in grief that she travels back in time to meet her dead husband in a previous life—only to find that he is a popular hero who has wrongfully been condemned to death. Can she save him? And can she twice surrender her heart to a dying man?

This pitch is better because it does not promise too much. It aims the novel at an appropriate market. It also downplays an aspect of the story—time travel—that may be problematic.

Pick a primary market, then sell that market a product that it, in turn, feels confident of selling to the public. Keep crossover elements in the background. For most crossover novelists, that is the way to win.

And what about marketing to the public? Here you need to coordinate carefully with your publisher. In all likelihood, you will continue to push your book in one category and let other readers discover it. That is what happened to a science fiction author that I represent, Richard Bowker. His great post-holocaust detective novel, *Dover Beach*, was published as science fiction and sold mostly to science fiction fans—or so we thought.

Only later did we discover that mystery readers had found it, too: the *Drood Review*'s annual reader poll ranked it one of the ten best mysteries of the year, along with books by Tony Hillerman, Sara Paretsky, Jonathan Kellerman, and James Ellroy.

Surprise!

Overall, though, be aware that crossover novels present many pitfalls. They can be slow to find their audience, and that can be dangerous in today's unforgiving publishing climate.

I doubt that today many novels would be allowed the long gestation period given the crossover novel whose plot I described at the top of this chapter . . . you remember, the one in which Satan hires a private eye? That is *Falling Angel* by William Hjortsberg.

The novel did not have an easy time of it. It was underappreciated when first published in the late seventies, and was slow to be reprinted. A few people today remember that it was the basis for the blood-soaked, nearly X-rated movie with Mickey Rourke called *Angel Heart*, but mostly when I mention it, people say, "Wow, it sounds good. Why have I never heard of it?"

So, new crossover writers, be bold but beware. You have a daunting task ahead of you. Think hard in advance about the problems you will face, and plan solutions. If you do, you may have a shot at success.

10

CHAPTER

Numbers, Numbers, Numbers

POP QUIZ

READY? HERE IS A PROBLEM TO TEST HOW WELL YOU understand book publishing in the nineties. Writer A received a $10,000 advance for his first mystery novel. Published as an original paperback, it shipped 32,000 copies to bookstores; 23,000 of those were sold.

Writer B's agent, on the other hand, auctioned her third mystery novel. Her hardcover publisher lost the auction and her paperback publisher bought hard/soft rights for $45,000. The hardcover edition sold 4,000 copies of the 8,000 copies shipped. Reviews were mixed, but the *Times* was positive. An independent Hollywood producer purchased a one-year option on movie rights for $2,500 (against an eventual pickup price of $150,000). Later, Writer B's publisher shipped 166,000 copies of the paperback to bookstores. Of these, 55,000 were finally sold.

Question: Which author has a brighter future, A or B? Take a moment to think. . . .

Okay, your time is up. Did you choose Writer B? If so you are wrong. The future of Writer B's fiction career is seriously in doubt. In fact, it may be over (under her real name, anyway). However, Writer A is looking good. He will prosper a while longer.

Surprised? I do not blame you. In the mixed-up world of book publishing in the nineties, numbers do not add up the way one expects them to.

When I began my career as an agent in the late seventies, the situation was somewhat simpler. If I sought to move an author from one publisher to another, for example, the prospective editor would ask, "How well does this author sell?"

Today the question is, "What are her numbers?" Decoded, the editor's question is about a range of figures and ratios. Each is important and worth examining in some detail.

SALES

Publishers still care about sales, that is, the number of copies actually sold. Sales are the main source of a given book's revenue (total funds received by the publisher). Sales are money in the bank.

Are you with me so far?

PROFIT

A publisher's profit on a given title is a fuzzy number. Most publishers do not even know how much money any given book has made. If that sounds bizarre, it is.

Profit is *not*, of course, a publisher's gross revenues from bookstores, mail-order sales, book clubs, subrights deals, and so forth. Not by a long shot. Out of gross revenues publishers must pay out royalties, production and printing costs, overhead, the cost of shipping (sometimes), taxes, and a hefty cut to distributors. *Then* maybe there is some profit.

Maybe. Who knows? Certainly not publishers. There is disagreement about how to assign, say, overhead costs to any given book. Publishers can usually tell you how much revenue your book brought in, but not how much they made. But they do make something.

That something can be increased, naturally, by keeping costs down. Paying a low royalty rate is one way. Doing without advertising and promotion is another. (Hey, when you launch hundreds of new products—sorry, books—every year you have to economize somehow.) Publishers, believe me, do control costs.

If profit is really a guess, then, that does not stop publishers from guessing. Indeed they must, especially before purchasing a new manuscript. That guess is called a P & L, a profit-and-loss estimate, and it is an editor's main money tool when cutting a deal. The P & L, which assumes a certain cover price, estimates revenues at different levels of sales. (Remember sales?)

The P & L is used in determining how much to pay an author in advance. Now mind you, the P & L says nothing about an author's earnings. Royalties are just a cost the publisher incurs on the way to profits. No, the P & L is really about the publisher's profit *level*, where it begins (or ends) given a certain cover price and a particular level of sales. If you, the editor, believe that you can sell X number of copies . . . well, good buddy P & L tells you how much money will be left over and that, in turn, gives you some idea of what you can pay the author up front.

Still with me? Okay, so it would seem that profits are an important measure of an author's value to a publisher, and are not unconnected to sales. Good profits equal good author for the publisher, right? Hold on! It is not that simple. These days, the numbers that most measure an author's performance are found elsewhere.

Besides, as I indicated before, no one in book publishing really knows what constitutes a profit anyway.

RETURNS

By the mid-eighties *returns* (copies not sold by bookstores and returned to the publisher for credit) had become more important than sales or profits as a measure of performance. Why? Because of an unexpected series of developments. First, in the early eighties sales per title, on average, dropped sharply. This may have been because books grew more expensive, or perhaps because the number of them published each year rose, thus spreading a static number of unit sales over more available titles.

Whatever the reason, this spawned another curious situation: the explosive growth of returns. (Well, hardcovers are returned to the publisher; paperbacks have their covers stripped off and *those* are returned.)

Now, you would think that higher returns would lead to lower print runs. Not so. Instead, publishers in the eighties began to pump out huge quantities per title, sometimes merely in the hope of creating enough "presence" in the marketplace for a given title to catch on automatically (which, at high numbers, they can).

A vicious competition for shelf space did not help. Soon, over-printing became the norm. A 50 percent return rate was the industry average, meaning that in most cases two books had to be printed in order to sell one. Sound like a dumb waste of paper? It is, and despite publishers complaints a 50 percent return rate is still the norm today.

To be fair, publishers do not like returns. Booksellers do not, either. Since every company's policy is different, returns are an administrative and paperwork nightmare for stores.

Some publishers have always sold on a nonreturnable basis (Dover Publications is one). But that policy works best with stores accustomed to buying nonreturnable wares: gift shops, toy stores, stationers, craft stores, art supply places, and the like. For book-stores, returns are still a helpful way to do business, though most booksellers say that nonreturnable orders—at the right discount—can be okay for certain books. Backlist, for instance, is not usually time sensitive and can be ordered on a nonreturnable basis. The category least appropriate for nonreturnable ordering? First novels.

Returns are understandably a big concern. In fact, by the mid-eighties, when I presented an author to a potential new publisher, the first question I was usually asked by the wary editor was inevitably, "What were the returns on his last book?"

But that, too, has changed. In the late eighties another figure began to overtake returns as the number of the moment. This one is a ratio.

SELL-THROUGH

This is the ratio of books actually sold to books shipped to stores, expressed as a percentage. (Returns can also be expressed as a percentage; sell-through is thus the inverse of returns.)

Take the case of Writer A, with whom I started this chapter. His publisher shipped 32,000 copies of his novel and of those sold 23,000. That puts his sell-through at 71 percent, which is excellent. If reorders warrant, his publisher will go back to press.

Writer B, on the other hand, sold 4,000 of 8,000 hardcover copies shipped. A 50 percent sell-through. Not especially good—and downright disappointing for a book that cost the publisher $45,000 to acquire! (A sale of four thousand copies is typical for a mystery, to be sure, but it is not the figure you expect for that kind of money.)

In short, Writer B is in trouble. Her situation gets worse, as well. Her publisher ships 166,000 copies of the paperback edition. Of these, 55,000 sell. Sell-through on that edition is 33 percent. Terrible! It means that three copies were manufactured and shipped for every one finally sold. A lot of waste there.

A 33 percent sell-through is so awful, in fact, that it completely offsets the good news regarding the movie sale, which to a discerning eye was never promising to begin with. The producer, for one thing, is not a major player but an independent with little chance of getting this book made into a movie. Plus it was an option deal, and that is a long way from movie-on-screen.

Still, though, Writer B's paperback edition sold some 55,000 copies, more than twice writer A's sale of 23,000. Does that not count for something? Frankly, no. In a logical world it might, but this is book publishing in the nineties. B's numbers may look better, yet to a publisher they signal danger, if not disaster.

Even if the publisher continues with B, the worry is that bookstores and wholesalers, noticing the 33 percent sell-through on this book, will balk when the next one comes along. Never mind that the next one is as good as or better than the last one. Few buyers will read it. Virtually all buyers, though, will check their computerized records and order it in lower quantities. Less exposure will mean fewer sales, which will, in turn, probably mean still lower orders on the book after that one.

In other words, this is the beginning of a downward spiral. So familiar is this pattern, in fact, that there is a term for it: *selling into the net*. Many publishers would be inclined to drop Writer B immediately. Why wait for the bad news to hit? Why not start over again with someone brand new?

Is Writer B's career over? Very probably, unless she cares to continue under another name. Can her hotshot agent save her? That is doubtful. In fact, Hotshot Agent is very likely soon to stop returning her calls. That is the power of sell-through.

In case you doubt me, think a little about sell-through from a store manager's point of view. If you have four copies of a novel on your shelf and sell three of them, that is an efficient use of your space. If, though, you have four and sell two . . . well, that is at least average. But if you have four and sell one—heck, what would *you* do? Would you stock that author again?

I rest my case. The jury finds that sell-through is the magic number of the moment.

VOODOO NUMBERS

Sell-through is by no means the only important number, though. There are others, some of which are used roughly to forecast a book's performance. These voodoo numbers, as I think of them, crop up frequently in my conversations with editors.

Voodoo numbers are a bit like your daily horoscope: they do not predict anything for sure, or necessarily anything at all, but just the same you hanker to know what the voodoo numbers say.

Here are a few:

Ship-in. This is the raw number of copies ordered by bookstores and wholesalers. It is an early number, and not particularly meaningful, but it does say something about how the future might go. A large ship-in bodes well—usually. It may mean that booksellers are behind the book and anticipate good sell-through.

Then again, it may mean that the book was overordered and will return in big numbers. At any rate, divide the ship-in figure by two and you will have the sales total, if this is an average book. As I said, a horoscope: it might be right, it might be wrong.

The "rate." This means the "reorder rate," the rate at which accounts are asking for additional copies of the book. Reorders are themselves a good sign, but it is the rate that is most telling. A good rate means soon going back to press. A low rate means that when the stock runs out the publisher will have to decide whether an additional printing will be worthwhile.

In the paperback business, where the rate matters most, a rate of three hundred to four hundred copies per month may be just enough to keep a novel in print. A five hundred copy per month rate is darn good. A rate of one thousand copies or more means it is time to break out the champagne.

The "six-week." The period varies from house to house, but whatever the interval, this number is a measure of early returns. Now, early returns are expected, but too high a rate of early returns can give publishers the jitters.

That normally does not matter. The die is cast and things will be clearer in a few months. However if there is a new book in negotiation, then the "six-week," or whatever, can take on a significance that outweighs its actual utility.

Aren't you glad you have Maalox on hand?

OTHER NUMBERS

Twenty-five thousand dollar advance! How many authors do you know who got exactly that much for a novel? Probably a few. If that is more than your largest advance then you no doubt envy them.

Well, you can stop. While $25,000 is a nice chunk of money, it does not automatically mean that a book is going to be a hit or that its publisher will get behind it. It does not even mean that anyone outside the editorial department will have heard of the book before it is published.

Why? Because in many companies $25,000 is the *discretionary limit*, that is, the most an editorial director can authorize an editor to pay. Sums above that level must usually be approved by a higher authority, often a committee or "Pub Board" (not, alas, a drinking club but a "Publishers Review Board").

When high-level approval must be obtained, curious things begin to happen. Corporate executives start to ask questions. They read. They get involved. The get excited, just like editors do ordinarily. The result is that the whole company, not just the acquiring editor, feels it has a stake in the book's success.

How unusual!

So, I hope you have put your envy aside. Your friends with the $25,000 advances are not on a level much different from yours. Like you, they are struggling to survive in the jungle.

One hundred thousand copy first printing! Do you read *Publishers Weekly*? If so, then you have probably noticed publishers' advertisements that hype forthcoming novels with the promise of things like "national advertising," "author tour," and "100,000 copy first printing." However, *promise* is the operative word.

Announcements like "100,000 copy first printing" are . . . well, let's not call them lies, exactly; rather, let us think of them as plans, hopes, good intentions . . . or maybe as that useful old publishing guff, "an expression of our enthusiasm."

Okay, lies. Ad budgets have a way of evaporating at the last moment, especially when orders are lower than expected. An author tour can become a single trip to the local Barnes & Noble. And first printings . . . well, everyone in the business knows that those are only a promotional gimmick. Real first printings are based upon early orders. One hundred thousand copies? That could be whittled down to half that number. Rarely does the figure go up.

Of much more interest to me is the ship-in (see above). While it is not a perfect forecast of a book's performance, it is more connected to the real world than that "big first printing."

Ten Weeks on the New York Times *Best-seller List!* Whoa, baby, that author must be getting rich, huh? Richer than most, to be sure.

But how rich is rich, exactly? The truth is that what puts a book on the list is not sales but the *rate of sales*; that is, not how much a book is selling (in total), but how fast it is selling. Also, the list is a relative measure of books against one another. The top-of-the-list rate of sales is many times that at the bottom of the list, and the August list probably represents greater sales overall than the January list.

And Christmastime? Forget it. The book industry does 25 percent of its business between Thanksgiving and Christmas. Just try to get on the list during the holidays! Only megasellers need apply in December.

FORECASTING THE FORECAST

What will the numbers of the future be? Will that old standard, sales, make a comeback? Will we need to understand algorithms?

Some observations: bookstores cannot shelve every title that is published. With fifty thousand titles coming out annually, that would be impossible. Even in the more limited arena of trade books—that is, consumer books that one would expect to find in a bookstore—there is not enough room. We have a glut of titles.

That means competition . . . fierce, back-stabbing competition. The prize? Shelf space; the opportunity to exhibit your books to the public, maybe even face out. And do not be mistaken: publishers take this contest for space very seriously.

Luckily for forecasters like me, publishing changes. One shift we are undergoing right now is a stabilization of the number of titles being published annually. It was 55,000 or so in 1990, sank to 44,000 or so in 1992, and has risen again to 50,000 or so, where the number seems to be holding steady (for now). Meanwhile, publishers are trying to control costs. They are printing fewer books, hoping to match supply more closely to demand.

On-demand printing is in the future, too. Will this new efficiency mean less competition for shelf space, or a longer shelf life for books? Probably not. Like lettuce, books will always be perishable; efficient use of bookstore shelves is here to stay.

Because of that concern, I believe that publishers and book-sellers alike will continue to look at the way that shelf space is allocated. New patterns will be tried. Indeed, the superstores are already stocking deep; that is, putting more emphasis on backlist and less on frontlist. (Well, somewhat less.)

The old days, when publishers would stuff stores with thousands of decorative copies of a book, are gone. No more will we see fifty copies of an author's new novel, but none of his backlist. Today, every inch counts. The current trend seems to be stocking more titles, but fewer of them. Backlist is your friend.

So, to my prediction: if this trend continues, the next significant number will not be a different form of sales, profit, returns, sell-through, or rates. I forecast that the next important number will be *the number of titles an author has in print.*

Think about it: with twenty novels on the shelf, half of which may not sell, the efficiency quotient is low. But with four copies each of five backlist novels stocked on shelves, all selling at a rate better than 50 percent . . . well, that means more profits.

Now, don't think too hard. If you do, you will notice that there is a very big *if* in the middle of my forecast: *if* those novels are selling! That in turn presupposes that authors will be writing book after book that their fans will want to read. That, friends, is a factor that only authors can control.

Aren't numbers fun?

11
CHAPTER

Self-Promotion or Self-Delusion?

BORN-AGAIN

YOU HAVE PROBABLY MET THEM AT CONVENTIONS. INDEED, they are hard to avoid. They are well-dressed, pushy, and hot on a mission. Before you know it, they are pouring statistics in your ear: over fifty thousand books a year are published . . . a typical big house does hundreds . . . only 5 percent of those get promoted. . . .

You nod in agreement. Your own last book received little, if any, advertising. As for promotion? Forget it. You know your place on the food chain. Only the big-name novelists and sizzling nonfiction books are sent on tour. What can you do?

Plenty, say your newfound friends, the born-again self-promoters: you, too, can take charge of your career. Show a glimmer of interest and they thrust upon you their handouts, press kits, bookmarks, buttons—see? You have to believe! Promote *yourself*! No one else will do it for you (though they can help).

Your eyes glaze over as the sermon grows more intense: they confess their former naïveté. They witness to the selling power of self-promotion. They beg you not to wait. They offer to put you in touch with their own press agents. They declare, "You can be saved! Put your trust in TV! You can be on cable!" Your brain feels numb. Their crazy rant is beginning to make sense.

Are they right? Should you break down and join the ranks of the self-promoters? Should you, too, be making cold calls to the talent coordinators at "Donahue" and "Oprah"? Should you send in your life savings to secure advertising space? What about signings? Satellite TV tours? What is effective? What does it cost?

Are you a numbskull for simply staying home and writing? Before answering those questions, let's first do a reality check and see how promotion is actually done by the pros in the book business.

HOW THE PROS DO IT

First, all publishers promote. They may merely mail review copies, or they may launch expensive, twenty-city author tours. Either way, the employee responsible for that stuff is the publicist.

Talk to a publicist and you will discover an alternate way of looking at publishing. Whether your book is good or bad may matter to your publicist personally—they are book lovers, too—but in the end the quality of it is immaterial to his job. More important is *you*. Are you attractive? At ease in interviews? Do you have a salable topic or personal story?

In short, are you "promotable"?

Let's assume the answer to that question is yes. Let's also assume that at your publisher's all-important marketing meeting, in which upcoming books and authors are culled, you and your novel are singled out for a push. What happens then?

Two or three months prior to publication you meet with your publicist. Here she determines your assets: who you are, what you do, whom you know, your level of experience with the media, and so forth. Are you an expert in forensic archaeology? Good. Are you married to a celebrity chef? Useful. Is your book especially appealing to scuba divers? Fine. All these suggest promotional angles.

A plan is formed. Depending on the budget for your book, a list of targets grows. The idea is to generate word-of-mouth about you among the readers most likely to fork over their hard-earned cash for your book. Fortunately, there are thousands of opportunities, from local newspapers to industry associations to specialty magazines to radio chat shows to "Geraldo." Press kits are mailed and pitches are made. You are "booked."

You hit the road.

Naturally, publicists have their own ideas of success. Big points are scored for booking authors on national TV. Handling a best-seller is status enhancing, too, especially if that best-seller was "made." Celebrity authors are the easiest to sell. Topical nonfiction is great, too. ("An Ebola book? Yes!") Guess which authors, though, are at the very bottom of publicists' wish lists? Yup, you guessed it: novelists. And last in line are first novelists.

Novels are not appealing to the media. When they must pitch novelists, most publicists focus on the author's own story. A check-ered past, a wacky personality, awards, odd writing habits . . . irrel-evant as these tidbits are, they are more likely to arouse people's interest than a novel's plot summary.

Looks, personality, and human interest are the key to media appeal. That brings me back to the main question: if you are a nov-elist, should you be promoting yourself? Does it even work?

There is plenty of anecdotal evidence, of course; talk to the born-agains. Heck, talk to me: I have a few clients who seem to have done themselves a world of good through self-promotion. Still, there is nothing like scientific proof that it works. Even so, most publishers like to see their authors try it. They may even offer support with local ads, posters, and such.

Self-promotion is better than no promotion. But how much better? Enough to make it worth all the time, trouble, and expense? That depends on several variables, each of which needs examination.

ARE YOU A CANDIDATE?

First, are you promotable? As a do-it-yourselfer, you alone must be the judge. (Obviously, don't ask your mother or your teenage kid; they are no more objective than you are.) Quiz yourself. Do you feel attractive? Do you like to meet people? Do you love to talk about yourself? Can you formulate a message and get it across?

Sure, you think. But most people feel that way. How realistic are you being? Ask yourself some extra questions. Do you know the name of your publicist? Do you maintain your own list of contacts? Do you already speak in public more than once a year? Have you ever been interviewed on TV or for publication? Can you, right this second, explain what makes your novel important?

Unless you answered yes to many of the latter questions, self-promotion may not come naturally to you. Chances are that you will be uncomfortable with it, and disappointed with the results.

Assuming you passed the promotability test, the next factors to consider are time and money. Self-promotion takes both. Do you live off your advances? If so, watch out. You cannot afford more than basic local, low-cost self-promotion unless your up-front money is much higher than average. If you have your own money to spend that is helpful. But how much should you invest? The reality is that at first self-promotion will probably not return in royalties the money that you put into it.

As for time, do you have a job? Young children? Church or civic commitments? Again, beware. Effective self-promotion can be a full-time job by itself. You will need free weekends and limitless energy.

The next factor is knowledge. Have you ever seen a press kit? Do you know the name of the talent coordinator on your local station's talk show? Does thinking about these things send you into a cold sweat? Relax, this part is easy. There are many books, contact lists, and newsletters that can help you get started. So can your publisher. Still, among my clients who have done well with self-promotion, several came from careers in advertising and public relations. Self-promotion requires expertise. If you do not already have it, you will have to get educated.

The final factor is commitment. Do you fervently believe in promoting yourself? You had better. Promotion builds in steps: local, regional, national. Each step takes years of sustained effort.

That's right, years. Think about it, unless you are a TV star or the daughter of a President you are not going to get to promote your first novel—or perhaps any novel—on NBC's "Today." Neither are you likely to be written about in the New York Times. Of course, you may get lucky. Your novel about a Soviet coup d'état may be released on the same day as the real thing. If so, get ready to move fast. Fame of that sort is fleeting.

So, if major media will resist you, how can you finally break through? The only reliable way is to build up a media following at lower rungs of the ladder. Publicity is a business of contacts. As feature writers become editors, book columnists go national, and TV producers move up to bigger and better shows, they may remember you. Over the years you will also be building a résumé, a clippings file—perhaps even a "reel," an audio sampler of your radio spots or videocassette of your TV spots.

All those things can be helpful later. Indeed, many national media bookers will not even consider authors until they have seen them on tape. Print media are also impressed by previous coverage.

Did you miss my passing remark about results? Be aware that your efforts may not soon be reflected on your royalty statements. That is why commitment is so important. Self-promotion is an act of faith. It is for those with a sense of personal destiny.

It is also for the humble. If speaking to a small reading circle of senior citizens at a town library two hours away is beneath you, stay at your word processor. True self-promoters will speak to anyone, anywhere, anytime. No booking is too small.

WHAT WORKS

Now, down to specifics. Assuming that you are sold on self-promotion and have the required personality, time, money, and faith, how do your formulate a plan? What actually works for novelists?

First, forget national TV. Forget satellite TV hookups. Forget four-color posters and postcards and promotional videos (unless you can get them done for free). And forget hiring free-lance publicists; they work wonders but cost as much as a typical first-novel advance, assuming a publicist would even be willing to take you on. To be treated by the media like a famous novelist, you must first become famous on your own.

That happens in slow stages. The first is local, which in time becomes a springboard to regional media. To go national, you will ultimately need lots of support from your publisher.

It is smart to start small. What do you write? SF? Mysteries? There is your core market, your initial audience. Go where they go. Locally, that means specialty bookstores and local conventions. Line up signings and appearances. Coordinate with your publisher. And always—always—send thank you letters.

Regarding your publisher, experienced self-promoters know that when their editors say they want to control the flow of information to their company's publicists, that can really mean that they want to keep you out of the publicists' hair. I cannot totally blame them. Publicists are busy. They have limited budgets and busy schedules. If you are not on their agenda (or in their budget) there is probably little they can do to help you.

Ditto the sales department. To get help you will have to break through those barriers, though slowly and respectfully. You need to make your publicist your friend. That means showing that you understand his job and, at least at first, doing much of the work yourself. When you do get results, send your publicist a letter and enclose a clipping or a tape. Send a copy to your publicist when you send your thank you letters. Show them you are a player.

Getting to know your local sales rep can be helpful, too, but once again it is important to be respectful of her time. Keep her informed, but do not expect her to do much more than make sure there are copies in a store when you go to sign—and remember that may require giving a month's advance notification.

One more thing: pray that your publisher keeps your books in print.

Once you've made your contacts and done your initial local promotion, you can branch out. Buttons and bookmarks are low-cost items that can be mailed to stores and left behind after signings. Design a press kit. This is a glossy folder that contains (depending on its purpose) a pitch letter, a press release, an author photo, tear sheets—i.e., reviews, articles, and interviews—and sample questions for media people to ask.

Now you are in a position to sell yourself to local newspapers, and to radio and TV stations. Always get in touch with the person best positioned to help you. At a TV talk show, that is the talent coordinator and/or producer. If your first contact is not interested in you, ask for the name of someone who might be. At radio stations, call the news director and ask about programs.

Radio, in fact, is one of the biggest secrets of book publicists. (Well, it is not terribly secret anymore.) Public radio, in particular, is well plugged in to readers. On the national level "All Things Considered" and, especially, "Fresh Air" are the holy grails of book publicity. Is there a local equivalent in your area? College radio stations may be a place to start.

Now, what is your angle? Remember, the media are not interested in your novel's plot. They are, though, interested in the book's subject matter, how it turned into a novel, and in your own personal story. Is there a local angle? Play it up. Something topical? Milk it. Do you have some personal link to your material—is it, say, based on family events or wartime experiences?

A word about advertising: there is much debate in the industry about the effectiveness of ads. Genre readers are thought to be primarily influenced by reviews and the glowing recommendations of friends. Besides, many genre novels sell well without ads, anyway, so why should publishers spend money on the *Chicago Tribune*?

Should you buy your own advertising? Generally, no. Ads in major media are highly expensive. In local media, promo can be had for free so why pay for ad space? Ads in trade magazines—*Locus*, *Romantic Times*, the *Armchair Detective*—are a judgment call. Since the purpose of such ads is mostly to let existing fans and stores know that your latest title is out, your publisher's "house ad" (group ad) might be sufficient.

Think carefully about paying for ad space in magazines that are sold mostly to other writers. Their publishers may bang the self-promotion drum loudest of all, but why preach to the converted, other authors? What you need are authentic readers.

You can also broaden your target list to include other special-interest groups. Do you write mysteries set in the world of insurance? A local association of insurance brokers may be interested in booking you. There may be other ways to exploit your specialty. For example, do you write vampire novels? Halloween may be an opportunity. Create an event (a vampire-bite clinic, or whatever) and get your local media in.

You can also set yourself up as an expert in your subject. Write articles; it is amazing how many local papers will print them. Also, let your local media know that you are available for comment. Try to keep your list of contacts current. And pay attention to timing. If you want publicity in a particular issue of a periodical, mail press kits six weeks in advance. Follow-up calls are made a week or two later. For media coverage of an event, call no sooner than the day before.

It is also possible to bypass your publisher, bookstores, and the media and go directly to your potential audience. The mechanism is the Internet. A Web page (Internet site) is easy to set up. It is like having a number that people can call to hear a recorded message, except that your Web page is visual and interactive. Some Web pages are stunning. To check out an exceptionally fine author's Web page, look at the one set up by fantasy writer J. V. Jones and her talented brother, an award-winning Web page designer. You will find it at this location:

http://www.imgnet.com/auth/jjones.html

Now, let us say that you have several books and several years of self-promotion under your belt. You have built a file of reviews and other clippings. You can begin to go regional, doing the same thing but farther away and in bigger markets. Contacts are harder to make, but there is help in the form of reference books like *Bacon's* and *Laramie's*, and newsletters like *Contacts*. Check your library, or with your publicist.

With luck, your story will someday be picked up by national media. It helps to have built a critical mass of publicity, but keep your expectations realistic. National media is celebrity driven. Even publishers find it tough to book authors on national TV. Still, certain avenues are open. Local bureaus of the Associated Press and the *New York Times* are helpful. USA *Today* is another that publicists love. True self-promoters will find a way.

Then there is the lecture circuit. For two hundred dollars a new service geared to midlist writers called Authors Unlimited will register you and book you anywhere from colleges to museums to cruise ships, retaining 25 percent of your fee in return.

Meanwhile, be sure to let your publisher know what you are doing. A brief letter giving a schedule of your appearances should go to your editor, the editorial director, the head of sales, and the chief publicist. They will notice, probably help, and maybe, eventually, when your sales and/or advances warrant, take over. (Maybe your agent will even be able to get you advertising and promotion guarantees in your contract.)

Even then you will probably have to do a certain amount of work yourself; for instance, thank you notes and follow-up. You may, at this stage, want to invest in coaching. For eight hundred to three thousand dollars, TV pros will spend four hours or so preparing you for TV exposure. It is expensive, but by now you should be reaping the rewards of the step-by-step work you have done over the years.

Is all this sounding like a lot of work? Are the born-again self-promoters beginning to seem like a bunch of amateurs in a sea of publicity-savvy sharks? Well, it is and they are.

Do you want to join them? The rewards can be great, but the truth is that few authors—and even fewer novelists—succeed at the self-promotion game. Perhaps you are one of the few who have the right combination of skills, savvy, and enthusiasm. Perhaps not. Whatever your path, though, be sure that your first priority remains writing irresistible stories.

Promotion is worthless if you have nothing to sell.

12
CHAPTER

Strategy Session II:
Midcareer Damage Control

PUBLISH AND PERISH

YOU MIGHT IMAGINE THAT, AS AN AGENT WITH A SOLID reputation, I am most often contacted by first novelists, newcomers who hope that I will pluck them from obscurity and somehow wave a magic wand and make them best-sellers. That is so, yet a surprising number of calls come from authors who have been published two or three times, but who suddenly have hit a brick wall.

Often their publishers have turned down an option book. Their current agents are not returning their calls, or have become oddly ineffective. They are confused: what has gone wrong? Readers adore their work, they swear, and their latest manuscripts are their best yet. However, they cannot seem to get things moving. Will I take them on? (Translation: Can I rescue their careers?)

Maybe, maybe not. These writers have fallen victim to a well-known phenomenon that publishing insiders call "publish and perish." Having been given membership in the club, so to speak, they are suddenly being pushed to resign. It is a desperate situation.

So, welcome to Strategy Session II. This chapter is all about what sends authors' careers off the rails and what can (or cannot) be done about it. If your career is going well you probably feel invincible. I urge you to read this chapter anyway. Just as senior executives at companies like IBM can feel the sudden sting of unemployment, so too can hot authors find their careers cooling off. It is a good idea to imagine the worst case.

Sadly, many authors bring fatal accidents upon themselves. On the other hand, that means that some career disasters can be prevented. So let us look at why midcareer authors perish.

FATAL ERRORS

Is there any way an author can predict that he is going to get zapped? If you have been paying attention to this book thus far, you have probably already identified some of the pitfalls.

A low advance, for example, is a certain sign that a novel will be brought out with little support. Bad covers can hurt sales, too. If in the middle of the publication process one's acquiring editor departs for another house, or law school, or an ashram, well, it is now nearly certain that sales—or, more importantly, sell-through—will fall below a sustainable level.

There is also the matter of switching canoes in the middle of the stream, by which I mean authors who, before they have reached the five-book threshold I discussed in Strategy Session I, radically change the direction of their fiction or change publishers. Those are risky moves. In the first case readers are lost. In the second, backlist is lost and intervals between books become irregular. Support from key accounts is then lost, leading to sales purgatory.

Some authors lower their survival odds still further by signing up with publishers who are known career-wreckers. Who are these publishers? They are easy to spot. They bring out twice as many genre titles as their competition. They adore first novelists, too, especially if they are not represented or have lousy agents. Theirs is the buckshot approach: fire lots of books at the market and hope that a few will hit the bull's-eye.

What happens to those authors whose books miss the target? If they are not dropped outright, they may be relegated to a kind of publishing limbo, where they neither move up nor are pushed out until in frustration they leave of their own accord.

Most new authors are caught by surprise when that happens. Is it any wonder? Caution and common sense can be the first things to go when one's first novel is accepted for publication. Indeed, many green authors describe their books as their children, and seem to have the same unrealistic hopes and dreams for them as first-time parents can have for their newborns.

A few first novelists even rush to quit their day jobs, especially if they managed to swing a large advance. It is accepted industry wisdom that getting big money up front means that one's publisher will be forced to work hard to earn it back. Sounds logical, but it ain't necessarily so. Even with massive support, a certain number of books are bound to fail. It also happens that publishers blow off high advances. Believe me, I have seen it happen.

Recipients of large first advances never imagine that disaster will happen. Indeed, hardly any new authors foresee it. While that is natural enough, it is also a good idea to take off one's blinkers and look to the right and left. The roadside is littered with the bodies of once-promising new careers.

Not long ago I received a call from a friend. A prize-winning short story writer, his first few novels had landed him on the fast track at a major mass-market house. He had often bragged that, slotted as high as he was on his publisher's list, the trip to the best-seller lists was nearly automatic. His agent, he had boasted, was "psychotic," the type of whom publishers live in fear. He had several high five-figure advances to prove it, too. With all that in his favor he felt that his success was assured. But then one day he called.

The "ship-in" on his new novel, he told me, was way down. Mistakes on his publisher's part had hurt him, he felt, although there was also a glut of novels in his chosen genre. Regardless of the causes, it was clear that his high advances and big-shot agent were not enough to protect him from the perish trap. He knew it, too, and glumly spoke of looking for a job.

Mistakes and groundless optimism are not the only reasons that authors perish. Publishers have added to this problem by their addiction to gambling. In the quest for the next Amy Tan, Scott Turow, Sue Miller, Whitney Otto——the Cinderella authors whose leaps into best-sellerdom seem nearly effortless——they repeatedly step up to roll the dice in a high-stakes craps game.

I am not talking about the seven- and eight-figure advances paid to established best-sellers. (They may deserve them.) I am talking about the periodic rush to pay six-figure advances to total newcomers. This addictive and at times destructive game only endangers other first, midlist, and genre novelists.

You would think that ego and gambling would have no place in the bottom-line corporate culture of book publishing in the nineties, but on the contrary gambling is its essence. The reason is *profit margin*. In publishing today it is not enough to make money; one has got to make serious amounts of money. One's corporate parent, after all, might be a cable TV giant used to an annual pattern of double-digit growth. That same cable giant may also be laden with debt. Either way, to win high margins a publisher must take big risks, i.e., gamble.

Whether or not the craps game produces the desired profits is debatable. (Remember, no one knows what profits in book publishing are anyway—see Chapter 10.) It is worth noting, however, that of the fifty-four novels that sold more than 100,000 copies in 1990, not one was a first novel.

Surprised? The surprise is that publishers continue to drain money away from proven money makers: midcareer genre and mainstream authors.

AN OUNCE OF PREVENTION

There are ways for new and midcareer authors to protect themselves. But to avoid the perish trap they must be informed, alert, and aggressive.

The first step—easy to say, hard to do—is to write a novel that readers cannot resist. That's facile advice, I know, but do not dismiss it out of hand. It is amazing how reluctant some writers can be to revise. Time and again I have seen it: validation comes and growth ceases. Having found acceptance, authors start to believe that ever afterward their publishers will purchase, even publish, their first drafts. They start to treat their advance checks as paychecks.

Another big pitfall traps new writers who are in a hurry to receive validation. Rushing to find a publisher is a mistake. New authors in a hurry tend to sign up with inferior agents, sell to career-killing publishers, and accept lousy deals on the flawed theory that any deal is at least a foot in the door. One way around this pitfall is to get the best agent one can right away (see Chapters 4 and 5).

The same goes for editors. Publishing conglomerates are political jungles in which only the strongest survive. In that atmosphere you need a knowledgeable and enthusiastic guide. If your editor does not know the ropes, or is not inspired enough by your work, then the thousand and one obstacles in your way become insurmountable.

WHEN THE AXE FALLS

Sometimes even a ton of prevention is not enough. The axe falls anyway, oftentimes through no noticeable fault of the author's. What can be done in these situations? Some ideas follow.

Being "orphaned" is a common and devastating disaster that overtakes midcareer authors. This problem is not preventable, but the odds of being abandoned are higher when a novel has been acquired by a junior editor. Junior editors tend to job hop, either for more money, opportunity, or escape from their mistakes—occasionally for all of those reasons.

When one's editor departs for another company, one option is to follow that editor to her new home. Indeed, when a powerful or exceptionally well-loved editor moves on there is often fighting over authors. When Henry Ferris, an editor known for spotting and growing young authors, moved from Bantam to Houghton Mifflin a few years ago, Bantam allowed two authors to go with him but prevented two others from following. The tug-of-war can be especially intense over best-sellers.

Should you stay or should you go? That is a tough question to answer. If you are inclined to go, consider the fate of your backlist. Backlist is crucially important in building an audience and cushioning large new advances (see Strategy Session III). If you migrate, will your backlist stay in print? If your books are doing well you would think so. It would be logical for your prior publisher to piggyback on your success with your new publisher by exploiting the books of yours that are tucked away on its list. That is logical.

Unfortunately, what seems logical is not necessarily what happens. History shows that publishers tend to sell stock on hand and then give up on most departed authors' backlists (unless a top bestseller is involved). Why? The reason may have to do with reprinting and warehousing costs. Those are less than original publication costs, of course, but reorder rates must justify the expense. For authors still building audiences, the "rate"—remember that?— may not be sufficient, especially when new titles are not driving reorders.

If you decide to stay, it is wise to consider the situation a major crisis. Decisive action is needed. I will illustrate with a story about Paula Volsky, a fantasy writer I represent. I had moved her from Berkley to Bantam for more than three times her previous advance money. Everything was looking good. Her new novel, *Illusion*, promised to be dynamite. The advance seemed to guarantee it lots of loving care—until her editor left. Her publisher then promoted an editorial assistant, Janna Silverstein, and assigned her the project.

My heart sank. This was a scenario for disaster. My first move was to phone the editorial director who had been in on the original acquisition and make sure he was still excited about *Illusion*. (He was.) I then arranged lunch with Janna, and pitched the project just as hard as I had the first time around. It worked. Janna—an editor of uncommon good taste—got fired up. Just to be sure, when the novel was finally delivered (all one thousand pages of it) I sent it to her with a box of Godiva chocolates and a note suggesting that some novels absolutely required that one have bonbons at one's side while being read.

Sound silly? Maybe so, but Janna ate the chocolates, read the manuscript, and discovered that she had a career-making novel on her hands. She promoted it fiercely in-house, fought to get a cover painting from the finest artist in the field, Michael Whelan, and arranged a number of clever, low-cost promotions. The book did splendidly. So did Janna, whose star rose at Bantam. (She also became, needless to say, one of my favorite editors.)

I hope I have made my point. When you are orphaned, it is fatal is sit around and wait to see what will happen. Take action. Sell the book all over again. A passive response allows your publisher to be passive, too.

Do the words "splendid cover" sound to you like an oxymoron? If so you have likely been stung by poor packaging. Recovering from that blow is difficult, sometimes impossible. If you have the chance to try again, however, be aware that there is a right way and a wrong way to influence cover decisions.

The wrong way is to rudely dictate your cover requirements to your editor. The right way is to politely suggest cover approaches that speak to your unique readers. It is also a good idea to make sure that your ideas reach your publisher's art director. This is the expert who knows better than anyone, even you, how to package books. On the other hand, you probably know your readers better than the art director does. Help him to find the right approach for your readers and you are doing yourself a favor. Dictate and you will be ignored.

I am sure that some editors reading this chapter are shuddering right now, because no one can alienate publishing professionals more quickly than an author. I agree, so again I will emphasize: keep your communications short and businesslike.

Once your book is published, what about the other pitfalls facing you? Suppose you are getting no advertising or promotional support? Self-promotion may be the answer for you. (See Chapter 11.) It is certainly better than sitting at home stewing.

More difficult to grapple with are problems like underprinting, overprinting, and overshipping with its consequent high returns. Remaindering too soon is another sore point. The only strategy to pursue in response to these problems is clearly to communicate your career plans to your publisher. That means identifying your audience, choosing the right format, and following up with a well-timed sequence of novels that will grow your readership. If your publisher understands your strategy, it may perhaps bring its own plans into line with yours.

Take overprinting: this commonly happens when a big advance has been obtained and there is hollow optimism about the number of readers really out there. A realistic appraisal of your potential audience—which can be achieved by making honest comparisons—may mean a lower advance than you would ideally like, but it can also leave you without the disaster of poor sell-through. Now, I am all for strong advances, but I am not for high returns. They benefit no one.

Keeping the advance level ambitious but within the realm of potential earnings is a smart strategy for many classes of authors. Genre novelists building slowly may not want to quickly push advances to unrealistic levels. One-shot mainstream novelists are another matter; if commercial enough, for them the sky can be the limit. Still, for me, sustainability is the truest measure of success, and step-by-step building of advances and sales is, more often than not, the best way to achieve that.

Another damage-control factor to consider is whether the plot of a particular novel plays into a short-term trend. If your new novel is a technothriller and those are suddenly hot, there are two ways to go: (1) exploit the trend to the hilt, going for short-term gain and accepting long-term risk; and (2) carefully disassociate your novel from the crowd, possibly losing sales but gaining potential long-term security by avoiding a trendy label.

Ideally, one's novels either immediately achieve and sustain a high level of sales, or show a pattern of healthy sell-through and rising sales. If this happens, there will be certain temptations. One of those temptations is to quickly become a full-time novelist. That has its dangers, though, so it may be a good idea to consider the "five-book threshold" and other measures of security that I discussed in Strategy Session I.

Another temptation is to quickly leverage up to bigger money. The danger here, as I mentioned above, lies in forcing a publisher to put out an unrealistic number of copies in the hope of earning back the unrealistic advance. Letting advances lag behind earnings is bad, to be sure, but big advances are not a safety net, either. I love doing large deals for my clients, but it does take some skill to keep a career from overheating.

In pursuit of big money, many agents and authors rush to change publishers. Our open and competitive market is a joy, to be sure, but unless there are obvious problems with one's current publisher it may be wise to be cautious about making a move. I have already mentioned the importance of backlist. There is another reason: if you look beyond the headlines in trade magazines, you will quickly find that most large leaps in advance levels occur in option deals; that is, they occur with one's current publisher. Strange but true. Ask around. You may be surprised.

A final temptation is that, having tasted early success, an author is seized with the desire to write the Great American Novel. Nothing is wrong with that impulse, but it is sensible to consider one's timing and one's audience. Think of the G.A.N. as a detour, or perhaps a vacation. Do you have time for it? Will your readers travel with you, or wait for your return?

If the answer is yes, bon voyage. If it is no, better stick close to home.

ENVY

When a writing career hits a crisis point, there is one event I can always count on: the author involved will fall prey to envy.

Misfortune breeds resentment, especially resentment of others' apparent success. The grass is never greener on the other side of the fence than when one's own lawn is dry and brown. Envy can spur action, I will admit, but it also clouds thinking and provokes emotional responses to situations that require cool heads, logical planning, and sangfroid.

Here are some common remarks that I hear from envious authors:

- My writing is better than 90 percent of the crap that's out there.
- I need an aggressive agent/editor/publisher.
- Publishers decide which books will be best-sellers.
- It's all about ego. Big egos get big advances.
- Why can't I have . . . ? (Choose one:)
  a) a bigger advance
  b) advertising
  c) hardcover publication
  d) mainstream status
  e) an auction
- This business really sucks.

I can hardly blame authors for these sentiments, but these ways of looking at their problems are not particularly helpful. The following are some of my responses to those envy-driven remarks:

- It may be true that your prose is better than 90 percent of the competition's, but can the same honestly be said of your storytelling? Maybe it is time to take a look at your plotting.

- What you need even more than an aggressive agent (or whatever) is a smart agent. Strategy beats brute force every time.

- Publishers do select certain books for best-seller treatment, but those decisions are based on certain criteria. Top among these is whether a given book really has the potential to sell widely to all categories of readers. That automatically eliminates most genre novels, first novels, and mainstream novels that have any kind of limiting subject matter, or unsympathetic protagonists.

- Sure, you can have an auction, advertising, hardcover publication, mainstream status . . . in fact, you can have whatever you want. But is this the right moment and is this the best novel for the strategy that you want to pursue? Let's think about it.

- Yes, this business sucks sometimes . . . but it sure beats managing a Wal-Mart.

If you actually feel that managing a Wal-Mart would be better than sticking with a writing career, then it might not be a bad idea to consider a change of occupations. Indeed, your health might improve.

If, however, you can get yourself over your envy, you may find that there are sensible ways out of your situation.

REHABILITATION

Suppose that in spite of all your caution, forethought, planning, and hard work, things nevertheless go drastically wrong. Can anything be done to help writers who are about to perish?

Some authors who felt they were treated unfairly have attacked the perish problem with a traditional American solution: they have sued their publishers for failing to advertise and promote.

A few have even won.

Indeed, the U.S. Court of Appeals, Second Circuit, has ruled that a publishing contract "implies an obligation upon [the publisher to make] a good-faith effort to promote the book, including a first printing and advertising budget to give the book a reasonable chance of achieving market success in light of the subject matter and likely audience." Sounds good, doesn't it?

Unfortunately, nothing much has changed. Neither is it likely to change quickly. The perish trap is bigger than, and beyond the healing powers of, any single author, agent, or publisher. It has to do with them, but also with powerful chain bookstores that (until recently) thrived on glitzy frontlist trash, with the antiquated returns system, and with many other factors.

So, while we wait for evolution to purge the publishing business of its inefficiencies, what can we do about crashed careers? Unfortunately, by the time I receive a call from most drowning authors it is, in many cases, already too late to rescue them. There are a few realistic options, though, and they go like this:

1. Switch genres.
2. Adopt a pseudonym and try again.
3. Hunker down and wait. The sting of bad numbers will fade in a few years.

Unsatisfying options, I agree. In fact, they are downright humiliating. But sometimes it truly is better to run away, the better to live to fight again another day. And there are other possibilities. These, however, require courage and clear vision on the part of both author and agent.

One strategy that works is to build a bigger and better mousetrap. I do not mean a novel that is just longer; I mean a novel that is much greater in scope, scale, quality, and ambition. Up and down the pipeline, this new book can then be presented as a great leap forward and, with luck and a change of category, the author's previous numbers may no longer be held against her.

There are pitfalls to this plan, chief of which is that many authors in crisis are bitter. Bitterness obstructs creativity. (If you do not believe me, just try to write when you are heat-of-the-moment angry. It cannot be done, or at least not very well.) Another common problem is that authors in crisis often cannot see their writing objectively. If they have developed bad habits or have grown lazy, they need to improve but the thirst for validation gets in the way. So, you may not want to attempt an ambitious leap forward until you are through your crisis and feeling more confident.

Changing publishers is also sometimes possible. In fact, it is sometimes the *only* option. If you have been stung by lousy numbers, though, making a switch can be difficult. As I mentioned in Chapter 10, when I pitch a previously published client to a new editor the first question I am usually asked is, "What are his numbers?" If they are awful, the new editor may be stymied regardless of her enthusiasm for the author's writing.

Switching formats can also help one get unstuck. A "perished" hardcover author can try a move into original paperback, and vice versa. There are drawbacks here, too, and it is a good idea to consider whether the new format really makes sense.

Finally, the most difficult advice of all to follow: if you have been marked to perish, keep alive your sense of adventure. You started writing because it is fun and highly fulfilling. If you lose that joy and let bitterness overwhelm you, believe me you will compound your troubles and slow your rehabilitation.

You need for your creative juices to be flowing. Why? Because creativity and confidence are what you are going to need to survive.

Damage Control Checklist

Warning Signs:
- ☐ Low advance
- ☐ High advance unsupported by royalty earnings
- ☐ Bad cover
- ☐ Bad reviews
- ☐ Low "ship-in"
- ☐ High returns/low sell-through
- ☐ Genre switch/new style
- ☐ Crossover novel
- ☐ New publisher
- ☐ Novel "orphaned" by editor
- ☐ Publisher a "career-killer"
- ☐ Poor distribution
- ☐ Backlist quickly out of print
- ☐ Option book declined

☐ Agent ineffective
☐ Agent not returning calls

Prevention:
☐ Revise novel
☐ Take time marketing
☐ Get good agent
☐ Find enthusiastic editor
☐ Find stable editor
☐ Tell publisher career plan
☐ Suggest cover approaches to art director
☐ Make friends with publicist
☐ Self-promote

Problem Solving:
☐ Follow editor to new house, *or* . . .
☐ Stay put, but "resell" novel in-house
☐ Seek realistic next advance, *or* . . .
☐ Push for high new advance
☐ Take time out to write Great American Novel, *or* . . .
☐ Stay the course
☐ Avoid envy, *or* . . .
☐ Take delight in self-pity

Extreme Remedies:
☐ Switch genres
☐ Adopt pseudonym
☐ Wait a while
☐ Write a bigger book
☐ Switch formats
☐ Switch publishers
☐ Switch agents
☐ Relax
☐ Have fun
☐ Manage a Wal-Mart

13
CHAPTER

The Bottom Line:
Storytelling

WHY TRASH SELLS

IT IS ONE OF THE ETERNAL FRUSTRATIONS OF PUBLISHING: exquisite stylists languish on the shelves while popular novelists like Harold Robbins, Sidney Sheldon, Jackie Collins, and Robert James Waller (*The Bridges of Madison County*) skyrocket to the top of the best-seller lists.

Why?

Before answering that question, let me clarify that I am not suggesting you write so-called "trash." I firmly believe that every novelist should follow his or her own destiny; nevertheless, it is undeniable and puzzling that trash sells. I believe that there is a reason, and in exploring it I think we all might learn a thing or two.

First, a statement of fact: trash does not sell because it is well written. It may be smoothly written, even deft at times, but wonderful word craft, haunting description, and deep and complex characterization are not among the attributes of trash. So why do people bother with it? An important point to accept is that people *do* bother with it. Millions of them do. Clearly it is getting through to them on some level. It must. If it did not, it would not sell. So, here is my main thesis: *What most people want from a novel is not fine writing but a good story.*

Many authors, I am sure, will disagree with my use of the word *good*. What is *good* about the plot of Sidney Sheldon's *The Other Side of*

Midnight? It is an unrealistic story about people who could not possibly exist. It is a fable, all black and white. Its plot strains credulity to the breaking point.

That is all true, and yet millions of people, myself included, could not put down Sheldon's novel. As incredible as its events were, they nevertheless got me involved. I think this was not only because Sheldon set an effective premise and then complicated it with ruthless single-mindedness, but also because he created characters to whom anyone could relate, and gave them problems that we all understand.

Stay with me here. First, about the characters: they may not seem like you or me, but that is not important. What matters is that there is something about them with which you and I can identify. Take the Aristotle Onassis character, Constantin Demiris. We do not identify with him because he resembles Onassis (although his wealth is attractive); we are drawn to him because he controls his own destiny and because he is driven by the all-consuming need for revenge. He not only feels a desire that we all have felt but also acts upon it successfully.

What is so great about that? Just this: we can see ourselves in him. He journeys somewhere that we all would like to journey, does things we all wish we were allowed to do. In him, Sheldon has magnified a common desire. Now, here is where many authors and critics differ with trash hacks and junk readers. Aesthetes feel that because a character, feeling, theme, plot, or moral is familiar, it is valueless, trite, overused; a spice that has lost its flavor.

Popular writers and their readers disagree. They say exactly the opposite: familiar characters, feelings, themes, plots, and morals are powerful precisely because they *are* familiar. They are durable. Time-tested. They are undeniably true. So, here is my second thesis: *Trash sells because readers want their values and beliefs affirmed in their fiction.*

You do not have to like that. You may be the sort of writer and reader who likes to see things in a new way, to be challenged by (or challenge in) a novel. If so, more power to you. However, it is pointless to deny that what you want from fiction is not what most people want. Generally speaking, readers want a mirror in which to see themselves as they would like to be; not as they are, but as they hope to become.

If you look closely at the work of trashy best-sellers, you will find that many of them tell moral fables with tried-and-true outcomes, full of time-tested observations. For example, money cannot buy happiness; ambition carries the seeds of its own destruction; greed is bad; love conquers all; anyone can be a hero. Sound simplistic? Such sentiments are, but they still have power because they reflect profound truths.

It is fashionable today to say that we have lost our values, that we are wandering, directionless, at the end of the millennium. I disagree. Look at popular fiction; it is full of morality. It brims with hope. It affirms for us again and again that the beliefs and values we hold dear are alive.

It would seem that *The Bridges of Madison County* is a huge exception to that principle; after all, it is a novel that celebrates infidelity. Indeed, no novel has caused as much puzzlement in publishing as that one. What do people see in it? Why did it sell? I am convinced that *Bridges* does affirm a belief for Americans: not that infidelity is good, but that going through life in a deadened state is bad. *Bridges* says that authentic feeling and true passion are worth great risk. The writing may not be brilliant, but the message speaks directly to our stressed-out decade.

The lesson in all this for novelists is not to dish tired plots on overcooked themes, but to think about what you want to say: your meaning, point, or moral. If it is something new, fine. If the message is familiar, then by all means put it across to readers in a fresh and exciting way.

The point is that to the extent that fiction validates our cherished ideals it will sell. To the degree that it condemns us as people, holding up the ugly mirror of truth but leaving us without hope, it will be shunned. Readers are largely optimists. They want to believe that human beings are fundamentally good. They love happy endings.

Those, I believe, are the main reasons that trash sells.

CHARACTERS: SYMPATHY VS. STRENGTH

The formula for all-purpose story construction has been boiled down to its essentials many times. One of the most effective breakdowns I have ever read is Dwight V. Swain's *Techniques of the Selling Writer*, but there are many other how-to texts from which to choose.

Virtually all of them begin the universal story recipe with some version of the following:

Take a sympathetic protagonist, and then . . .

Stop right there. I am interested in that phrase *sympathetic protagonist*. What exactly is meant by that? Many green writers want their readers to *like* their main characters. While it is indeed pleasant to enjoy the company of the character with whom you will journey for four hundred pages, likability is not a primary reason for identification. Indeed, characters who are merely nice can quickly grow insipid.

Other writers often try to make their characters sympathetic by causing the reader feel sorry for them. To be sure, evoking pity is effective. Characters who are down on their luck, or who struggle with inner demons, may win my good wishes. That is *sympathy* in the ordinary sense, but not in the technical sense. Our type of sympathy is something different.

Sympathy in the technical sense is the identification between reader and character. It is the reason for their bonding. If I say that I sympathize with Scarlett O'Hara, it means that I see in her something of myself. She is a reflection of me. I appreciate her qualities and care about her fate since in a way she *is* me.

Now, you are probably wondering what I have in common with the heroine of *Gone with the Wind*. Actually, apart from having been born in Georgia, Scarlett and I have little in common. She is a woman; I am not. She has a sharp tongue; I wish that I did. She makes dramatic gestures; I generally just read about them. Nevertheless, when lost in that classic novel I bond with Scarlett O'Hara. I sympathize with her. We become one.

That happens because I project myself into her. She has qualities that I would like to have: courage, willfulness, pride, ego, wit. One word that can sum up all of that is *strength*. If nothing else, you have to admit that Scarlett O'Hara is strong. Indeed, I believe it is most often the strength of protagonists that draws us to them. Not niceness, not vulnerability. Strength.

Dozens of objections doubtless leap to mind. But stop: think for a minute. Strength is not only a physical quality, but an inner quality, too; thus frail, elderly Miss Marple is strong. Strength is also not the same as goodness; if it were then Patricia Highsmith's criminal protagonist Ripley would not be a hero (anti or otherwise). Neither is strength the ability to take action; if it were, corpulent and sedentary Nero Wolfe would not attract us.

Indeed, what unites all the detectives I just mentioned is their brains. They are, quite simply, a lot smarter than anyone else around them. That is their strength, and that makes them protagonists with whom we mentally bond, with whom we sympathize. We would all love to be as smart as Sherlock Holmes.

Strength is so fundamental to sympathy, in fact, that it explains why sometimes the most memorable character in a story can be the villain. Everyone remembers Sax Rohmer's Dr. Fu-Manchu, but who remembers the nominal hero of the Fu-Manchu series? (It was Nayland Smith.) The same goes for the jailed serial killer Hannibal Lecter in Thomas Harris's *Red Dragon* and *Silence of the Lambs*. He is the most sympathetic one in those books because he is the strongest, despite being sociopathic and locked in prison.

Having established the relationship between sympathy and strength, we can begin to catalogue the different kinds of strength and thus determine in advance the degree of sympathy that our protagonists will evoke. There is physical strength: Conan the Barbarian. There is endurance: James Bond. There is cunning: George Smiley. There is integrity: Howard Roark. There is love: Jane Eyre.

What is the greatest kind of strength? Many authors would argue that it is *principle*, a protagonist's beliefs. Indeed, holding principles dear can redeem much else that is unpleasant in a character. Case in point: Raymond Chandler's Philip Marlowe. I would like to argue, however, that there is one quality—or perhaps call it an ability—that is even more supreme: self-sacrifice. The willingness to give of oneself, maybe even to offer one's life for another, is a strength that goes beyond muscles, brains, or heart. It is a strength of spirit.

If that sounds religious, so be it. There is a reason that the stories of Moses and Christ have inspired people of faith for centuries. Their strength came from beyond personal convictions; it came from above. Authors who look for sources of sympathy for their characters could do worse than to find examples in the protagonists of our most enduring storybook, the Bible.

If you would rather stick closer to earth, there is certainly no shortage of strength in historical characters. Who knows? If we look hard enough we may even find strength in people around us today; if not in our leaders, then at least in our friends. And that is a thought that wins my sympathy.

CONFLICT: THE BIGGEST PROBLEM OF ALL

Seventeen years as an agent makes one accustomed to handing out rejection. I do not like to turn away authors, but it is part of my job—a big part. Sadly, there is one oft-recurring reason that manuscripts do not make the grade. It is so common, in fact, that I have a number of different ways to express it:

- Your novel gets off to a slow start.
- It takes too long for your novel to get into gear.
- The tension level in your story is low.
- Your protagonist's central problem is not strongly focused.

All of these comments in some way refer to the engine that drives any story: *conflict*. Authors use a variety of terms to describe this quality: tension, the "problem," the "obstacle," friction, suspense. Whatever the term, it is the encounter between characters and whatever blocks them from their goals or happiness.

Conflict keeps us reading. When a character about whom we care, or even with whom we simply identify, runs up against a problem, a block, an obstacle, we want to find out how things will turn out. If everything is fine and dandy, who cares? It is conflict that stops us in our tracks and forces us to pay attention.

Indeed, there is something almost mathematical about the effect of conflict upon a reader. It can even be expressed as an equation: "The degree of believable conflict contained in a story or scene (x) is directly proportional to the level of reader interest in that same story or scene (y) and the span of the reader's attention (z)." Not for nothing is the news on TV always bad.

One of the tritest, but truest, pieces of advice one reads in how-to-write-fiction books is "Establish conflict early." Other expressions of this same principle are "Hook your reader right away" and "Grab your reader's attention and don't let it go." They all mean the same thing: a reader will not become fully engaged in your story until conflict appears.

The fear most authors have about putting conflict on page one is that it may be too obvious. They imagine that if they set up the central problem right away then their novel will read like an action-packed pulp magazine yarn, or like an overheated confession article of the type found lying around in cheap beauty salons. Most authors want to be taken seriously. They want their novels to exhibit craft, to elicit admiration.

For that reason, many authors begin by setting the scene, using long, mostly visual descriptions to put us in the right mood. It is hard to argue with that kind of opening. Some great writers have opened their books that way; Charles Dickens, for example: "It was the best of times, it was the worst of times."

The truth is that it takes enormous skill to pull off a descriptive opening. The same is true of openings that first set up character and give us all the background to the story. The latter approach is essential to novels in which a cast of players must gather in one place, but as with the openings that are purely descriptive there is a trick to them, and it involves infusing the opening with some alternate type of tension.

Take another look, for instance, at the opening line of A *Tale of Two Cities*: "It was the best of times, it was the worst of times." The dichotomy in those ideas is striking. Their juxtaposition carries tension. We want to know *why* the times were both good and bad, and for the next six hundred pages or so Dickens tells us.

A more complicated opening situation occurs when it is essential that a certain event be included because it sets up the components of the conflict to come. Take the opening scene of John Grisham's *The Firm*. It is a job interview. In it, the novel's young lawyer protagonist, Mitch McDeere, is being scrutinized by several partners in a prominent tax law firm. They want the right man for the job, and Mitch very badly wants the job, too. The scene is ripe with tension.

Later on we discover that the firm is crooked and that McDeere is in danger, but first it is necessary for Grisham to establish that McDeere badly wants this particular position. It has to mean a lot to McDeere; otherwise the whole premise falls apart, since as a top

Harvard Law School graduate McDeere could have had any job. The novel's main conflict is still chapters away, but Grisham wisely fills this opening scene with intermediate conflict.

Intermediate conflict is a temporary conflict that keeps the story going while it is on its way to the main source of tension.

Let me illustrate with an example from an entirely different sort of novel, Anton Myrer's *The Last Convertible*. Myrer's is a generational novel: it tells the story of a group of five friends, beginning at Harvard during World War II and ending in the present day. The action of the novel moves back and forth in time, as well. As the characters grow and change, lose love and find it, we come to care for them deeply. (Trust me.) Now, where do you begin a novel like that? What is the story's inciting incident, its first moment of change?

Myrer opens the novel at his narrator's family breakfast table. *At the breakfast table*? It might seem that there is nothing dramatic about that, but it serves several functions. First, it introduces two of the main players, George and Nancy, and gives us an opportunity to hook into the loving hurly-burly of their family. Sympathy is established. So is the novel's unifying symbol, a classic green Cadillac convertible called the Empress that once belonged to the five friends and now sits up on blocks in George's garage. The story is foreshadowed.

The real reason that this opening works, though, is that it is shot through with intermediate conflict. There is friction between George and Nancy. They are at odds over their daughter Peg's boyfriend, Ron. Nancy judges him harshly; George not at all. And then there is the Empress: George loves it, but Nancy wants to wish it good riddance. You see? Conflict.

Needless to say, sustaining conflict throughout a novel is important. Raising its level is also helpful. Mystery writers, for example, will drop several bodies on the way to the solution. Thriller writers frequently set their action against a ticking clock, creating a "countdown to doom." A good romance is darkest before the dawn.

But before any of that comes the novelist's first job: putting conflict on page one.

SETTINGS: IT'S ALL IN THE DETAILS

A story is not a story unless it is set in a place that is both believable and absorbing. Who wants to go somewhere flat? Now, do not get me wrong: there is no reason that a novel cannot be set in, say, Kansas. However, in order for Kansas to live as a setting it will need to be described in a way that makes it a living, breathing thing, a character in its own right. The method for doing that involves selecting the right details.

Details that are the most effective at describing a place are telling or representative. It is easy to be heavy-handed that way, of course. If a choice of detail is too obvious, too symbolic, it will puncture the illusion of place. The reader's disbelief will suddenly let go and fall from the high spot where it was previously suspended.

On the other hand, ordinary details selected with no concern for their value in establishing mood, time of day, or location—those details are no good, either. Details must add value.

Now, how much description is too much? How much is too little? Believe it or not, most beginning novelists err on the side of too little detail. Perhaps they are afraid of losing their readers' attention, or perhaps they have been influenced by the shorthand techniques of movies and TV, but whatever the reason much novice fiction feels like it is set in Nowhere Land.

The opposite problem often crops up in science fiction and fantasy manuscripts. Here, the world in which the story is set is unusual. It is necessarily different from ours, and the reader must understand the way it operates—its rules, if you will—in order for the action of the novel to make sense. Thus, in SF and fantasy manuscripts I often find long prefaces or clunky passages that explain why things here are not the same. More effective is *demonstrating* that things are not the same. Frank Herbert did that brilliantly in *Dune*, as did Tolkien in *The Hobbit*.

Happily, there is one technique that experienced SF and fantasy writers use that may have some utility for everyone: world-building. This is the practice of cataloguing all the different dimensions of an alternate society: government, religion, economy, the arts, science and medicine, class structure, and so on. In short, everything about a place and *what makes it different*.

Gifted world-builders can not only construct a logical alternate place, but also invest it with inner conflicts and contrasting sides.

For instance, in a well-built alien civilization there is not only religion, but warring sects; not only rich and poor but rival minorities and ethnic hatred; not only industry but declining resources.

What is the lesson in this for writers whose stories are set in our world? In searching for details that will bring a place alive, one can look not just at what may be seen, touched, heard, or smelled but at what may be feared, enjoyed, misunderstood, forgotten, blessed, or buried. A place is more than its externals. It is a collection of aspects, the depiction of which will make that place either real, vivid, and exciting or blurry, dull, and uninvolving for the reader.

Settings are packed with potential. The details are up to you.

TWISTS AND TURNS

Little is more disappointing than a novel in which nothing seems to happen. I do not mean that a story has to be action-packed. I am talking about characters that grow, a plot that swings in new directions (or even reverses), the offstage revolution that suddenly puts onstage events in a whole new context. I am talking about variety, plot shifts, twists, and turns.

Causing a plot to shift is often a matter of breaking free of linear structure, or allowing the characters to make a mess. Spring the unexpected. Suppose, for instance, that in your coming-of-age story the hero's house burns down or his mother suddenly commits suicide. What would that do? Shake things up?

Well, there you have a shift. If your shift also manages to permanently change the direction of your story, you have a full plot turn.

Plot twists are surprises that connect story threads, or perhaps tear them apart. They provoke the response, "Ah-ha!" The disclosure of a killer's identity is usually, one hopes, a twist. Other ways to initiate a twist? Suddenly elevate the status of a minor character, or kill off someone essential to the plot.

Scary? Then perhaps your story is too tame.

Sometimes turning the whole ship is a good idea. Blow a hurricane into the middle of a romance story. What would happen to your detective's investigation if all of a sudden the state legislature passed the death penalty? Are you in the middle of a fantasy quest? What if magic spells suddenly did not work at night?

You see what I am getting at: impose a big change in the rules, or in the social, political, or economic background to your story. Shake things up. Assassinate your president. See what it does.

Some of the most effective twists and turns are those internal to characters: the creep who suddenly turns good and grows up; the beauty who is disfigured and begins hurting others; the loner who discovers that friends can betray; the jokester who one day can find no reason to laugh; the upbeat invalid who unexpectedly recovers; the widow who learns that she is happy alone.

Consider putting your characters through some changes. Isn't that what a story is for? One of my favorite novels is Irwin Shaw's *Bread upon the Waters*. In it, a high school history teacher and his family receive ever-growing gifts from a rich gentleman whose life was saved by the teacher's daughter. Far from improving their condition, the rich man's rewards tear the family apart and nearly ruin the teacher's life. To cope with his blessing, the teacher must recognize that he is cursed.

Irwin Shaw knew how to put his characters through changes. And how to hold my attention.

SCOPE AND SCALE

What are the stakes in your novel? Life and death? Sorry, that is not enough.

What do you mean? you ask. *What can be more important than a person's life?* Plenty of things: the health of the economy, the fate of democracy, the integrity of the Church, a person's honor, the trust of children, the course of history, the outcome of war . . .

Life and death is easy. Every wanna-be suspense writer can come up with a premise that puts somebody's life at risk. (Come read my slush pile and see the evidence.) What not all can do is to devise a premise in which a whole lot more is at stake: large issues that matter to us all, not just a few. A premise that transcends ordinary concerns in this way is said to have *scale*.

Here is one of my favorite large-scale stories of recent years: Roger MacBride Allen's science fiction novel *The Ring of Charon*. As the novel opens, gravity experiments are being carried out on Charon, a moon of Pluto. Mere hours before the facility is due to shut down, a gravity wave is at last successfully sent toward Earth. The researchers watch on a view screen as the wave breaks back home . . . and Earth winks out of existence.

A tiny gravity wave should not have done that. Where did Earth go? And why? Can they get it back? The answers to those questions make for an exciting novel, and one in which the stakes are not merely life and death but are the very fate of Earth itself.

Even if you prefer your stakes pitched on a more credible scale, consider how your story can become about something more, something larger. One can start by asking what principles are involved. Are codes of conduct called into question? Are there concerns that go to the bedrock of the institution on which one's story is built? If not, *can there be*?

If *scale* measures the weight or importance of a story, then its breadth is measured by *scope*. Scope is a story's range of view. It can be narrow or wide-angle. If a novel moves freely across society, taking the reader high and low, or spans years, decades, or centuries, then it is said to have scope.

Some novels demand a narrow scope. A category romance, for instance, is most effective when it is narrowly focused on the hero and heroine. Their interaction is the cake, and everything else is frosting. Most romance readers do not want too many layers (unless we are talking about a wedding cake at the end).

Novels that demand wide scope are those such as historical sagas, epic fantasies, space opera, and satires. *Satires*? Yes. Consider *Catch 22* or *The Bonfire of the Vanities*: both of these classic novels show us a range of people, humble to high. Human folly knows no bounds, and using that range is one important requirement of a satire. (Without scope satire becomes parody, lampoon, or burlesque, and those are difficult forms to sustain over the length of a novel. Try it sometime.)

More often, though, when we think of novels with scope we think of *Dr. Zhivago, War and Peace, Gone with the Wind, One Hundred Years of Solitude, Hawaii, From Here to Eternity, David Copperfield, Les Miserables, Don Quixote, Dune, The Lord of the Rings*, and so on. These novels range up and down society and/or carry us across great spans of distance and time.

Can you extend the scope of your story? Thriller writers can add interest by adding characters; however, adding time to their story lines will weaken suspense. In thrillers, usually the shorter the time frame the better. So, too, with novels like Joyce's *Ulysses*, which takes place all in one day (or night).

For just about every other author, though, there are usually ways to increase a novel's scope. One technique for doing so involves creating a cast that has variety and some pairings of opposites. Obvious choices are good/bad, rich/poor, weak/strong, pretty/plain, smart/smarter, centered/chaotic, crafty/naive. Pairings do not need to be terribly obvious. The point is to create contrast in your cast and give it texture.

Historical writers have unlimited opportunities for scope. Readers of historicals love broad-ranging casts and a sense of sweeping change and passing time. Indeed, to portray another era with anything like accuracy one is practically forced to have scope.

In fact, one of the secrets of adding scope to a story premise is to set that story against a historical backdrop, preferably war. For example, take any simple love story, mystery, or tale of family conflict and plunk it down in the middle of World War II. See what happens? It gets bigger, doesn't it? Instant scope.

Unfortunately, World War II is overused as a backdrop. There are plenty of other exciting eras, but the farther back one goes in time the harder it becomes for modern readers to relate. That limits the choices. Ambitious authors are always looking for settings that are less obvious but that still contain broadly significant social currents that make for powerful scope.

Figure it out. There is always a way to heighten your story's scale, or enlarge its scope, or both. Writers who bother to do so will ride the whirlwind and reap the rewards of powerful storytelling.

14
CHAPTER

Collaborations

THE POWER OF TWO

I BEGAN MY CAREER AS AN AGENT AT A LARGE, WELL-KNOWN firm. Its list was hundreds of clients long and was divided into equal portions that were assigned to several "desks." Agents came and went, but each desk's list of clients stayed more or less the same.

That was how, at the very outset of my career, I found myself representing one of the most successful collaborative teams of all time: the pair of cousins who wrote under the name Ellery Queen.

I was ecstatic at first. As it turned out, though, there was little for me to do. Only one of the cousins was still alive. My job for the team, I discovered, was mainly to write the letters that accompanied the checks that were cut for them almost daily. Those checks, however, proved to be an education in themselves. Some of them were huge, but the one that impressed me the most was one of the smallest. It was a check for the sale of "Zulu language rights" to two Ellery Queen titles.

Zulu language rights! Can you imagine? How many authors do you know who have sold Zulu language rights? Not too many, I will bet. One thing I learned from those checks was that collaborations can be highly profitable. Before you rush out to hook up with a collaborator, though, let me tell you another story.

This one concerns a successful nonfiction author. One day her publisher had a bright idea: why not write a novel based on her area of expertise? A suspenseful premise was inherent in her subject, so she agreed to write a proposal. After struggling with the difficulties of novel construction, this author decided to join forces with a collaborator. She figured that the proposal would get done in half the time and be twice as good.

Such was not the case. A violent disagreement over the story broke out between the collaborators. Soon they were tape recording each other's phone calls and paying enormous hourly fees to intellectual property lawyers in order to settle the question of the story's true ownership. All of this, mind you, over a proposal that was never very good and that, to my knowledge, finally went unsold.

Collaborations, then, may make you rich but they may also make you paranoid and poorer. Are they worth it? If you are planning one, how can you know whether or not it will be a success?

PREDICTORS

Believe it or not, one factor that does *not* predict the success of a collaboration is that of complementary skills; that is, working with a partner whose strengths are your weaknesses. Obviously, that is a welcome by-product of any collaboration. Indeed it is natural, since no two writers are exactly alike.

A far more accurate indicator of success is friendship; that is, working with someone whom you've known long and well. Why? Because good communication is crucial to the process, as is the ability to resolve disputes. Two friends are more likely to compromise than two acquaintances. Friends care for each other's feelings. They have a relationship to safeguard.

Indeed, a good way to judge whether a possible collaboration will work is to ask yourself this question: "If the worst happens and we ultimately waste each other's time, will we still be on speaking terms?" If the answer is yes, then your partnership may have a chance. If no, you might want to rethink.

Another positive indicator is a comparable level of skill and experience. There are exceptions to this rule, but generally working with someone on your level of development, whether that means beginner or long-time best-seller, will yield better results. Two writers at the same stage are in balance. An unbalanced pairing, however, can produce feelings of inhibiting awe, impatience, or resentment over the unequal contribution that each makes. (And believe me, it is not always the experienced one who works the hardest.)

I mentioned exceptions to this rule. One is the "master/slave" collaboration, which is now common in the science fiction field. In this arrangement an established pro either outlines a story or defines the premise and parameters of a series. The less experienced writer, the slave, then executes the outlined novel or writes a novel that he himself has outlined (with the pro's approval). Pros can thus milk their past success without troubling to write whole new novels of their own.

Such novels, however, are usually work-for-hire projects set up by a packager. Thus, they are not true collaborations even though the pro may approve or even polish the completed manuscript. The slave is a hired hand, paid for her time and rewarded with an inferior share of the profits. (Who gets the biggest cut? The packager.)

I recommend such collaborations only for new writers who want to learn on the job, or who are devotees of the "master" in question.

Perhaps the most reliable indicators of success are three of the simplest:

First, a willingness by both collaborators to work hard. In no case should you assume that a joint effort will involve less time and effort than a novel of your own. The workload is the same.

Second, a lack of ego. A successful collaborator always sees problems as his own; after all, that is how it is with his own fiction. He also will not collaborate on a story that he feels he could write by himself. (Why should he? A partner would just get in the way.)

Third, a shared passion; that is, a strong agreement on what makes a good story and what the partners want to say in their work. Without that, believe me, any collaboration is doomed from the start.

PRACTICAL CONSIDERATIONS

Suppose you have got all that. You have found a collaborator at your level, you are buddies unto death, you are in complete sync on style, and you have got a hot story mapped out and ready to go. Should you start word processing? Not just yet.

There are a number of practical considerations to deal with before beginning. It may save trouble and heartache later to clear them up now. Many collaborations have been wrecked by procedural snags that could have been settled at the outset.

First, there is the *collaboration agreement*. Okay, you trust your partner. Furthermore, you are not a lawyer. Your inclination is to let a formal agreement go for now since, after all, you have not produced anything salable yet. Plenty of time to write a collaboration agreement later, right?

Bad idea.

Anything you have not calmly discussed ahead of time, believe me, you could well wind up screaming about later on. Get it in writing now. Your agreement does not have to be in incomprehensible legalese. It does need to exist, however, and it should address all the possibilities that might come up. There are a number points to cover.

Who will do what? How will proceeds be split? Usually the work and the rewards are split fifty-fifty. However, there are exceptions. If the work to be written is to be based upon a prior work by one of the collaborators, that underlying work may have a value that you will want to have reflected in the ultimate payout.

What about rights to sequels? Usually this is no problem: the collaborators write sequels together. But that is not always possible or practical. One partner may have prior contract commitments, or may simply be bored with the project. What happens then? Unless your agreement spells out a procedure, there could be delays, sore feelings, and lost income.

So work it out. Be generous. If one of you wishes to continue but the other does not, why not let the series go forward? Some authors are afraid their children will grow up into monsters that they cannot control and do not recognize, but if you are that hung up on control why collaborate in the first place?

Others are worried about money. They feel they should benefit from what they helped to make. Well, why not? Work out something equitable. Cut your partner in even if she cuts out. That is a lot better than not being able to profit at all.

It is a good idea, though, to keep it simple when it comes to splits on sequels. Things can get pretty slippery when you start to consider, say, down-the-road movie sales. For instance, suppose you and your partner write one book together, but then your partner drops out. You continue the series, write nine more, and then an option deal for movie rights to one of them appears.

What sort of cut does your collaborator deserve in that instance? Fifty percent? Five percent? One percent? Ten books down the road, it would seem that your collaborator would be entitled to only a small share, but the "pick-up price" built into movie deals can be mouth-watering enough to make Mother Teresa feel greedy. If the collaborators have previously agreed on a simple formula—five percent of all future revenues, say—then there will be no problem. Get it on paper now.

Another possibility for splits on sequels is to draft a new collaboration agreement as each book comes along. That pattern has some pitfalls, though, one being that if future opportunities to negotiate fall at times of strain between the partners the negotiations could turn into nasty, no-win fights.

As I said, keep it simple. You may want to agree that either partner may kill the series if there is disagreement about its future direction. Better to quit while you are both ahead, no?

What about logistics and rules? You would think that in these days of phone, fax, and e-mail logistics would not be a problem. Collaborators can live as far away as Anchorage and Atlanta, can they not? Alas, it is rarely so. High-quality communication is called for in a collaboration, and that is difficult to achieve unless two people are face to face.

Many collaborators live close to each other for another reason: it is easier to keep track of things, such as which draft is which.

Whether you are close or far away, however, it is wise to agree on procedures. Who writes what? How much rewriting is allowed? What are your time limits? (This is not a hobby, after all.) Who will pay the paper, printing, and manuscript mailing costs?

Also, how will you settle disputes? It does not matter, really, so long as *some* procedure is set up; for instance, partner A gets his way the first time, partner B the next—no exceptions. Alternately, you could split the project into areas of supremacy. For example, you have final say in all decisions about plot, while your partner has final say in some other area, perhaps one that you care little about, like dialogue.

Finally, when the book is done who will do the final pass to establish consistency of tone? In a well-written collaboration it should be impossible for the reader to tell who wrote what.

Put your agreement in the form of a letter that both of you sign or, if you like, get a lawyer to draft something formal. The most important thing is to work it out in advance.

You both will thank each other later if you do.

AGENTS

Together you have written a dynamite book. Both your agents are happy, right? Not necessarily. If your partner is represented by a different agency you may find that you have bought yourselves ringside seats for the clash of the titans.

Now, most agents will handle this situation coolly and professionally. Regarding commissions, the usual arrangement is that each agent takes her 10 or 15 percent from her client's share of the revenues.

So far so good.

When disagreements arise, it is often over which agent will control the work; that is, who will sell it, market sub-rights, receive payments—and, incidentally, receive credit for the sale. No doubt about it, what is at stake here is a lot of ego. If your agents cannot reach agreement, suggest that they equally divide responsibility. That is, if one cuts the book deal, the other handles all sub-rights including TV and movie.

If all else fails, the Association of Authors Representatives—of which both your agents are members, I hope—has an Ethics Committee, one purpose of which is to settle disputes between member agents behind the scenes. Get your agents into arbitration.

Now, suppose your agent is dead set against the collaboration. What should you do? First, listen to him. His reasons may make sense. Your proposed collaboration may not fit into your career plan, or might endanger a solo series that you already have underway. Why compromise a successful line of business just for the thrill of trying something new?

If your agent's reasons do not make sense, though, you have a problem. It may be that your agent places her control and income ahead of your career. In that event, examine your options.

And remember: you come first (after your readers, of course).

PUBLISHERS

A great novel is a great novel, and if there is one thing publishers want it is great novels, correct? Again, not necessarily.

Your regular publisher may feel threatened by your collaboration. A new author and, possibly, a new agent have entered the equation. Will they get to keep you? And if they do, how will they sell their accounts on this new product line?

Collaborations can also embroil publishers in problems. Take the issue of cover credit: whose name goes first? Don't laugh! This issue is so troublesome that the boilerplate of most contracts already addresses this point. (It gives the publisher control over the order of cover credit.)

The stickiest problem for collaborators, though, comes when their publisher does not treat them equally. Indeed, a publisher may sign a collaboration team not because it is enthused about their novel, but because it wants to add one of them to its list. Keep your eyes open. If you feel you are being ignored in favor of your partner, you may be getting squeezed out.

By now you may have decided that it will be easier to work alone. Perhaps it is. Successful long-term collaborators are a special breed.

Still, you do not necessarily need to make a career of collaboration. If you and your potential partner trust and respect each other, you may discover that you can write both together and apart.

Will your collaboration be profitable? That is up to you both. When all is said and done, readers do not care whether the cover of your novel has on it two names or one. What your readers want from your collaboration is what they want from any novel: a good story.

15
CHAPTER

Packagers and Work-for-Hire

GIFT WRAPPING?

FROM MY AGENCY PHOTO ALBUM, HERE ARE SNAPSHOTS OF three career novelists:

1. Writer A is smiling. Her earnings from a best-selling novel based on a popular TV show are running into six figures.

2. Writer B appears worried. After finishing thirty action/adventure novels under another writer's name he is having trouble: publishers are not interested in his solo fiction.

3. Writer C looks grim. A new writer who went full-time too soon, she has been dropped by her publisher. Desperate for a new advance, she is writing an outline for a YA (young adult) horror series.

What is the factor that these snapshots have in common? Each of these writers is involved with some form of packager. Are packagers helpful to career novelists, or do they exploit them? Is Writer A right to feel happy? Is Writer B's career in big trouble? Is Writer C making a smart career move or a dumb one?

First, let's see what packagers actually do. Simplified, a packager is an individual or company that has an idea for a book. The packager pitches that idea to a publisher, obtains a contract, then hires a writer to execute the text. Then the packager may or may not (depending on the deal) rewrite the manuscript, edit it, and supply everything from illustrations to cover art, mechanicals, film, marketing support—even finished books.

Packaging is an old profession. Its roots are in nonfiction. Art books, textbooks, heavily illustrated medical and scientific books, and the like are the province of the packager. A more recent trend is the rise of the packaged trade book. Titles like *The Joy of Sex*, *The Way Things Work*, and *New York Public Library Desk Reference* are successful examples.

Fiction, too, has long been packaged. Earlier in this century, Edward Stratemeyer and his syndicate created the Bobbsey Twins, Tom Swift, the Hardy Boys, Nancy Drew, the Dana Girls—overall, 125 juvenile series. More recently, Lyle Kenyon Engle's company Book Creations generated the best-selling *Kent Family Chronicles*, *The Americans*, and *Wagons West*.

Publishers can also become packagers, as with movie novelizations and Star Trek titles. It can be argued that whole genres have been packaged: the steamy contemporary romance, for example. This category was not invented by any single author, but evolved out of a competitive quest for new product lines during a war between Harlequin and Silhouette Books.

Today, the science fiction field is overloaded with novels connected to movies, TV shows, computer games, role-playing games, and comics. Packaged product is encroaching, too, on the mystery field. Celebrity mystery "authors" are taking up slots, and publishers are even filling up their lists with mystery series created in-house and owned outright by them. What next?

To see what tomorrow may look like in a packager-dominated genre, one has only to look at the mass-market YA and middle-grade categories. Here, packaged series abound. In the eighties it was girl-oriented YA series like *Sweet Valley High*. Nowadays it is a flood of copycat middle-grade horror series. Such books can be delightful, but what happened to single authors? They are still around in hardcover, but fewer and fewer are making it in paperback. Packagers rule the YA racks.

Why do publishers buy from packagers? The reasons are not difficult to understand. For overburdened editors in our downsized industry, it is tempting to believe that packaged product will be easy to publish. Preedited manuscripts! Cover art in place! Of course, the reality is that packaged books can be twice as much work as those of single authors, but history never stopped anyone from taking a shortcut.

Another reason publishers like packagers is that they come up with strong commercial ideas. Clever hooks are the packager's ace up the sleeve. It is hard for editors to resist a cute idea, especially when that cute idea can easily be sold to the boss.

Packagers also have the knack of linking novels with licensed brand names. Spiderman? Sure! He's a natural bet for a novel, not because he is an especially rich or complex character (although he is more interesting than some), but because he has a ready-made audience—in theory. In actual fact, the packager who convinced Marvel Comics to go ahead with Spiderman novels hedged his bets and recruited a client of mine known for her quality writing, Diane Duane, to make the idea more foolproof.

Indeed, so many packaged novels and series have failed that publishers are growing wary. They are also getting smart: in some cases they are beating the packagers in the race to link up with top licensors. (That packagers make a healthy profit by exploiting young writers has not escaped their notice, either.) The packaging road rally is gathering speed.

RATIONALIZATIONS

So what does all this mean for authors? Opportunity? Danger?

The first truth to grasp is that in obtaining contracts from publishers, packagers do not generally get better terms than authors. Packagers claim that they do, and in some cases they are correct. But usually a packager's advance is no more than an author could get for the same project. Now, let's do a little math.

Is 100 percent of that advance money going to be paid to the work-for-hire writer? Are you kidding? The packager is going to take a healthy cut, usually 50 percent. What value do packagers add to a fiction property to justify this split? Ask and they will say: their ideas, outlines, editing, and reputations. (Cover art and production services do not count; those are paid for by the publisher in a separate transaction for an additional fee.)

If a licensor is involved, they too get a big slice of the cake, per-haps 25 percent. So what is left for the poor writers who execute the actual books? Often less than they might have gotten for novels of their own. Indeed, some authors are working for pitifully small pay. I have heard of some who wrote full-length novels and were paid as little as a flat $1,500. Advances like $3,500 and $5,000 are quite com-mon in the packaging game.

Does this add up? Are ideas and outlines (when packagers them-selves trouble to write them) worth the 50 percent that they skim off? I wonder. Still, there is no shortage of authors willing to accept deals for this kind of money. In fact, so many authors need work-for-hire assignments these days that it is getting quite difficult to obtain them unless you already have several solo novels under your belt. Packagers are getting picky.

Why are authors dying to write work-for-hire? The most common reason is the desperate need for income. For others, it may seem that this is the only chance they will have to see their writing in print, a fear that grows more valid as packaged product multiplies.

Of course, most writers do not see themselves as desperate or exploited. They convince themselves that writing work-for-hire nov-els is a really good idea. One attractive illusion is that work-for-hire contracts are easy to get, and so it may seem at first. For frustrated authors-in-waiting, being offered a contract with no delays and lit-tle up-front work seems like a sort of paradise. (Needless to say, this paradise is not all that it appears, but more on that in a moment.)

Another reason that authors clamor for work-for-hire is that they may believe it will help them to build an audience. That is quite wrong. One's name may appear on the cover of a packaged novel, but that is not why the public will buy it. They will buy it for the *other* names that appear on the cover: licensed characters, TV shows, celebrities credited as "author," and so on.

Readers will not necessarily follow authors from their work-for-hire novels to their own fiction. In fact, the evidence suggests oth-erwise, despite the lucky few who have managed a successful tran-sition, such as Margaret Weis and Tracy Hickman or R. A. Salvatore, all of whom wrote for TSR (creators of "Dungeons and Dragons").

Most writers-for-hire move on to their own fiction only to find themselves left high and dry.

Generally, publishers assume that work-for-hire will have no impact on the sales of an author's own fiction. They may use work-for-hire success as a selling point within the trade, but rarely do they try to sell new work to the public on that basis.

Another faulty rationalization that authors employ to justify accepting work-for-hire contracts is that such work will buy them time to write their own fiction. This is rarely true. Packagers pay for a writer's time and, believe me, they extract good value for their money. Usually a work-for-hire advance gives an author just enough breathing room to finish the project in question—and many work-for-hire deals do not even provide that much air.

As a result, work-for-hire authors who accept such assignments to fill in gaps in their income can find that at the end of the day they are in the same fix they were in at the beginning. With no new solo novel ready, and no new contract in sight, they are still short the rent money. What to do? Get a job? That is unlikely, especially if another work-for-hire contract is handy. If they are not careful, that income gap will turn into a chasm that they will never get across.

Those who fall into the work-for-hire trap frequently allow themselves this consolation: at least they are getting paid quickly. While that can be true, it is also often the case that there is a rush on for the manuscript in question. It is common in the packaging game for authors to finish their assignments around the same time that their signing advance arrives.

Younger authors sometimes also rationalize that writing work-for-hire fiction will allow them to learn on the job. This reasoning, at least, has some basis in fact . . . that is, if you are dying to become the kind of writer whose fiction appeals mainly to consumers of comics, computer games, TV shows, and movies. It is not that packaged novels are necessarily bad; it is just that they inevitably shape writers in a certain way. It is wise to consider whether one wants to be that type of writer before one gets too deeply into work-for-hire writing. It can be tough to undo the writing habits learned on that particular job.

Recognize, too, that producing packaged novels all day will satisfy your craving to write. When the day is over, what are you likely to do with your evenings? Go back to work, or turn on the TV and relax? Your own fiction can become a low priority when you have money in the bank and a brain that needs a rest from writing.

Face it; there are really only two good reasons to write work-for-hire: money, or the love of a particular project (or perhaps of the media property on which it is based). Several authors I know want to write "X-Files" novels simply because they love the TV show. Other authors of my acquaintance are dying to pick up where Ian Fleming, Rex Stout, or Erle Stanley Gardner left off.

For them, work-for-hire may be worth it. For everyone else, given the generally low pay and exploitation involved, the only reason to write work-for-hire is to pay the rent when there is no other choice. However, a work-for-hire contract can also, I admit, soothe an ego that has been beaten down by the industry. Many authors succumb for that reason alone.

INS AND OUTS OF WORK-FOR-HIRE

The concept of work-for-hire is derived from the most recent revision of U.S. copyright law in 1976. The new law created several categories of work-for-hire, that is, a situation in which the writer is not the creator of a work, but a contributor to a work created by another person or entity.

For instance, if one writes a foreword to a textbook, a translation, test questions, or compiles an index, those are instances in which a writer is contributing to a larger work. Her writing is occasioned by the larger work, is dependent upon it and subsidiary to it. The law says that the owner of such a larger work may copyright the whole. Employees who create documents in the normal "course and scope" of their employment—technical writers, for example— are similarly covered (or *uncovered*, I suppose). Such employed writers are also entitled to legally mandated employee benefits, though, unlike free-lancers.

With work-for-hire fiction, a different legal definition generally comes into play. Here, work-for-hire is any writing that is especially "ordered or commissioned"; that is, it is work created *after* an agreement has been drawn up between a packager and an author. In this instance the law also allows the packager to hold the copyright. What the writer is owed for his creative effort is defined entirely by the deal that he strikes.

In other words, if a novel-to-be has been commissioned, then the author's rights and compensation can be fixed rather than open-ended, as with royalties. Needless to say, work-for-hire horror stories abound. I know one science fiction author who wrote the text to a kids' picture-book version of a well-known SF movie. Her book sold some 750,000 copies and was the second best-selling hardcover of its year, surpassed only by a novel by James Michener. Her fee? A flat $6,000. (Later, her publisher did pay her a small bonus. Whoopee, huh?)

Let me tell you an even more horrifying story. There once was a well-regarded literary novelist—let's call him "Tim"—whose writing was much admired by the editor of a certain science fiction imprint. One day at lunch a packager heard this and later called Tim. He suggested that he package a novel to which Tim would write the text and for which he would commission a cover and interior illustrations. A deal might be obtained, he suggested. In fact, he already knew an editor who might like it.

Tim went for the deal. He wrote a proposal—the concept was entirely his—and sure enough the packager turned around and sold it to the editor who admired Tim's work. Now, this same deal could have been done by Tim's agent for a mere 10 percent commission; the publisher would have provided illustrations and art for free. Instead, the packager inserted himself into the situation and both took a large chunk of the revenues and kept the copyright.

Granted, in most cases the packager contributes more than that, but you can see how a writer can get ripped off in a work-for-hire situation. (By the way, Tim does not think that he was ripped off. He considers the packager his friend, and is grateful for the contract. I must admit, it did result in a terrific fantasy trilogy that might not otherwise have been written.)

What do you think? Was Tim ripped off? Is the packager entitled forever to control the copyright to Tim's work, not to mention his revenues?

It is possible that someday the law will be revised to disallow certain of the more abusive forms of work-for-hire contracts. Indeed, an attempt was made in Congress in 1993 to strike the work-for-hire provisions from the copyright law. (The effort died when the congressional term ended.) The next year Senator Thad Cochran of Mississippi tried to reform the work-for-hire provisions to curb specific abuses. For example, magazines might demand work-for-hire status for articles *after* they had been written, often with a waiver stamped on the back of the writer's check exactly where the writer would endorse it.

Reform is certainly needed, but on what legal basis will it be built? One remote possibility is a concept in European law called *droit moral*, meaning "moral right." *Droit moral* says that authors have the right to be credited as creators of their work (or not, at their election), and further, that they have the right to prevent work from being altered in ways that compromise its artistic integrity. Moral rights are weak under American law, but the concept gained some strength when the U.S. in 1988 became a signatory to the Berne Convention, an international copyright treaty. True reform, though, is still in the future.

Naturally, as weak as it is, packagers have noticed *droit moral*, and so you will find in nearly all work-for-hire contracts language in which the author waives all her possible rights and future claims to her work, including *droit moral*. Once signed, such agreements will be impossible to break no matter what Congress may do.

Should authors fight the terms of work-for-hire contracts? Should they insist, for example, that the copyright transfer to them after a certain period of time?

That depends. In most cases, packagers simply will not agree to let writers keep copyright control. Why should they? Too many authors are willing to sell it. The project may also involve licensors or others who have their own interests to protect. Disney would be foolish to cede any control of its character Mickey Mouse, for instance. However, in cases where an author's novel is wholly original to the author, and is merely being included in a product line trademarked to the packager or publisher—certain romance imprints have fallen into this category—then it is entirely reasonable that the copyright remain with the author or, at the very least, that it return to the author after a period of time, or once the book is out of print. In no circumstances should the copyright be relinquished when a novel is wholly the author's.

Now, what about compensation? Are flat fees ever fair? Should an author be due a royalty regardless of who controls the copyright?

Again, that depends. The law allows packagers to pay as little as they can get away with paying. When a flat fee is offered, take a look at what the project might earn down the road. The back-end revenues might be good (or bad). Look, too, at the sub-rights possibilities. The packager may not agree to a royalty or sub-rights split, but it never hurts to ask.

When given, royalties in a packaged deal are generally less than royalties for an author-owned work. Royalties of 1 and 2 percent are fairly meaningless unless the work sells better than most. Where that is unlikely or just a remote possibility, I usually try to get my clients at least 50 percent of all revenues, half of the prevailing royalty and half of all sub-rights income. I do not always get it, though. Packagers know how cheaply some writers are willing to sell themselves.

OTHER CONTRACT POINTS

Two other important points to consider in work-for-hire contracts are creative control and approval of the completed manuscript.

Generally speaking, packagers will want the ability to change what you write, to add to it, subtract from it, and to edit or rewrite it as they see fit. If your name is going on the book's cover this may be an issue of some concern. If so, you will want to be certain that your contract grants you absolute control, or at least approval of the changes that the packager makes. If *that* cannot be obtained, then secure your right to remove your name from the book at your option.

If the work in question is largely your own, and no third parties beyond the packager and publisher must approve it, then there is a strong case to be made for author control of any changes. However, the situation alters when the loop includes a licensor. The licensor probably has its own creative concerns, as well as an interest in protecting the integrity of its underlying property. DC Comics does not want some rogue fiction writer killing off Superman. (They reserve that privilege for themselves.)

Reasonable that may be, but where the licensor has approval of the manuscript there is room for tremendous abuse of the writer's talent and time. A job that was supposed to take ten weeks can stretch to ten months—for no extra money, either. Acceptable work can be turned down for the vaguest of reasons. Unless authors have first obtained contract protection, revisions can be forced upon them endlessly.

Do such abuses occur? In my experience they happen in 50 percent of all cases where a licensor is involved (and that is *not* an exaggeration). The reasons are plain enough: licensors who are the creators of stories or characters can be control freaks, or simply possessed of strong ideas about how stories based upon their work should feel to a reader. I sympathize with them, but at the same time comic-book writers and movie directors may have little idea of how a novel goes together, or, indeed, of what makes a novel good.

Novels that are overcontrolled by their licensors can wind up reading like comic books. Their characters can become as shallow as those in movies. Licensors have the right to do this, but when it comes at the author's expense the situation is abusive.

Nowadays, I insist that my clients work from an outline that is preapproved by the licensor; any revisions required of them may not go beyond the scope of that approved outline. I also insist that the author be given a minimum period of time in which to complete the manuscript. That lesson was taught to me the hard way. Once, a licensor waffled about my client's outline until just two weeks before her manuscript was due to the publisher. When the approval finally came I said to the packager, "Okay, let's negotiate a new delivery date."

"Nothing doing," said the packager. He had agreed to a publication date that was just months away; the novel had been announced, orders had been taken, a press run had been scheduled, and the covers had been printed. If he did not get a novel inside those covers on time he stood to lose big bucks. He said, "The contract says delivery in two weeks, and two weeks it shall be."

The licensor was at fault, but in this case it was the author who got squeezed. On top of that, the whole process had dragged on for so long that the author's advance, which previously had seemed good, became less and less adequate.

Building in a time limit for revision requests and final approval is also a good idea; that is, revision letters should be sent within a certain period after delivery, and approval of the revised manuscript should also come in a timely manner. And what if the final manuscript is, for some reason, unacceptable? A contract that calls for the author to return moneys previously paid is unfair. In work-for-hire projects writers are being paid for their effort, not for the final product, which, after all, the packagers can rewrite to their satisfaction.

If a manuscript is finally disapproved, I contend that it should be returned to the author (together with outlines, drafts, and computer disks), and no further use of its content should be allowed. If the packager *is* going to use even a portion of that "disapproved" manuscript, then it is fair to say that the author has done his job, at least in part, and is entitled to payment that reflects the time and effort he has put in.

Further, if the rejected manuscript is returned to the author, the author ought to be able to make use of any ideas, plot lines, characters, or places that are not proprietary to the packager or to a licensor. That is only fair, especially if payment is to be revoked.

Cover credit is something that most writers want on their work-for-hire novels, but there are cases in which an author may not want it, such as when the novel has been rewritten by another. Nowadays most packagers will agree to remove an author's name from the finished book if she desires, provided that the request arrives in adequate time.

Hopefully, everything will go well, the novel will be a success, and everyone will make money. If so, the author may want to write any future sequels. However, nothing obligates the copyright holder to use the author again unless it is spelled out in the contract in advance. If you want it, ask for it.

Finally, be sure the contract provides you with author's copies, and allows you to audit the packager's accounts and records as they relate to the work. If you have been paid a flat fee that is one thing, but if you have a royalty due or a cut of sub-rights revenues then your interest in the work is as material as if it were a novel of your own. Protection is your right.

In any event, it is wise for authors to push for as much as they can get in work-for-hire contracts. Packagers are hard-nosed people, and one can be sure that an unchallenged work-for-hire deal will be a bad one. Get a fair contract.

A FINAL LOOK AT THE ALBUM

Before closing, let's take another look at the snapshots from my agency album.

Is Writer A right to feel satisfied with herself? Since her earnings are running into six figures, it is hard to say that she should not. However, there is a potential danger for her: if she becomes too dependent on work-for-hire income, or compromises her work creatively for too long, then she is taking chances.

A full-time work-for-hire writer is not an independent author, but is rather a franchise manager, one with fewer rights than most employees. There is no security, and while the pay may be good it ultimately has upward limits. Such writers will never get really rich. Packagers have no reason to let them.

What about Writer B, the one who is trying to launch his own fiction after doing someone else's writing for many years? The only problem this writer has is one of self-perception. He feels like a pro, but in practical terms he is a first novelist. Readers have never heard of him. In selling to publishers, he actually faces only the same problems that all first-timers face. If Writer B will relax and let his career unfold as if from the beginning he will be okay.

Writer C, on the other hand, is heading down a slippery slope. In scrambling to get work-for-hire to pay the rent, she is setting herself up to get snared in the trap I described earlier. What should she do? If she does wind up writing that YA horror novel, she will have to accept that she is really only taking another sort of day job. Her own fiction will have to be done as it was before: late at night and on weekends.

Her biggest mistake was going full-time too soon. If she had waited she might not be in this situation now. Oh, well. At least she will build an audience and get paid quickly. That, at any rate, is what she is likely to tell herself.

16
CHAPTER
Contracts and Income

CONTRACT HOT SPOTS

IT WOULD TAKE MORE THAN ONE CHAPTER TO EXPLAIN THE intricacies of a publishing contract. Luckily, there are a number of excellent books out there that are wholly devoted to this subject. Career novelists should seek them out and read them. Contracts matter. Be sure you understand the fine print, for if you do not you may inadvertently sign away pieces of your future.

Happily, what I can do here is alert authors to some of the hottest points of contention in contract negotiations in the nineties. One of the hottest, as you may already know, is the scope and control of electronic rights. Indeed, this subject is so controversial and complicated I will devote the entire next chapter to it. Meanwhile, here are a few other hot spots:

Termination. About the last thing one thinks about when signing a book contract is the eventual end of that book's life. Nevertheless, it is a topic about which authors should be concerned.

With publishers reluctant to do reissues these days, it may seem that getting your rights back once your novel has gone out of print is not an urgent matter. But it is. Think of it this way: if your car dies by the side of the highway, you quickly get it towed. You keep control of it even though it is not running.

The same principle applies to novels. While you may not be able to convince another North American publisher to reissue, rights might still be sold overseas. Also, movie rights to out-of-print novels are sometimes bought, and if they are the chances of bringing that novel back into print go up dramatically.

It is a good idea to revert your rights as soon as possible. These days, however, there is a potential obstacle to doing that: electronic editions. If your novel is offered on-line or on disk, it may technically still be on sale and "in print." Never mind that it is not in stores and nobody will buy or read it in electronic formats (unless they want to go blind), your publisher nevertheless may be satisfying the strict letter of the contract.

To prevent abuse of this potential loophole, many agents are negotiating into termination clauses the phrase "out of print in its *printed and bound* edition," that is, your book in book form. Leave no doubt in your contract about when your novel is no longer on sale and all the rights should revert to you.

Bankruptcy. Here is another subject that authors do not like to think about: the possibility of their publisher going belly up.

Most contracts have comforting clauses that assure the author that if such an unlikely event should occur, all the rights to their novel will automatically revert. I am sorry to report, though, that those clauses have got it all wrong. If your publisher goes into bankruptcy, your book and any rights granted with it are legally considered assets that the publisher owns just as surely as they own the desks in their offices. Such assets can be seized, sold, and the proceeds paid to the publisher's creditors in an order fixed by a bankruptcy judge.

There is more to this than just collecting royalties that you may be owed (which, by the way, you may have but a snowball's chance in hell of getting). What is at stake is the control of your book, its overseas and audio rights, and any other rights that you may have granted your publisher in your contract. In bankruptcy, those are gone. Poof! The receiver appointed by the court is free to dispose of them as he sees fit. If you want any money that is rightfully yours you will have to wait in line.

A practical demonstration of this principle was given a decade ago when a publisher called Pinnacle went under. Its entire list was acquired by Zebra, and scores of authors suddenly found that they had a new publisher—one that some of them did not care for.

Amazingly, nothing has changed since then. Not a single publisher has dropped or modified this clause in its contract. Agents are not attacking it, either.

One remedy to consider is becoming designated in the contract a "secured" creditor in the event of a bankruptcy proceeding. That puts you in the same class of creditors as investors in the company, and puts you closer to the head of the line for handouts of recovered money. Unfortunately for us, there are few examples of authors obtaining secured creditor status.

Huge multinational media conglomerates may not seem candidates for bankruptcy, but who knows? If it can happen to airlines and auto companies, it someday might happen to the media giants.

Manuscript approval. Check your last contract: you may notice that whether or not your completed manuscript is acceptable is entirely up to your publisher. If that seems reasonable, think again: when no standards are given and no criteria are defined, it means that your publisher can reject your manuscript without any explanation whatsoever. They can just say no.

That may not seem like a big problem now, but what if your editor departs or your imprint is shut down? Suppose your novel is suddenly unwanted inventory on your publisher's list? For no good reason it can be declined, and on top of that most contracts state that you will then have to return your advance.

To be sure, publishers and agents disagree over the meaning of advances. Publishers claim that they are loans against future royalties. Agents, aware that authors must feed their families somehow while they create products for publishers to exploit, tend to regard advances as a form of payment or investment. Whatever the rationale, after perhaps a year of work it can devastate an author's life if she suddenly has to cough up twelve month's worth of income. Can one guard against this possibility?

This inequity in American publishing contracts was highlighted in 1991 when many British publishers signed a so-called Minimum Terms Agreement with two British authors' associations, the Society of Authors and the Writers Guild. This agreement sets out rules for rejection and the handling of advances. It states that a manuscript must be "professionally competent, ready for press, and in accordance with the original proposal and any matters or changes subsequently agreed in writing." When rejection occurs for any reason other than failing to meet those criteria the author keeps his advance, including any unpaid balance.

One of the signatories to the Minimum Terms Agreement was Penguin U.K. Authors published by its sister company, Penguin USA, realized that their contract terms were not as favorable. Angry over that, twenty-eight of them (including Joe McGinniss, Gloria Naylor, Jessica Mitford, Ariel Dorfman, and Dave Marsh) sent a letter of protest to Penguin USA. The response was frosty.

Fortunately, U.S. courts have ruled in favor of authors in cases relating to rejection. Conservative senator Barry Goldwater sued Harcourt Brace Jovanovich when it rejected his autobiography without explanation. He won. The court stated that Harcourt had "breached its contract [with Goldwater] by willfully failing to engage in any rudimentary editorial work or effort."

A similar finding went in favor of a novelist, Julia Whedon, who sold Dell a novel on the basis of a twelve-page outline. The first half of the manuscript was approved, but the complete manuscript was rejected for vague reasons. The court ruled that Dell's contract contained an implied obligation "to offer Whedon the opportunity to revise the manuscript with Dell's editorial assistance, to bring it up to publishable standards." Whedon kept Dell's advance and resold the novel.

For authors, this means that procedures and time frames for revision requests, acceptance or rejection, and rights to be returned to the author on rejection should be clearly spelled out. These days, publishers such as Bantam are even allowing authors to retain a sum—albeit a small one—out of their advances when their work is rejected. That is better than nothing.

Clearly we have a long way to go before book publishing contracts will equally balance the interests of publisher and author. Still, by focusing our attention on the hot spots we may yet make some progress.

ROYALTIES, RESERVES, RIP-OFFS

For decades, authors and agents twice a year received incomprehensible accountings of sales and moneys due. Full of strange numbers, odd-sounding designations, and debits and credits arranged in bizarre ways, these reports were called "royalty statements." CPAs and other financial experts found them appalling.

In the last five years authors and agents have begun to rebel. Writers' organizations have called for reform and have devised model royalty statements. A committee from the AAR has visited with executives at major publishers to encourage them to reformat their royalty statements and provide more information.

These efforts have produced results. Slowly but surely, publishers are beginning to issue more logical and complete statements. Simon & Schuster and Penguin USA, formerly two of the worst offenders, now send statements that are far easier to understand . . . which is not to say that they are simple. Far from it.

To be fair, it must be said that accounting what is due an author is not a breeze. There are many different ways for books to be sold, varying royalty rates, many types of rights and subsequent splits to keep track of, all of which makes the royalty department's job cumbersome. Antiquated systems do not help. Many sub-rights departments, for instance, still keep track of sales on index cards, and record payments by hand.

In this age of computers and automation, though, there is no excuse for shoddy accounting. Besides, publishers have a contractual obligation to accurately pay authors what they are due.

Even with the improved statements, there is a lot of artfulness in royalty reports. The chief reason for this is the returns system, that is, the ability of bookstores to return unsold copies. Thus, while 100,000 copies of a book may have been shipped and billed, until all the returns are in no one can know for sure how many copies were actually sold.

To guard against this potential hit, most publishers hold a "reserve against future returns" when reporting sales. Formerly, the numbers of copies printed, shipped, returned, and held "in reserve" were secret. Today, reformatted royalty statements usually include most of that information. Even when those figures are absent, authors and agents can request a "reconciliation to print," which is a fancy way of saying "figures that tell the whole story."

For authors, the crucial question is *What is a reasonable reserve?* British contracts sometimes spell out a reserve formula that allows for a gradual release of moneys withheld. In the U.S., the matter must be settled on a case-by-case basis. Generally, at the end of the first complete six-month period of sales it is sometimes not unreasonable to accept a sizable reserve (keeping in mind that average return rates run around 50 percent).

Even then, however, there are cases when a high reserve is not justified. Not long ago I received the first six-month statement for an author whose first novel seems to be a big success for Warner Books. The novel had gone back to press several times, and had appeared on genre best-seller lists. Sure enough, the Warner statement showed a healthy total of copies shipped. Sales were assumed to be good, too, and attached to the statement was a check for several thousand dollars. Not bad. The reserve, however, worked out to a whopping 55 percent. I felt this was too high. The novel's "rate" was strong, and therefore its "sell-through" was likely to be extra high (see Chapter 10). I called the royalty department and argued with them. They agreed to drop their reserve to a more realistic level, and a few days later I received a check that doubled the author's royalty payment.

This kind of haggling goes on all the time. In fact, as publishers have become more conscious of their bottom lines, reserve levels have increased. Over the last year I found myself challenging as many royalty statements as I had over the previous fourteen. Royalty statements are not scientific. Be alert.

One nonfiction author became suspicious of her royalty statements when she began receiving two of them for the same book each period. The duplication was especially weird since each statement showed different results! After attempts to get information from her publisher, HarperCollins, proved fruitless she and her agent sued, supported by the AAR, the Authors Guild and the American Book Producers Association (a packager's group).

High-powered auditors were brought in to scrutinize the HarperCollins records. Their findings were astonishing. Not only were the company's reporting procedures antiquated, large chunks of sub-rights income were not being credited to authors at all. The problem was not that the publisher was dishonest, but that it was sometimes quite difficult to properly assign all the different sums received. Large book-club payments, for instance, might arrive with a statement one thousand pages in length. Sorting out all that data is an overwhelming task for an understaffed sub-rights department.

Worse, the audit suggested that at many major publishers author payments that are returned because of address changes or errors may simply be bankrolled. One house, which went unnamed, is said to be sitting on a pool of $13 million! No doubt the writers to whom that money is due could use it, yet it just sits.

The author who sued HarperCollins won her suit, needless to say. She was paid back earnings with interest, plus her legal and auditing fees. Her name? Judith Appelbaum. Her book? *How to Get Happily Published*, a classic reference in the field that is now in its fourth edition. If that is what happened to her, you can imagine what happens to authors who are less savvy.

So, back to my earlier question: what is a reasonable reserve? Generally speaking, eighteen months or two years after publication it is fair to assume that most of the returns are in. Any reserves should be fully released by that time. New reprintings may occasion new reserves; the problem for authors is then knowing where old printings run out and new ones begin. Once again, obtaining complete and accurate information is important.

When should you audit? When large sums are at stake it may be worth bringing in the big guns. There are lawyers and accounting firms that specialize in publishing audits and lawsuits. Contact the Bar Association or the AAR. For authors of modest means, many writers' organizations offer assistance, as does the AAR.

One caution: most contracts contain a "lookback" period, after which you can no longer challenge a given statement. If you are concerned about your royalty report, do not let that period of time go idly by. Take action. The only sure way to get a fair accounting is to demand it.

THE GREAT CANADIAN ROYALTY RIP-OFF

Now that Congress has passed NAFTA, the way is open for a true North American free-trade zone. This is good news. Tariff barriers will fall. Goods and services will flow freely between the U.S., Canada, and Mexico. Some critics fear that employment may suffer in some sectors but that drawback, it is thought, will be more than offset by an overall improvement in our joint economic outlook.

What, though, is the outlook for authors? Lower royalty rates on Canadian sales are a publishing institution. When I challenge them, some U.S. publishers are still incredulous. How dare I question Canadian royalties? They have been that way for . . . well, forever.

Will NAFTA improve this situation? Sorry to say, probably not. An informal survey shows that few in our industry expect any change in royalties on Canadian sales. Canadian authors are angry about that, but U.S. authors and agents accept the status quo and publishers flatly declare that change is impossible.

Here are the facts: duties on U.S. book exports to Canada are already gone. Furthermore, Canadian cover prices are higher than those in the U.S. Despite that, authors' royalties on Canadian sales are significantly lower. What is worse, there is no uniform standard. Some contracts stipulate two-thirds of the U.S. royalty rate; others only 5 percent of the cover price. Still other publishers pay authors a simple 5 percent (maybe 6 percent) of the publisher's net Canadian receipts, which, after deducting a 44 percent trade discount and commissions to independent Canadian sales reps, can mean very small sums indeed.

What's going on here? And is this issue really worth fussing about? Sure, Canadian authors have a right to be sore, but for the rest of us how much money are we actually talking about?

It is impossible to know exactly how much more authors would get if royalty rates between the U.S. and Canada were equalized. Nevertheless, Canada is a huge export market for U.S. books. In 1992, U.S. publishers shipped $702,174,000 worth of books to Canada, more than the total shipped to their next *eleven* largest foreign markets combined. Even small royalty increases would obviously still buy authors quite a few extra pencils.

Take a look at individual authors and books, and the potential payoff becomes even more dramatic. Canadian sales can be anywhere from 5 to 15 percent of a given book's volume. I have seen that figure go as high as 25 percent. The ratio tends to be especially high for Canadian authors who, of course, publicize, promote, and find a large following in their home country.

Clearly the time has come for us to reexamine this issue. Unfortunately, my talks with publishing executives while preparing this chapter—most of them, by the way, requested anonymity— show that current attitudes are just about set in stone.

The biggest rationale that publishers give for lower Canadian royalty rates is the higher cost of making Canadian sales. Many U.S. publishers do not have Canadian sales forces, and instead work through independent Canadian reps. These reps take a commission (up to 10 percent) off the top of the publisher's revenues.

Transportation is also a factor. While shipping books to Canada may actually involve shorter distances than shipping within the U.S., transfer to a Canadian carrier at the border is often necessary. This transfer also hikes up costs.

Publishers also point to inefficiencies in Canadian distribution channels. In remote areas of the U.S., independent distributors service small accounts but that is not so in Canada, one publisher told me. Another said that Canadian return rates are higher. All the publishers I spoke to cited the country's bilingual population and a customer base that is both smaller and more spread out than that in the U.S. Canadians are just tougher to reach.

It all adds up, publishers say, to smaller sales that cost more to make. Canada, I was told, is a truly an "export" market. On top of that, several publishers also claimed that Canadian authors often withhold their Canadian rights anyway. Never mind that U.S. publishers can do a better job, they sniffed; Canadian authors are a chauvinistic lot, so why cater to them?

Are the publishers right? Canadian authors I've heard from have plenty of counterarguments. While many of them can and do work with publishers north of the border, many cannot. Authors of science fiction, for instance, have little choice but to sign contracts with U.S. companies. In addition, they counter, many U.S. publishers insist on keeping Canadian rights.

Currency fluctuation is also a phantom issue, Canadian authors say. The lower value of the Canadian dollar—generally 15 to 20 percent less than the U.S. greenback—is more than offset by higher Canadian cover prices, which on average are 30 percent more.

Surely that compensates for higher shipping and commission costs?

Canadian authors are also under the impression that Canada's Goods and Services Tax ("VAT" elsewhere in the world) is also a rationale for lower rates, even though no U.S. publisher mentioned it to me. In reality, the GST is paid only by Canadian customers at the cash register. Canadian sales reps pay it, too, but can get it refunded. GST may somewhat inhibit sales, but its direct cost to U.S. publishers is nil.

As for low population density, Canadian authors point out that 80 percent of Canadian sales are made in the province of Ontario. Much of the rest come from a few metro areas like Vancouver. Thus, the cost of a given unit sale should be no more than in the U.S.

They have a point. Now, as ever, U.S. publishers treat Canada exactly as what they claim it is: an export market. They do not want to do business there directly simply because they are not used to it. Frankly, their Canadian operations are wastefully inefficient. No wonder they perceive their costs as high.

Will that change? Yes. It must. Canadian sales are edging toward, indeed may already be over, three quarters of a billion dollars annually. That is big bucks. Agents and authors cannot afford to overlook this source of revenue, and neither can publishers.

The first step for everyone is to look at Canada in a new way. Canada is not across the ocean. It is right next door. Getting there is easy. Most Canadians even speak our language.

Indeed, looking at Canada in a new and more creative way is the whole point of NAFTA. It is time for authors to demand equal royalty rates on Canadian sales. Publishers are actually less and less surprised when I raise this issue, and it is possible that if everyone keeps hammering at it, things will eventually change.

Until then, though, I maintain that authors are victims of the Great Canadian Royalty Rip-off. Arguments for unequal rates do not hold up. And anyway, it is time to stop seeing Canada as the same as any other foreign country. It is not; Canada is America's number-one trading partner. The sooner publishers start doing business there in a normal way, the sooner we will all make more money.

SELLING SUB-RIGHTS

At first it appears that every novel contains a secret source of wealth: subsidiary rights. Why, then, are so many authors disappointed with their sub-rights revenues? Why is it that agents and publishers so often seem unable to sell audio rights, or movie rights?

It is worth taking a look at the complex sub-rights market (not to explain how to sell each of these rights—that is another whole book) to spread some information about what makes rights salable in some cases but not others. I hope that once given a realistic overview, authors may feel happier.

A few examples follow:

Audio. Books on tape are not exactly a huge business, but to an early-career author whose income is meager, it is a big deal to get an extra five thousand dollars for audio rights. So why are they so tough to sell?

The reality of the audio business is that for the publisher of an abridged recording, the kind most often seen in bookstores, there must be a minimum sale of about ten thousand units for the audio edition to be profitable. Now, since audiocassette sales average about one-tenth of those for their hardcover parents, that means for an audio edition of a novel to be feasible the hardcover must sell, at rock bottom, 75,000 copies. (That number still makes the audio a gamble, but if the novel has some special appeal then it might be worth a risk.)

Now, your average first mystery novel is not going to sell anywhere near 75,000 copies; in fact, even 5,000 would be nice. For that reason, it is usually the best-sellers that get picked for audio.

Having said that, I must also point out that there are exceptions. Smart audio companies like Brilliance have found out that there can be a decent market for audios of genre novels, provided that the purchase price is low and not a lot is spent on celebrity readers or other fancy production costs.

There is also a small but interesting market for unabridged audiocassettes; that is, the whole book read on multiple cassettes with not a word left out. Some of those companies are also willing to take a chance on novels below best-seller status. Small and regional audio companies also exist, though dealing with them can be similar to dealing with small presses: little money up front and lots of headaches later on.

Serial rights. Once upon a time, novelists could count on selling excerpts of their work to magazines like the *New Yorker, Vanity Fair, Esquire, Playboy, Cosmopolitan*, and the like. While that market still exists, it is today quite a bit smaller, as is the money. Nonfiction authors still have a healthy serial rights market, but for fiction writers this source of revenue is waning.

Chances of a sale are much better for novels that are episodic in structure, where portions can be lifted out and remain satisfying when read on their own. A self-contained scene or glued-together subplot can also sell, but there is fierce competition and not all novels are suitable for all magazines. As with so many sub-rights, best-sellers have the best shot.

Translation rights. Here, too, first-time and early-career authors are disappointed. So many countries! So many languages! So few sales . . . how come?

The reason is fairly logical: consumers in foreign countries are like consumers anywhere. They buy what they want, what is safe, and what is familiar. Best-sellers are big. That goes as much in Italy as it does in Iowa. Are you at all surprised?

First novels are especially hard to sell overseas. So are genre novels, except for established authors whose work is at the top of their field. American settings work in some countries but not others. Poland and Japan, for example, are mad for American culture, but the British hate to buy any mystery *written* by an American, let alone set in the U.S. And the French . . . well, who can tell what they will like? For them, the more intellectual and outré the better.

Another reason beginning novelists may find their work unwelcome overseas is that much of the selling of translation rights is done at the Frankfurt Book Fair, a one-week long rights extravaganza held in Frankfurt, Germany, every October. This whirlwind event puts a premium on big books that have universally appealing hooks (*The Hunt for Red October*) or prestige value (*The Name of the Rose*). As ever, best-selling American authors command a premium; unknowns go begging. In the crush, it is tempting for a rights director or agent to dismiss any novel that does not have obvious international appeal.

Fortunately, genre authors can often find information about overseas genre publishers in their trade publications. One can go directly to them and bypass the Frankfurt madness. It is worth a try, anyway.

Movie/TV. "Your book would make a great movie!" I wish I could take every novelist's friend or family member who ever said that, arrange them in a line, and give them each a good smack.

Most people have no idea what makes a novel attractive to Hollywood. Heck, even most movie insiders cannot tell you! Despite that, fiction authors can work themselves into a frenzy when seized by the suggestion that there are big bucks waiting for them in Tinseltown.

When an author is in such a state, it is no use pointing out that few novels are optioned and even fewer make it to the screen. That only whets their appetite. The only thing that will satisfy them is getting their novel on Steven Spielberg's desk or into the hands of Whoopie or Winona or whomever.

The situation is only made worse by the periodic book-buying binges that seem to grip studio executives. One such period was the late seventies, when it seemed for a time that any book that wasn't nailed down was sold. *The Island* by Peter Benchley sold for $2.1 million. *Thy Neighbor's Wife*, Gay Talese's tour of American sexual behavior, sold for $2.5 million. (*Thy Neighbor's Wife* was never made, and *The Island* was a box-office bomb.) Then, just as suddenly as it began, the buying binge was over. "Pimple movies" became the ticket, and for years afterward anything not geared for teenagers was impossible.

So what *does* make a novel a hot item in Hollywood? To understand that, one has got to look beyond the obvious. Every novel seems to unspool like a movie in its author's head, but what primarily causes moviegoers to buy tickets is a star. Stars are fundamental to movie economics, and stars must be fitted into roles. Needless to say, not every novel protagonist translates into an interesting and actable role. Larger-than-life characters, flawed heroes, and unusual real people types (like Forrest Gump) are often the most appealing to actors.

Tight plots and easy-to-explain hooks are also big pluses in Hollywood. Here, at least, the commercial novelist is on familiar ground. Still, Hollywood has bandwagon syndrome as badly as New York, so if one's novel does not fit neatly into a hot category it can be difficult to sell it to nervous execs. Then again, anyone can be wrong: courtroom movies were thought to be a box-office snore until *Presumed Innocent* came along. Go figure.

Another fact of moviemaking is that it is entirely visual and exterior. Inner monologue, flashback, and gorgeous description are useless, even deadly, in a movie. Action is a help, but that does not necessarily mean car chases. It means that character qualities must be demonstrated, and story lines should not require too much explanation. The stakes must be high, but at the same time the conflict must be resolved in one hundred minutes.

Not many novels can offer all that. Movie people know instinctively what works on screen, even if they cannot articulate it well to others. They have a "nose," and their judgments are final.

So, *if* Hollywood is in a book-buying cycle, *if* a book contains highly appealing roles, *if* it fits neatly into a hot category, *if* it has a contemporary setting, *if* the story will play well overseas and on video, *if* the novel is in hardcover, *if* it got great reviews and has snob appeal . . . oh yes, and *if* it also happens to tell a good story, well maybe then, you can confidently say, "This book should be a movie."

Finally, let us suppose that it should. (And in spite of everything I have said, you are probably convinced that yours fits the bill.) What happens then? Again, a certain disappointment may be in store. Movie rights are rarely sold outright; mostly they are *optioned*, which means that less money is paid and you, the novelist, agree not to sell the rights to anyone else for a period of time (usually a year, which is automatically renewable twice more for additional payments).

During the option period the option-holder—a producer, director, star, or writer—develops a script and attempts to sell it to a studio or obtain financing in some other way. TV and cable movies have similar life spans. Eventually, some projects are "picked up," financed, shot, and shown to the public. The commencement of principal photography is usually the trigger for payment of the big sums one hears about in connection with movie deals.

After that? Well, some movies turn into hits. Some gross hundreds of millions of dollars. Authors of underlying novels are entitled to a share of the movie's net profits, but studio accounting is so creative that even the highest-grossing movies never—and I mean never—show a "profit." To obtain their due compensation, most novelists must threaten to sue. Paramount has been threatened and sued more than once recently.

On top of that, ideas are routinely stolen in Hollywood. Your manuscript might be stolen, read, passed around, and turned down before your Hollywood agent ever lays eyes on it. Hollywood is also filled with sharks and phonies. The industry has seduced novelists for decades, and ruined many of them. Glamorous, isn't it? Welcome to the wonderful world of filmmaking. Don't you wish you had stayed home in bed?

No, probably not.

17
CHAPTER

Electronic Rights:
Power Source or Static?

THIS MEANS WAR!

AFTER A FEW SKIRMISHES IN THE EARLY NINETIES, FULL-SCALE war broke out in the skyscraper-lined canyons of Manhattan in October, 1993.

The opponents: book publishers vs. authors and agents.

The issue: electronic rights.

The inciting incident: the appearance of a new Random House contract with a killer electronic-rights clause. A full legal page long, this shocking clause enumerated every known form of electronic publishing and granted control of each one of them (plus any yet to be invented) to Random House. Worse, the revenue share assigned to authors was a paltry 5 percent. Worse still, when agents called Random House to complain they were coldly informed that there could be no changes to this awful clause. None. Never. It was in every case, they said, a deal-breaker. Needless to say, technology-savvy agents and authors hit the roof.

War erupted.

Quickly, authors' organizations fired off batteries of statements in support of authors. The Authors Guild and the American Society of Journalists and Authors issued a joint statement that November urging authors to hang on to their electronic rights, and recommending stiff contract language for cases in which they were forced to sell. The National Writers Union also shot off a position paper the following April, this one concerned with works originally created in multimedia.

Agents were already armed for the battle. In May of 1993 the AAR had issued a position paper outlining a division of electronic rights into two classes, and calling for a set of protections for authors with regard to exploitation of those rights. Nevertheless, Random House would yield no ground. Encouraged by their stance, other publishers stiffened their electronic rights clauses and took hard-line positions in negotiations.

The battle raged.

The high ground was fought over by two generals, Alberto Vitale, the CEO of Random House, and a senior executive at the William Morris Agency named Robert Gottlieb. Gottlieb cited the sad experience of a former William Morris client, the actor Spencer Tracy. Tracy's contracts with movie studios did not cover the broadcast of his films on television. When studios began to make millions selling them to TV, Tracy and his heirs lost out.

Vitale, on the other hand, had been stung by the near-loss of multimedia rights to the works of Dr. Seuss, which Random House had published for fifty years. Angered that the company that had made Seuss a household name had nearly lost an opportunity to profit from his work, Vitale swore that Random House would never again relinquish electronic book rights, and would henceforth insist on a first-look option on multimedia rights.

The fight went public. Gottlieb let it be known that Random House was now at the bottom of his agency's submission list. Vitale fired back that William Morris was not serving its clients well. Finally, the two generals squared off in a panel discussion at the "Multimedia Now" seminar in April, 1995.

Sponsored by *Publishers Weekly* and SIMBA Information, "Multimedia Now" was perhaps a turning point. For one thing, multimedia products had then been on sale for two years. All day long experts from publishing houses, software companies, booksellers, distributors, and computer magazines testified to the bright promise, but generally disappointing results, of multimedia.

The war was clearly winding down.

What happened at the panel discussion? How has the war turned out? Before answering those questions, it might be useful to examine what we actually mean when we talk about "electronic rights."

THE ELECTRONIC FUTURE

As soon as you scratch the surface of this issue contradictions appear. For example, some see electronic rights as an exciting new source of income—especially publishers, who are fighting furiously to hang onto them. Others say the printed book is dying. My fellow agent Richard Curtis even said in a recent issue of *Publishers Weekly* that "we are living in the twilight of the print age."

Both sides cannot be right. If money is being made in the sale of electronic rights, does that not imply that electronic publishers are, in part, counting on a healthy and growing book sector to be a source of their product?

What gives?

Common sense tells us that the printed book is not dying. As I established in Chapter 2, book publishing has never been bigger or more profitable. Further, all projections are for steady growth. Nevertheless, new ways of transmitting data are en route. Surely some of those will whittle away at the preeminence of the book?

Yes. In fact, certain types of publishing have already changed forever, for example, reference publishing. If you have a spell-checker on your computer then you have already seen the tip of that iceberg. Also transformed are publishers of law, medical, accounting, and other types of professional books.

Scholarly journals, believe it or not, are a hot center of controversy. A huge philosophical debate is under way. Should electronic access to, say, scientific research be limited? Is it right that scholarship be available only to those who can afford to download it? Should the Internet be free or commercial?

Good questions, but our focus is on trade publishing. Are commercial books vulnerable to the electronic invasion? Yes, they are. Many nonfiction books have already appeared in, or been acquired for, electronic editions: tax help, video guides, Spanish lessons, photography how-to's, and cookbooks.

You name it, it is coming to a screen near you—an interactive screen, I should say, and fiction is not immune. *Jurassic Park* has sold, as have Random House's extensive Modern Library editions, John Steinbeck's backlist and Terry McMillan's best-seller *Waiting to Exhale*. Getting nervous? I do not blame you. Few thoughts can make authors feel as awful as the idea that someone else is making easy money while they are just sitting around.

Before you rush to call your agent, though, take a moment to learn exactly what you are trying to sell and how much money can be expected for it. Let us start by looking at the devices ("platforms") in which your novels might be used electronically.

PCs. Personal computers have been sitting on desktops for years. Writers use them to create novels, so why can't readers use them to read those same novels? Well, they can. Plenty of companies publish novels on disk. Their products are available.

Novels are even available on-line. A new program on the World Wide Web called Dial-a-Book allows you to browse through the table of contents and first chapter of a book for free in its Chapter One service. If you like what you see you can access the Download Bookstore and capture the entire book including the cover art and internal graphics. (Or, if you like to read your books the old-fashioned way, you can have a printed copy sent to you.)

Dial-a-Book is a serious service offering titles from, among others, Addison-Wesley, Houghton Mifflin, Little, Brown, Morrow, Thomas Nelson, Pantheon, Putnam, Random House, a host of university presses, as well as the Newbery Award winners from the past two decades. (Go to http://dab.psi.net/Dial-A-Book/)

But a question: do you currently read any novels on disk? (Besides your own, I mean?) I thought not. Neither do I. Come to think of it, few of my clients have ever sent me their novels on disk, which is perfectly okay with me. I prefer print.

Some cutting-edge theorists contend that a strong market for PC-viewed novels has not arisen because few novels fully utilize the PC's capabilities. Of course, interactive print novels offer various paths through the story, even multiple endings. But that is not what these theorists mean. They are talking about nonlinear novels, *hypertexts*, to use the preferred term.

In hypertexts the whole idea of beginning and ending is thrown out. Users become fully interactive with the text, creating their own stories and experiences. And who knows? Someday a hypertext best-seller may appear and spawn a whole new business.

However, such a product will be fundamentally unlike a conventional novel. Despite all the high-flown talk, it will actually be more like a game. And its market will always be small, I imagine, for two major reasons: (1) people like endings, especially happy ones; and (2) people would rather be told a story than write one themselves, even with computer help.

Believers in hypertexts claim that their tomorrow is bound to dawn because today's children—with their Nintendos and classroom computers—relate to information in a whole new way. Oh yeah? Then why does kids' television thrive? And why are children's books the biggest growth sector in publishing? Reading is a habit, and today's kids are catching it very young.

Let's look at other electronic book formats that have come along.

CD-ROM. This is the big one. Already this new technology has made a larger dent in book sales than the PC made in a decade. CD stands for "compact disk." ROM means "read-only memory." CD-ROMs are disks that can be inserted into drives in a desktop computer, or sometimes into lightweight handheld units. Whatever the device, a laser beam inside scans the disk's digitally encoded data and sends images to a screen.

Several handheld CD-ROM players are on the market. The best known is Sony's Data Discman. As you might expect, the most popular titles for the Discman are reference works like the Bible, encyclopedias, language translators, wine guides, and so forth. Another proprietary handheld device is Franklin Electronic Publisher's Digital Book System. Franklin has sent its stock price soaring by finding niche markets for electronic reference books for doctors, nurses, lawyers, and so on.

By far the biggest market for CD-ROMs, though, is for those played on personal computers. PCs have the largest "installed base" of any electronic platform, in both offices and households. Many old PCs are already hooked up to CD-ROM drives, and you can hardly find a new PC without one already built in. InfoTech of Woodstock, Vermont, reports that there are 26.9 million CD-ROM drives in use around the world; an analyst for Link Resources puts the U.S. number at 6 million (at the end of 1994). Annual sales of CD-ROMs in the mid-nineties were around $600 million.

What are CD-ROM products like? If you have not tried one, pre-pare yourself: CD-ROMs combine text, pictures, sound, and moving images in really cool ways. You can tour London's National Gallery, play exotic musical instruments, study Beethoven's Ninth, look up any phone number in any phone book, call up the street atlas for any city or town, comb baseball stats and highlights, play Myst or Doom or Iron Helix, fight the Battle of Gettysburg, visit the rainfor-est, tour outer space, go to the San Diego Zoo, check into the Mayo Clinic, interact with the Grolier Encyclopedia, and a whole lot more.

No one really knows exactly how many CD-ROM titles are avail-able. U.S. estimates range from 3,500 to 10,000. InfoTech says that by the end of 1994 there were 11,837 worldwide, and that world unit sales for 1994 were 91.8 million. Ingram, the U.S. book wholesaler, stocks about 1,500 titles and ships to 1,200 stores.

Sad to say, though, the development costs of these products are high, and experts pretty much agree that fewer than two hundred CD-ROMs have been profitable. On top of that, the best-selling CD-ROM titles have mostly been games like Doom II, Myst, Sim City 2000, Seventh Guest, Nascar Racing, and Wing Commander IV.

Depressing, huh? It gets worse, because there is another catego-ry of platform: electronic devices linked to television sets.

CD-I. This device works much like CD-ROM devices; it just isn't hooked up to a computer. Phillip's CD-I machine plugs into any TV set in the world and looks somewhat like a VCR. In addition to CD-ROMs it plays audio CDs and Kodak PhotoCD disks. It can show real moving images instead of the herky-jerky QuickTime found on other players. It costs less than a PC, too, around six hundred dollars.

The "I" in CD-I stands for interactive. Games and golf (the sixteen most challenging courses in the world!) are some of CD-I's better available disks. There's also a photography course that lets you snap pictures, choosing your F-stop, exposure, and other settings; it then develops your "film" on screen. Like CD-ROMs, CD-I disks also offer a museum tour, in this case the Smithsonian, complete with moving images and the ability to rotate objects—even to turn them upside down to see what their bottoms look like. There's also a tour of the sunken Titanic, including the dance music that played while the liner sank.

Poor cousins of the Phillips CD-I player are game systems made by companies like Atari, Nintendo, and Sega. Products for these are kid- and game-oriented. Think sports and Sonic the Hedgehog.

You may have noticed that our discussion of these "new media" has wandered pretty far from fiction. I will come back to that point, but before I do let us gaze into the electronic far future.

Full-motion CDs, virtual reality, the data superhighway, and beyond. The problem with CD-ROM is that film-quality moving images are not possible, never mind TV-quality stuff. In fact, the moving pictures on CD-ROM are not even as good as animated cartoons.

The reason for this is that moving images eat up vast amounts of disk space, even with today's data compression. But tomorrow . . . ! Get ready.

And, in fact, tomorrow may not be very far away. New breakthroughs in full-motion CD are rapidly heading our way. Two rival alliances were formed to develop this new technology, and for a while it seemed that a new Beta/VHS-type format war was in the wind. Luckily, the rivals have agreed to common standards, and that means we will soon have movies on CD.

Interactive movies, no less! Actors are already part of PC games (catch "Baywatch" beauty Yasmine Bleeth in *Maximum Surge*), and interactive movies for theatrical release have already been tested. But movies on CD is something new. It means not only a new and better way of playing feature-length movies, but a whole new category of interactive entertainment.

Imagine having a drink at Rick's in *Casablanca* and chatting with Humphrey Bogart, or trading wisecracks with James Bond, or hunting for clues and discussing the evidence with Columbo. These are only some of the possibilities for the souped-up devices of the future. A CD player is coming that will plug into any screen—TV, PC, anything. It will play games, education-ware, CD-ROM-type programs, and whole new classes of user-controlled experiences with the lifelike quality of TV.

Farther down the road we may encounter laptop, palm-top, and maybe even credit-card-sized machines that will do it all: compute, play music, receive TV programming, run full sound-and-motion interactive programs—and, yes, even let you read novels.

Now, look farther. Imagine you can plug your device into fiber optic telephone or cable TV lines and access all the on-line data bases and services in the world. Sound good? Okay, now throw away your hardware and put on a helmet with a visor screen, and wired-up gloves. Now you can walk, float, swim, or zoom through this vast virtual universe, your finger pointing the way.

What will our electronic future be like? Travel is obsolete. Global business leaders sit down together in picturesque surroundings—all without leaving their offices, or rather, homes. (Offices are now obsolete.) Safe sex? No problem. Want to visit Disney World during the busy season? Do it at home. Shopping for a new house? Don't leave your chair. Want a good novel? Fly around the stacks at Barnes & Noble or Borders.

Actually, most electronic forecasters don't see a place in their brave new world for the novel. To them, novels will be quaint relics of a bygone era. And novelists? If any survive they will be fringe entertainers, similar to poets or oral storytellers.

Luckily for us, that day is still far off. How far off is difficult to say. For the moment, though, let us stick to what exists now and what is likely to happen in the next five years. What are the key issues for novelists? What is selling in the electronic marketplace, and for how much?

THE ELECTRONIC REALITY

First, what are the formats that work for fiction? PC programs on floppy disk and CD-ROMs are, for now, the only possibilities.

Prices? The news is not thrilling. One of the largest electronic-rights sales to date was for a nonfiction title, J. K Lasser's *Your Income Tax*. A natural for electronic editions, its rights sold for nearly $500,000. That probably sounds good, but let's look deeper. Rights to eight Betty Crocker cookbook titles went for a total of $30,000. The Baedeker Guide rights went for $15,000. Hmmm . . . not too impressive. And those are nonfiction titles, too.

In the fiction field, prices are generally very low. They start at five hundred dollars (maybe less, for all I know) and creep up from there. Not very exciting, is it? The worst news of all is that outside of the children's book field, very little fiction has sold at all.

So, what about the Steinbeck backlist? What was that all about? Good question. Examine the situation and you will see that the Steinbeck books had several advantages that made them right for electronic editions. First, almost all of the backlist was in the hands of Steinbeck's publisher, Penguin. Second, the historical elements of his books lend themselves to electronic enhancement. Finally, Steinbeck's novels are big in schools.

The Modern Library, which I mentioned earlier, also has an electronic rationale because it is a unified body of work with a brand name. It lends itself to electronic anthology editions.

It still remains to be seen whether fiction of any type will sell profitably on CD-ROM. For that matter, many wonder whether CD-ROM itself will survive. Christmas sales in 1994, the first big season for multimedia, were generally fairly lackluster and they have not improved much since. Granted, many retail issues have yet to be sorted out. Price, packaging, display space, demonstration modules, and a host of other factors are all still in the development phase.

Nevertheless, most industry observers agree that CD-ROM product is mostly a collection of lifeless derivatives—or "repurposings"—of movies, TV, comics, books, and the like. Our early CD-ROMs are also beset by technical glitches. They are hard to run. Picture quality is poor. Film clips are the size of stamps. Fonts look fuzzy. User interfaces vary. No wonder games and content-oriented titles like *The Way Things Work* sell best.

CD-ROM content is a long way from its potential. Very few disks seem artistically exciting. There are exceptions. *Johnny Mnemonic*, one of the first titles to use full-screen video creatively, is one, but it was developed by Propaganda Films, producers of "Twin Peaks" and *Wild at Heart*. Several Inscape titles like *The Dark Eye* are also promising. (That one explores the mind of Edgar Allan Poe using a phrenologist's cranial map. It was animated by Doug Beswick, who worked on *Beetlejuice*.)

Are you seeing a pattern here? Innovative CD-ROM material is not springing from licenses of novels. It is coming from movie studio–style production teams, and that process is producing its own stars. Writers working in the multimedia business will tell you that the way to get ahead is not to license old novels but to write original material. Multimedia writers are the new screenwriters. And—sorry—the leading writers are already in place.

RIGHTS, CONTRACTS, REVENUES

Nevertheless, back at home novelists must still deal with the contract mess and battle with publishers who want to sew up their electronic rights. What to do?

The first issue is copying. New technologies always bring new fears for authors, since they mean that their works can be copied more easily. Is this fear justified? To a point. For that reason copy protection needs to be built into electronic-book products. When licensing or granting rights to electronic versions to your book publisher, be sure that copy protection is part of the deal.

Copyright itself is another issue. Current copyright laws do not cover cyberspace. President Clinton has proposed new legislation that would make transmission on-line a right belonging to a work's copyright owner. He has also proposed new rules regarding "fair use" copying by libraries, with exemptions for nonprofit organizations that supply material to the blind. Hacking devices for disarming safeguards would also be outlawed.

Issues remain. For one thing, cyberspace is worldwide. Can U.S. laws really protect intellectual property on the Net? The most recent GATT (General Agreement on Tariffs and Trade) also left in its wake many unanswered questions and nightmare scenarios. Innovative forms of tariffs and trade protection are now possible. Much has yet to be done. For the time being authors should at least be sure that electronic-rights agreements stipulate strong copyright protections for their work.

Two other points to negotiate when selling electronic rights are (1) the means of display; and (2) the term of license. The first is important because there are so many ways of presenting a book electronically. If your buyer can produce only one format—say, read-only floppy disks for PCs—then what is the point of selling him rights to all other formats (though licensors will want them anyway)? Similarly, broad grants in publishing contracts, such as "in all media whether now known or hereafter devised" should be modified.

For the same reasons, you will probably want to grant only a short term of license. New technologies are coming out all the time. Where they compete, exclusive licenses will be more valuable than nonexclusive ones. To protect the value of your properties, place strict time limits on their exposure. If granted any electronic rights, your book publisher should keep them only for a short time after publication, especially if the publisher is unable to license those rights or exploit them in house.

Next, a question of more immediate interest to genre novelists and their agents: to whom can I sell my electronic rights? Slow down, though. You cannot sell them if you do not control them. That is the main issue over which the current war is being fought.

What stance should you take? The AAR position paper identifies two types of electronic rights: electronic versions of the book ("electronic books" or "text-only" versions), and enhanced versions ("multimedia"). The position paper states that nondramatic rights—that is, versions without adaptation, audio, or visual components—are simply different forms of the printed book and may be controlled by the publisher in the same way that they normally control paperback, book-club, and similar rights.

A problem arises, though, with regard to electronic anthologies, which in high-storage-capacity CD-ROMs can be enormous. Authors should be able to control the context in which their work appears; therefore the position paper states that authors should be given approval of any electronic use or license.

Multimedia rights should always be controlled by the author, just as are film, TV, stage, and radio rights. Now, most publishers are today insisting upon at least a first-look option on multimedia rights. Whether or not to grant that can be a dilemma. In authors' defense I must point out that there is no reason to expect that book publishers will prove better at creating and selling multimedia products than, say, movie studios. In fact, so far the most successful publishers of multimedia products are software companies. Why should book publishers, then, have a favored position when it comes to licenses?

In addition, the AAR position paper also points out that traditional royalty rates may be inadequate in the face of the lower costs and higher margins involved in electronic versions. For that reason, royalty rates should not be fixed just yet, nor should a fifty-fifty split of licensing moneys be automatic.

Finally, since publishers may not want to license electronic versions if they will compete with their books (especially on the basis of price), authors and their agents should be informed promptly of any inquiries or offers for these rights.

Got all that?

Okay, now to money. What can you get for electronic rights? There are few precedents, but here are some rough guidelines:

Electronic books offered on-line usually involve payment to authors based upon net receipts. Here, authors must evaluate the product and its price structure. What will the version cost the consumer? How many units does the vendor expect to sell? Where the profit margin is high, the author's cut should be high, too. Research it. Find out what other authors are getting.

Where a work is being adapted into a multimedia format, it will probably wind up being but one component of the whole. Directors, actors, composers, designers, and other creative talent will be involved. CD-ROMs are also sold in outlets other than bookstores. Royalties may give way to a share of net profits. A 5 percent share for the author seems to be an emerging standard.

Stay tuned for further developments, though. This is all still pretty new.

PEACE TREATY

Not long ago I asked a Berkley editor how many sales of electronic rights the company had actually made out of the hundreds of cases in which they demanded control of those rights. She could think of only one sale, for science fiction writer William Gibson.

There is a lesson in that: as with most any subsidiary right, the greatest value will rest with the author, series, or character that has established for itself brand-name recognition.

So, back to the battlefront . . . what happened at the "Multimedia Now" square-off? Well, Alberto Vitale and Robert Gottlieb aired their differences. Each made strong points, but the whole debate had a lot less heat under it than it had a year earlier. The reason? Multimedia has not yet turned into the expected bonanza.

In fact, some publishers are already getting out of the electronic publishing game. The Putnam-Berkley Group sold its electronic division in April, 1995, and others are sure to follow. Who can blame them? The capital investment is huge (usually six-figures per title) and so far a mere handful of CD-ROMs have made money.

The rights battle has cooled off a lot, too. Most publishers will agree to table the issue of royalties on electronic versions, or at least to give authors the highest prevailing future rate—whatever that may turn out to be. They are also mostly settling for a first-look option on multimedia.

Soon, they may not even care about that. The war is ending not because one side or the other scored a decisive win, but because fast-changing media technologies may be rendering the whole ugly debate pointless. That is progress for you.

Electronic Publishers

Book publishers like to claim that they are content providers in all media. There is some truth to that assertion, but in the race for electronic-publishing leadership it is too early to say who will win. Book publishers are up against scores of start-ups, software developers, TV networks, movie studios, and even telephone companies. Many of the most promising are to be found not in New York, but in San Francisco's "Multimedia Gulch." Here is a partial list of current contenders:

ABC-CLIO
Adams Media
Allegro New Media
Anjujar Communication
   Technologies
Applied Optical Media
Arnowitz Studios
Arome Interactive

Attica Cybernetics Inc.
Big Top Productions, LP
Books That Work
Bowker/Reed Reference Electronic
Broderbund Software Inc.
Bureau of Electronic Publishing
   Inc.
Carole Marsh Family CD-ROM

Charles River Media
Claris Clear Choice
Cliffs Notes Inc.
Compact Publishing
Compton's New Media
Corbis Publishing
Creative Multimedia
Creative Wonders
Cyan
Davidson & Associates
Dearborn Trade
Delrina Corporation
Discovery Channel Multimedia
Disney Interactive
Dorling Kindersley
Ebook
Eden Interactive
Edmark
E.M.M.E.
Enteractive
Facts on File
Fairfield Language Technologies
FlagTower Multimedia
Fox Interactive
Grolier Electronic Publishing
HarperCollins Interactive
Headbone Interactive
High Text Publications
Houghton Mifflin Interactive
Humongous Entertainment
Hyper-Quest
IBM Multimedia
Infobusiness Inc.
Interactive Factory
Interplay Productions
IVI Publishing
Kaplan InterActive
Knowledge Adventure
The Learning Company
LucasArts Games
Lunimaria
Macmillan Digital USA
Magnet Interactive Studios
Maris Multimedia
Maxis Software

McGraw-Hill Professional Book
  Group
MECC
MediaVision
Meridian Data
Merriam-Webster
Microsoft Home
Mindscape
Multicom Publishing
National Geographic Society
NTC Publishing Group
Oryx Press
Penguin Electronic Publishing
Phillips Home Media
Byron Preiss Multimedia
Primary Source Media
The Princeton Review
Queue
Rand McNally New Media
Random House New Media
REMedia
RoundBook Publishing
Sanctuary Woods
Scholastic New Media
Sierra On-Line
The Software Toolworks
Soleil
Sony Imagesoft
Spectrum HoloByte
StarCore
Sumeria
Sunburst Communications
T Maker
Time Warner Interactive
Turner Home Entertainment
  Interactive
Unidisc
Universal Interactive Studios Inc.
Viacom New Media
Videodiscover Inc.
Visible Link Interactive
The Voyager Company
John Wiley & Sons
Workman/Swifte International Ltd.
Yano Electric Co.
Zelos Digital Learning

18

CHAPTER

Strategy Session III: Managing Success

CLIMBING TO THE TOP

THIS IS THE FUN PART. YOU HAVE QUIT YOUR JOB, BUT NOT TOO soon. Your royalty earnings are healthy. Sub-rights sales are becoming a regular event. Your agent returns your calls promptly. Your editor is sending you birthday cards. Even your family no longer feels that this writing thing is a fluke.

Life is good. So what next? Is this as good as it gets? Welcome to Strategy Session III, where we will examine some of the issues and challenges that face midcareer writers as they come into the fullness of their talents and try to climb higher up the ladder of success. There is no one right way to do this; all writers must find their own paths. Nevertheless, there are certain common issues and concerns that deserve discussion.

Chief among the problems of midcareer novelists is hitting a plateau. That happens when sales stall out and advances reach a ceiling. It can make some authors crazy. If they get too frustrated or too envious of others they can be moved to ill-considered actions—such as leaving a good and supportive publisher—all just to relieve their anxiety. A few may leave their spouses. Some might even leave their agents!

What can one do to get off the plateau and get back on the mountain trail? That is a complex question, and the answer, naturally enough, often leads back to one's fiction itself.

BREAKING OUT

Break-out Book: that term is bandied around a lot in publishing, but what does it really mean? It has different definitions for different people, but generally it refers to any book that moves an author a giant step upward in sales or name recognition. If a novel leaps onto the best-seller lists without warning, you can be sure everyone will be calling it a "break-out."

Are break-out books "made," or do they just happen? To be sure, few books can get on the best-seller lists, or stay on them once there, without strong support from a publisher. You would think, then, that break-outs are planned, but that is not necessarily the case. Soaring reorders can take publishers by surprise. When that happens publishers may have to scramble to keep copies coming.

Whether planned or a surprise, however, there are certain circumstances that usually accompany a break-out. One of them is a leap in an author's writing. A move out of genre fiction into mainstream, a plot newly large in scope and scale, a deeper-than-usual theme . . . any of those factors may elevate an author's newest novel and make it a candidate for break-out.

Of course, there are those break-out books that are simply the reward of accumulated good writing and long-term word-of-mouth. Anita Brookner's Hotel du Lac, which was a best-seller in 1985, was not a significantly bigger novel than her former ones. It did win Britain's Booker Prize, which did not hurt (but which also does not necessarily help a novel in the U.S.). In truth, Brookner's time had simply come. The public was ready for her.

Did you catch that phrase word-of-mouth? That means a devoted and passionate coterie of readers who are talking up an author whom they love. Such authors are said to have a "cult following." A loyal readership is truly the launching pad for a break-out book, but I think that many people in our industry do not realize how manageable word-of-mouth may be. It can be cultivated.

Authors who spend years doing signings, interviews, convention appearances, and the like are not just indulging themselves. (At least, let us hope not.) They are connecting with readers, making friends, winning converts, getting bookstores behind them so that each new novel will be hand sold to customers. There is nothing accidental about that. It is all calculated and deliberate and enact-ed over a long period of time. *Cult following*? I think *cultivated following* is a more useful term.

One trap for authors is getting cozy with their long-time fans and failing to reach out to potential new readers. True, it can be boring to speak the same message over and over; conversely, it can be comforting to surround oneself with people who already under-stand one's work. Smart authors strike a balance: they neither neglect fans nor quit selling themselves to new readers.

Another circumstance that often attends a leap out of category or off the midlist is a new format, as with the paperback novelist who goes hardcover, or the hardcover novelist who has a splashy new trade paperback. A new cover look can also help, such as an "up-market" design, an all-type cover, or simply the placement of the author's name above the title.

New formats and stylish packaging are not by themselves enough to make a book break out, however. The book must "be there," as insiders like to say. In plain English, that means the break-out book must be good—damn good. It is natural for authors to believe that of their most recently completed novels, but it is quite another thing for everyone who reads those novels to agree. A break-out novel is a two-part equation: first, writer; second, readers.

With luck, one's agent, publisher, publicist, and sales force will all recognize the break-out book when it arrives, and will all shift into high gear. A better advance, nicer packaging, blurbs, bound gal-leys, ads, publicity . . . any or all of those may come into the equa-tion. But in the end there is one group that matters more than any other when it comes to breaking out.

They are . . . well, you know who.

ADVANCES

A moment ago I mentioned advances. No doubt about it, there is nothing like a large advance to get everyone's heart racing. A big advance not only calls attention to a novel but also strongly moti-vates the publisher who is paying it; after all, suddenly its number-one job is to earn back all that dough.

Or so says the theory. In reality, large advances can actually be profitable for a publisher, in the short term, anyway.

How's that again?

Okay, here's how it works: let us use as an example an advance of $1 million. Authors reading about such deals are prone to think, "Shoot! That writer just got a million bucks!" But did she?

Probably not. Over time she will get the full amount, of course, but most publishers spread the payment of megasums over as much time as possible. The author's on-signing portion of that advance is likely to be somewhere around $200,000. That is still a lot of money, but look at what happens next. The publisher, which now has a hot novel on its hands thanks to the publicity given the deal, also acquired world rights—that is, all rights in all languages—to this property.

World rights? Of course. How else do you think the agent got $1 million?

Okay, so now the publisher takes the novel to the Frankfurt Book Fair. Remember that? It is the huge rights marketplace that convenes in Frankfurt, Germany, every year in October. Foreign publishers attending the fair are all excited about the $1 million novel. Their U.S. scouts have told them about it, maybe even snuck them stolen copies of the manuscript.

Auction fever begins. Everyone is hot to buy translation rights to this $1 million wonder. (And, probably, the novel is pretty commercial if it got that kind of money.) So, the selling begins. The Brits pay the equivalent of $100,000. The Dutch pay $50,000. The Germans, who love American culture, fork over $225,000! And the Japanese go nuts: they cough up a cool half mil.

When the dust settles, the U.S. publisher has raked in $1 million in overseas sales. The book is paid for, right? Noooo, actually the publisher has turned a profit of about $800,000. (Remember, so far it has paid the author only a paltry $200,000.) True, some of that $1 million in overseas moneys will eventually have to be split with the author, but not until the author's first royalty statement is due, which may be two years from then.

Nice racket, huh?

Now you also know one dirty little secret of seven- and eight-figure deals: To obtain money like that, agents often sell all world rights to their clients' books. That is just what happened in 1990 when HarperCollins promised Jeffrey Archer what was said to be in excess of $20 million for three new novels. In that instance, Harper got not only world rights, but movie/TV rights as well. (Archer's agent got his whole commission on one deal. Nice for all concerned, don't you think?)

Did you read about the $800,000 paid to unknown first novelist Carol O'Connell for *Mallory's Oracle* in 1994? That was a world-rights deal, too. Naturally, not all big deals are for world rights. The $12.3 million that Ken Follett got for two new novels—just one week before the Archer deal—was for the U.S. and Canada only. Same thing for the $14 million Clive Cussler got from Simon & Schuster for two new ones in 1994.

Is selling world rights a good idea? Ask the authors who get the millions: they think so. World rights really become an issue at lower advance levels. How low can you go and still justify it? The answer really depends on what you want to accomplish with a deal. I had a case a few years ago in which an author, previously unpublished, insisted upon selling his first four novels—they were linked—all at once. I told him that to bring off this nearly impossible feat I might have to sell world rights. He said, "Do it." I did. He got his four-novel deal, but somewhat less than seven figures.

Was he sorry? Not a bit. He knew what he wanted. So, what do you want out of your next deal? Is it worth giving away world rights to obtain it? Interesting question!

THE IMPORTANCE OF BACKLIST

Speaking of big deals, negotiating with the publisher who has your backlist can make it much easier to get huge up-front sums.

The logic behind that should be obvious. "Backlist" is previous novels that are still on sale. They are paid for. Their cover art is paid for, too. There are no expensive author tours to worry about, and the reviews are in. In fact, the only cost a publisher has to shoulder now is the price of reprinting and warehousing. Of course, even that may be too dear if the "rate" (see Chapter 10) is not high enough, but if that is the case then the novel is probably out of print anyway.

You do not hear about backlist selling much except in the mystery field, where the only strategy that works is doing series. Nevertheless, for adult trade books backlist sales can be 25 percent of a publisher's business. That figure more than doubles if you add in children's and reference books. So why aren't publishers paying more attention to backlist, you wonder?

Actually, they are. Now and then publishers notice the gold mine they are sitting on and get serious about selling it. In 1995, for instance, Random House kicked off a year-long backlist promotion with a cross-imprint catalogue that grouped backlist titles according to category. They also offered bookstores extra co-op advertising, better terms, and special display stuff if they would put on a minimum number of category promotions during the year, hopefully using Random House titles.

Publishers also like to repackage classic novels. Backlist like that gives them prestige, not to mention easy profits.

So, back to advances: if your publisher has your backlist, which is paid for and earning profits on a regular basis, then needless to say the potential risk involved in a lofty new advance is lessened. It has a cushion.

And so do you. For instance, suppose you spend all of your big new advance, but then your "break-out" novel does not pan out? Ouch. What will you do? If you have backlist, then at least you will be able to look forward to your twice-yearly royalty checks. That will be some consolation, I hope.

BEST-SELLER LISTS

The ultimate measure of success is appearance on the best-seller lists, particularly the one appearing in the Sunday *New York Times Book Review*. "The list," as everyone calls it, has tremendous power and reach. Many stores use it to highlight current offerings, and it clearly accelerates the pace and broadens the nationwide exposure of any book lucky enough to get on it. The *Times* list is a big deal.

The list is also the best publicity a book can have. Readers associate it with quality. For stores it means sales. For agents it means prestige. For editors it can mean a job promotion, even their own imprint. For publishers it means profit. All parties want their books on the list, and when there is a chance of that happening—baby, watch out. People get aggressive.

Many authors suspect that the list is somehow rigged. They believe that there is a way to manipulate it by shipping heavily to, or buying from, the right stores. And do you know what? They are right.

Well, they are right to a point. While publishers regularly try to pack those outlets known to be polled by the *Times*, and also send authors to them for signings, it is still notoriously difficult to "buy" one's way onto the list. About the best one can hope for is to increase the odds.

Still, that does not stop authors from trying to force their way on. For years attempts have been made, and a few may have been successful. Most recently, the two authors of a business book, *The Discipline of Market Leaders*, laid out big bucks to buy 10,000 copies of their book through stores known to be polled by the *Times*. When exposed the authors protested, saying their purchases were legitimate buys for clients and potential clients of their consulting company. Uh-huh.

Whether legitimate or not, *The Discipline of Market Leaders* appeared on the *Times* list for fifteen weeks. Now, that is a lot of money to spend for those results. Charles McGrath, the editor of the *Times Book Review*, said at the time that such a stunt—he called it "not impossible"—would be so expensive that one would need a reason beyond boosting sales to do it. The authors of *Market Leaders* have a consulting and lecture business, and I do not doubt that it is doing nicely.

So, what is the lesson in this for novelists? Simply that manipulation of the list is a costly gamble with an uncertain chance of success and a hard publicity slap if one is caught.

It is worthwhile studying how the *Times* list is put together. The *Times* issues a form every week to 3,050 chain bookstores, independent bookstores, and wholesalers. From the completed forms the list is tabulated, though it appears in the *Book Review* several weeks after the data are recorded. A lag that long is still not long enough for many publishers, who need to plan extra printings, advertising, and promotional activity.

The form that is sent out became the focus of a lawsuit brought by author William Peter Blatty (*The Exorcist*) in 1983. He claimed that his novel *Legion* had sold enough to qualify for the *Times* list, but did not get on because the snobbish editors of the *Book Review* left it off the all-important form. Appearances of *Legion* on the lists of the *Los Angeles Times*, the *Chicago Tribune* and *Publishers Weekly* gave his claim some weight. He called the *Times* negligent and said they had denied him a possible business advantage that he was rightfully due.

Blatty's case went all the way to the Supreme Court. They refused to hear it, though, and let stand a lower court ruling against him. It is tough to fight the *Times*. It may at least make authors feel better to know that the way the list is tabulated, especially the weighting given to certain stores, is intended to give the *Times* list a more literary tone than that of other lists. In other words, certain books are not going to get onto the *Times* list no matter what. (That is especially true for Christian books, children's books, and computer titles.)

Luckily, there are other lists. While not as powerful as the *Times* list, the best-seller lists of USA *Today*, the *Wall Street Journal*, and *Publishers Weekly* are all closely watched by insiders.

The USA *Today* list is interesting because it does not separate sales into paperback and hardcover categories. It instead simply ranks the nation's top fifty titles by raw unit sales. This yields some surprises. Novels by juvenile author R. L. Stine, it seems, outsell many best-sellers for grown-ups. The USA *Today* list is also timely. The newspaper receives figures from chain stores and independents early in the week and publishes its best-seller list that very same Thursday.

The *Wall Street Journal* list has some influence with upscale readers partly because it is they who buy the newspaper, and partly because the list is limited to hardcovers. The disadvantage of the *Journal* list is that it is tabulated entirely from numbers supplied by the four biggest chains.

In many quarters the *Publishers Weekly* list is thought to give the most accurate picture of what is happening out there in retail land. While its sector samples are not as broad as those behind the *Times* list, the way its figures are weighted may give a more accurate reflection of mass-market tastes. In fact, when best-seller bonuses are negotiated into deals, some agents and authors these days are choosing *Publisher's Weekly* over the *Times*.

None of the lists that I have just mentioned, however, poll specialty stores or book clubs. (Only one, the *Times*, polls price clubs.) Genre novelists, whose sales can be the strongest in specialty stores, are therefore at a bit of a disadvantage. Fortunately, the monthly best-seller lists in trade magazines like *Locus* and *Mystery Scene* make up for this lack since they are based entirely on sales in selected specialty stores.

Genre editors and agents use these specialty lists as maps to which authors are finding acceptance among a given genre's hardcore fans. Look at these lists and you will know who is up-and-coming.

Are you still hoping to learn a surefire way to climb aboard the best-seller express? Sorry. No easy way exists. If you want to improve your odds, however, I can offer a helpful hint. In 1993, 87 percent of the *Publisher's Weekly* hardcover best-sellers, and 81 percent of its paperback best-sellers, were published by seven corporate groups (the "seven sisters"): Random House, Bantam Doubleday Dell, Simon & Schuster, Putnam-Berkley, HarperCollins, Time Warner, and Penguin USA.

Lesson: if you want to be a best-seller, then you should probably be published by one of the major media giants in New York City.

GETTING OUT OF OPTIONS

Ahem . . . if you are an editor or a publisher kindly skip this section.

If you are an author with no backlist to keep together, and who is convinced that the time has come to make a break from your current publisher, read on. There are ways out of your option clause.

Sometimes, of course, trickery is not needed. That is especially true if things are not going well. Your publisher may turn down your option proposal. You might even have an honest talk with your editor and arrange an amicable parting of the ways.

The problem arises when you want to go, but your publisher wants you to stay. Your option clause does not absolutely lock you into selling your next book to your current publisher, but it may grant them the right to acquire that novel on the same—or slightly better—terms offered to you by someone else. If they "top," then you are stuck. So what can you do?

The safest bet is simply to come up with an offer that is so much higher than the sum that your current publisher is willing to pay that they cave in. The initial offer they make for your option book will give you a hint of what they think your book is worth.

A sneakier way to slip out of an option is to offer your publisher a book about which you care nothing. That was done by the author known as "J," who wrote the best-sellers *The Sensuous Woman* and *The Sensuous Man*. She wanted more money, but her killer option clause said that her publisher, Lyle Stuart, could obtain her next book on the same terms as the first two.

What did she do? She offered Lyle Stuart a guide to Florida golf courses. While this turkey was in preparation she went ahead with a lucrative new deal with another house. This plan will not work, though, if your option is for "the next in the series."

Actually, the best way out of a bad option clause is not to get into one in the first place. Never agree to "same terms." Resist "matching," which means the ability to match or top another's offer. You have the right to publish with whom you wish.

KEEPING UP THE QUALITY

Probably the biggest challenge faced by authors who are climbing to the top is that of writing good new novels. It is so easy to slip.

Temptations abound. One is to recycle old material. That can be a joy, but it can also ensnare you in stories that are smaller in scale and weaker in substance than your readers now expect.

It is also tempting to enjoy the many distractions that are available to successful authors. Writers' conferences, guest faculty spots, ABA (the American Booksellers Association annual convention in June), leadership positions in unions and authors' organizations, TV appearances, literary feuds with other novelists . . . any of those will eat up mountains of time if you let them. Sadly, some authors make a second career out of distractions. (Norman Mailer and Truman Capote come to mind.)

Writing quality can suffer. Of course, that is not always the author's fault. Best-selling authors whose editors are top executives can find that these "editors" do not have time to work properly on their authors' manuscripts. Junior editors may be assigned the task, or maybe no one will do it at all. That happened to Kurt Vonnegut. It could happen to you.

If it does, how can you cope? Demanding quality editing is one way; going to book doctors is another. They can be expensive, but they can also prove invaluable to authors who need major help in whipping their novels into shape. In fact, it is amazing to me how big the book doctoring business has become.

THE DARK SIDE

A final—and gentle—word is owed to authors who are plagued by blocks, the bottle, pills, depression, or thoughts of suicide. Who would have thought that the writing life could involve such pain? But it can. For some it does. If you are an author having problems like these, know that you are not alone.

Blocks are common. I had one myself, for about a year. It was excruciating. In my case, I rewrote the same opening to a novel over and over. It was depressing and destructive. I got over it with the help of an excellent psychotherapist, to whom I will always be grateful. What I learned about being blocked is that it has nothing to do with one's ability to write.

The ability to write does not diminish. What blocks it, though, is anxiety. Anxiety may be fueled by money worries, or by a crisis of confidence, or by external factors like a lousy marriage. Whatever the reason, anxiety stops the flow and makes writing a misery.

There are many ways through a block, almost as many as there are blocked writers. The main thing is to seek help. Not talking about the problem is one of the most painful conditions of all. You will probably find your editor sympathetic. I have several times seen blocks overcome when an author and editor agreed to substitute one novel for another.

Unfortunately, research suggests that there are links between creativity and madness. According to a study done in Britain, artists, writers, and poets are thirty-five times more likely than the average person to seek help for serious mood disorders. And we are not talking about crummy artists, either. The British study was done on fine artists who were members of the Royal Academy, playwrights who had won the London Critics' Award, and poets who had received the Queen's Gold Medal.

Episodes of intense creativity may also be partly attributed to manic depression, according to that same study. Curiously, people in a mildly manic state think more quickly, fluidly, and originally. In a depressed state people are more self-critical and obsessive. That makes manic-depressive syndrome a seductive illness for writers: when you need to write, just get manic. Need to revise? Get good and depressed.

Depression and suicide are even more serious plagues upon the writing profession. It is horrifying to contemplate the talent we have lost. Sylvia Plath. Anne Sexton. Ernest Hemingway.

William Styron has chronicled his struggle with depression in his book *Darkness Visible*. With regard to the specific disorders manic-depressive syndrome or depressive illness, writers are ten to twenty times more likely to suffer them than the general population, according to an American study.

Extremely serious problems—and hauntingly beautiful writing—can result when authors make their illness their subject. Sylvia Plath, John Berryman, and Robert Lowell all did that. Suicide can sometimes become an attractive theme, too, especially when it seems like a possible resolution of one's own life story.

If you are addicted, depressed, manic-depressive, or have thoughts of suicide, please get help. Your life is precious. I also believe that nothing so easily treated as an addiction or a mental disorder is worth the sacrifice of a writing career. Please stay with us. We need you.

19
CHAPTER

Staying Alive in the Land of the Giants

MEGA-MERGERS

IT IS A BALMY SATURDAY. YOU ARE HAVING A BARBECUE IN YOUR backyard with your family. Suddenly, a two-hundred-foot-tall colossus, blind in both eyes and drunk as a skunk, comes staggering through your neighborhood, crushing station wagons and doghouses under his massive, hairy feet. Worse, he is heading for your picnic! What do you do? What else? You run for your life and then, hopefully, wake up.

Unfortunately, if you are a career novelist, this nightmare may have a familiar feel. Giant media conglomerates are lurching through your neighborhood, spreading paranoia and crushing whole publishing houses as they go. They may be drunk with power, hung over on debt, or maybe too nearsighted to see beyond the bottom line of their next quarterly report. It does not matter. The effect is the same: writers' careers are getting trampled and there is no waking up. This is the land of the giants.

You don't believe me? Take a look at the business section of your newspaper. The merger mania of the eighties is still alive today. Simon & Schuster's owner, Paramount, has been sold to Viacom. Little, Brown's corporate parent, Time Warner, is merging with Turner. Hyperion's sugar daddy, Disney, is merging with ABC. MCA's publishing stepchild, the Putnam-Berkley Group, formerly owned by Matsushita, is now controlled by a distiller, Seagram, that wants to get in on the media action.

History shows that the aftermath of these mergers can be devastating. One day in 1990, the enormous U.K. publishing corporation Penguin (itself owned by Pearson) wiped out its 137-year-old U.S. subsidiary E. P. Dutton, except for its children's division. Twenty people were fired by the hatchet man, New American Library chief Robert Diforio, who was himself told a few days later that his contract would not be renewed. Dutton survives today as a hardcover imprint linked to the NAL imprint Signet, but it is a pale shadow of its former self. And there is worse.

The economic downturn of the early nineties led to some wholesale slaughter. In 1990 McGraw Hill cut one thousand jobs from its payroll. The same year Simon & Schuster, which was digesting Prentice Hall, announced a $140 million pretax write-off against earnings. A few of the most sinister events of that downturn occurred at the top; for example, the long-time CEO of Random House, gentlemanly Robert Bernstein, was forced into retirement and replaced by Bantam's aggressive Alberto Vitale.

Random House was the focus of another controversy in 1990. André Schiffrin, the managing director of the highly acclaimed hardcover publisher Pantheon, was forced out. Four top editors resigned in protest. Editors and authors, outraged in advance over the expected decimation of a distinguished list, took up signs and picketed Random House's headquarters on East 50th Street.

All over our industry, once-proud publishers have been reduced to imprints. Imprints are blending together in the corporate soup. Editors are on edge. Their eyes are being forced to the bottom line. Despite that, many titles take huge returns because people out there do not want to read them. Everyone in the industry says, "It isn't like it was in the old days."

I do not need to tell you what all this means for the career novelist: nothing good. Sure, you may think, but I am okay. I write fantasy (or romance, or mystery, or whatever). Mega-mergers have nothing to do with me.

Really? Well, let us take science fiction as our example. There are ten publishers who are sufficiently experienced, big, stable, solvent, and smart enough for me to place my clients' work with them. *All ten* are either owned by, affiliated with, or distributed by a huge publishing, media, or entertainment conglomerate. Further, the conglomerate is as likely to be global as it is to be based in America.

The situation is the same in the other genres. Thus, if you are a career novelist you are, like it or not, almost certainly squirming under the huge, hairy foot of a media colossus. Not a comforting thought, is it?

Should you be worried? Can you do anything practical about it, short of selling to a small press or giving up altogether and going to work as a CPA? How did this mess get started, anyway?

THE URGE TO MERGE

Let us back up for a moment. Understanding the history of this situation will go a long way toward putting you back in control. First of all, conglomerates *per se* are nothing new. During the go-go years of the sixties, large corporations regularly gobbled up smaller companies, regardless of whether they had a logical connection to their core business or not. Bigger was better, and earnings proved it.

The conglomerates of today are somewhat different. An early forerunner in the communications area was CBS. Under William Paley, CBS acquired or started up entertainment-related businesses like Ideal Toys, Steinway pianos, Fender guitars, magazines, cable networks, and film studios. But the regulatory climate in the Paley years was working against conglomerates.

Things really got cooking in the heady, deregulated atmosphere of the eighties. Mergers and acquisitions (M & A's) were, until recently, the hottest game on Wall Street. Bigger became—and still somewhat remains—better thanks to a tax system that favors debt. The fall of the dollar, a move engineered by our own government in the Plaza Accord of 1985, attracted foreign buyers such as the moguls Maxwell and Murdoch, the German giant Bertelsmann, and the Dutch firm Elsevier.

I mentioned science fiction imprints . . . for the record, here are the big ten, along with the colossus that owns, controls, or distributes each:

Ace: Seagrams (via MCA and Putnam-Berkley)
AvonNova: Hearst, a U.S. publishing conglomerate

Baen: Viacom (via its distributor Pocket Books)
Bantam/Spectra: Bertelsmann
DAW: Pearson (via Penguin USA)
Del Rey: Advance Publications, the Newhouse family publishing empire
HarperPrism: HarperCollins
NAL/ROC: Pearson (via Penguin USA)
TOR: Holzbrink (via St. Martin's Press)
Warner/Aspect: Time Warner

So that's the history. Whatever the reason for M & A activity, M & A's ultimately continue only with the consent of the conglomerate's shareholders. They expect to earn higher dividends because of them. But how? Especially when so much debt is involved?

The first rationalization is obvious: economy of scale. A conglomerate can, supposedly, boost earnings by fusing certain functions of separate companies. For instance, when the payroll and benefits departments of two subsidiaries are merged into one small unit, money is saved. The shareholder gains.

Then there is bigness itself. More products equal more profit, provided those products are the type that produce a steady cash flow—like cable or books. But this rationale does not fool anyone anymore, really. Shareholders know that M & A's must be paid for. The conglomerate must either raise the capital by issuing new stock, thus diluting earnings, or by taking on debt—junk bonds, for instance, which are nothing more than corporate credit cards with outrageously high rates.

The biggest rationalization for M & A's is the concept of vertical integration; that is, the conglomerate's ability to market an entertainment property simultaneously in many markets and media, perhaps even in many countries around the world. Disney is masterful at this. Well before a film like *The Lion King* is released, tie-in products of all kinds show up in stores. When the film finally hits with a media blitz, the company is poised, sponge-like, to soak up every bit of loose revenue.

Or take Time Warner . . . consider *Sports Illustrated*'s highly popular swimsuit issue. In the old days Time made money on this. Today

Time Warner makes a mint. *Sports Illustrated* publishes the magazine and licenses the calendar. A Warner division might make a video-tape and that, in turn, can be aired over the cable network HBO. See? The colossus wins in several ways.

Plenty of other conglomerates practice this strategy, too. Viacom owns Paramount Studios, which makes Star Trek TV shows and movies . . . and Pocket Books, which publishes Star Trek novels and books . . . plus Simon & Schuster Interactive, which markets a CD-ROM called *Star Trek—The Next Generation Interactive Manual.*

To discover the hidden "vertical" value of a publishing company, you have only to look at what they own. Warner owns D. C. Comics. Simon & Schuster owns Nancy Drew and the Hardy Boys. You fol-low? Publishers follow, too. So do financial analysts. They like to call vertical integration the creation of "synergies."

Thoughtful authors will have noticed a hidden danger to them in the drive for "synergies"; namely, the giants can make big money from a property only if they own it outright. With fiction, that means they must control the copyright. They may settle for trademarking a series title and logo, or even for mere merchandising rights (the ability to license a property or its contents for use in or on other products such as, say, toys).

Great. Just great, you say. As if we do not have enough problems already! Not long ago, publishers tried to grab audiocassette rights. Then came their drive for "world English" rights—remember that? And then there was the big electronic-rights war. (That one is still going on, come to think of it.) And now you are telling us publishers will want to own our copyrights, or at least control of all rights throughout the world? How long does it take to become a CPA, anyway?

Do not panic. The situation is not as bad as it looks. For one thing, synergies ultimately will not remain a threat since they are not the magic bullet that will rid the giants of their debt problems. (Although it must be said that some synergies—like the coupling of Disney's programming with ABC's TV network stations—will proba-bly produce big new revenues.)

For another thing, in the world of fiction most copyrights are held by individual authors, who are not going to give them up lightly. Selling world rights is tempting in certain situations (see Strategy

Session III), but even that is not so bad. At least the copyright is still held by the author.

The other saving grace for career novelists is agents. A good agent rarely or never surrenders subsidiary rights, let alone copyright. Agents know that to maximize their clients' earnings they must shop around and set licensors—movie studios, for example—against each other in competitive bidding.

In the short term, then, while conglomerates may seek to raise earnings through "synergies," leaving less room for individual authors on their lists, in the long run the financial benefits will reach a limit. As a result, some of the most heavily debt-burdened conglomerates will probably fall apart in the nineties, selling off their pieces either to raise cash or to streamline and more sharply focus their operations.

Indeed, divestiture by media conglomerates is already happening. Simon & Schuster grew huge buying Pocket Books, Prentice Hall, Ginn & Co., Silver Burdett, and finally Macmillan and its subsidiaries (Scribners, Atheneum, etc.). In 1995 S&S sold off Simon & Schuster Young Books, Prentice Hall Professional Software, and two publishers of legal and financial books. The reason? To sharpen their focus, they said, on their twin goals of globalization and educational technology.

I have no doubt that other divestitures will follow. Hearst recently tried to sell William Morrow and Avon, shaking the companies' morale and causing massive staff defections. (A planned sale to Putnam-Berkley grew close, but fell through.)

Who will be next? Read tomorrow's business section.

OFF TO THE ORPHANAGE

Sell-offs and restructurings raise another fear inherent in the mega-merger trend: the possibility of having your novel orphaned. This may occur if you are under contract but your editor is gone, if your imprint is in peril, or perhaps even if your publisher is on the chopping block. It happens. Pinnacle, Pageant, and Lynx are a few of the publishers that have gone under in the last decade.

Here again, however, the author and agent are actually in control. Or should be. It is your agent's business to place your work with editors who, one hopes, will stay in place. Measuring the health of a publisher can be trickier, but for seasoned agents it is not hard to notice when changes are coming.

In the science fiction field, we have been fortunate to have a core of editors that has remained in place for nearly ten years, but as I write, a new shuffling of the deck is underway. I do not know how far it will go, but I know the players and the jobs that are open, and I can at least make some educated guesses.

As for publishers, it can pay to be an industry observer. Start-up publishers have a high attrition rate. Hardcover-only houses are a dying breed. Certain big media conglomerates are built on shakier foundations than others; for them, the necessity of divestitures will come sooner or later.

Keep your eyes open. You are sure to stumble if you walk around in the dark.

ESCAPE FROM THE LAND OF THE GIANTS

Probably you are wondering if there is any foolproof way to avoid getting trampled.

Is selling to small presses the answer? It can be. Lots of agents are singing the praises of small presses these days. The problem with small presses is that they can be as volatile as conglomerates. They can have cash-flow problems, too. Few small presses have any mass-market paperback clout, either, and that is a negative. Career novelists grow most in paperback.

One helpful thing to remember is that the situation may not be as bad as it seems. Just because you hear rumbling does not mean that you are standing on top of a publishing fault line.

Take Simon & Schuster's $140 million pretax write-off in 1990. If you had been reading the business section you would have known that S & S's then corporate parent, Paramount, had sold a large financial services subsidiary to Ford in 1989. The huge cash payment this generated was due for a giant tax hit, unless offset by a big loss. Hence the write-off.

Likewise, Alberto Vitale's arrival at Random House: many feared a bloodbath, but most Random House divisions were running a healthy profit. "If it ain't broke, don't fix it," goes the saying, and that is what happened at Random House. No bloodbath ensued. (Not among the editorial staff, anyway, but the war that Vitale began over electronic rights is another matter.)

Another point to remember in the land of the giants is that genre and commercial fiction are generally left alone in the wake of large-scale changes. The genres are low-cost profit centers, not unlike daytime soap operas for TV networks. There is no way Disney is going to cancel "All My Children," and it is doubtful that any purchaser of the Time Warner book publishing companies would mess with the Mysterious Press.

Furthermore, genre publishing is a specialty. It has arcane ways and terminology. Outsiders are, I think, a little bemused by the insiders. In many ways that is a problem, but during the aftershocks of a mega-merger it can be a hidden blessing.

Finally, the most important fact to remember is that the ultimate customer of the career novelist is not conglomerates but readers. Serve them well, make yourself a profit center, and you will not need to fear the heavy tread of the giants. In fact, you may become one of the very reasons that they are worth millions.

Now there's a comforting thought to take with you to the picnic.

20

CHAPTER

The Economy and Publishing

BATTEN DOWN THE HATCHES

AN AGENT NEEDS NERVES OF STEEL, AND LUCKILY I DO NOT easily panic. Still, the 1987 stock market crash raised my eyebrows a notch. I phoned the publisher of a large paperback house. What effect, I asked, did he think that the suddenly looming recession would have on that industry? Little, he replied: the paperback business usually fares well during hard times. Paperbacks are, after all, a cheap form of entertainment.

As everyone in the fiction game surely knows by now, he was wrong. Paperback publishing, and the book industry in general, is not recession-proof. During the worst of the last storm, in 1990–92, publishing profits plunged and layoffs seemed to go on without letup. The total number of titles coming out also dropped, from 55,483 in 1988 to 1990's nadir of 44,218.

Numbers do not quite express the anxiety and trauma experienced by authors. Option books were dropped. Editors, newly "productivity-enhanced," grew tough to get on the phone. Ad and promo budgets, never generous, were badly slashed. Interminable negotiations and lags in the delivery of contracts and payments became common. Authors racked up credit-card debt.

The experience of the 1990–92 recession leaves us with this question: how sensitive, really, is publishing to large economic swings? Which indicators will forecast an upswing? In what ways will the nineties differ from the eighties? And what can you do?

In short, are there strategies for surviving storms in the economy?

STORM WARNINGS

As a career novelist you may feel that you are being mercilessly tossed on the economic seas, but luckily it *is* possible to foresee and prepare for both ups and downs in the business. In September, 1992, I attended a lecture given by James W. Haughey of Cahners Economics called "The Economic Context of Publishing." I am indebted to him for much of what follows. (Of course, any errors or misleading suggestions are mine alone.)

First, good news on the current weather: we are out of the recession of the early nineties, and although a slowdown may arrive from time to time, the outlook for most of the decade is mildly sunny. The government's index of leading indicators may swing up or down, but generally the trend is up. We are in a period of slow growth.

If you want to become an economy watcher, here are some indicators to follow: investment in manufacturing, overtime hours and new unemployment insurance claims, export levels, manufacturing output and orders, and department store sales. When we are emerging from a recession, rises in those indexes are early signs of recovery.

Another big indicator to track is consumer confidence. Books are impulse purchases, and those are made when people feel good about their financial prospects and future. A rise in confidence usually follows a rise in employment. When folks get jobs, they buy books; when they get fired, they economize.

Still another indicator to watch is holiday sales. Publishing does 25 percent of its business in the period between Thanksgiving and Christmas. Strong holiday sales bode well for the next year. Weak holiday sales mean publishers (and, later, authors) will feel the pinch.

As I said, the long-term outlook for the nineties is not too bad. It will not be like the boom of the eighties, but growing exports and a steady dollar all augur well for the U.S. economy. Stock prices, especially in the technology sector, are on a roll, too. The GNP is likely to swerve up and down in short, shallow cycles, but the general trend is upward.

Now, what of publishing? The first point to grasp is that publishing swings wider in either direction than the overall economy.

Second, publishing turns upward later in the economic cycle than many other industries. Why is that? Well, books are technically "durable" goods, since they last more than three years (though not, I must say, on bookstore shelves). But consumer book *spending* patterns are more like those for nondurable goods. Nondurable sales rise late in the economic cycle. In fact, book sales may grow right into the start of the next recession. Thus, auto and home sales will go up first. Sales of frivolous stuff like books go up only later.

On the other hand, when book sales go up it is usually with greater oomph than for sales in other sectors. It is not surprising, then, that while our overall economy is growing at a 3 percent annual rate, book publishing is growing at 6 to 8 percent.

Looking more closely, we find that adult trade hardcover sales will generally hold steady more than paperback sales. That is because hardcover customers have higher and somewhat more reliable incomes. Paperback sales, though, are naturally more sensitive to employment and income swings. However, when paperback sales swing up they rocket up sharply. Paperbacks boom or bust.

Unfortunately, most of the growth we are experiencing is coming from higher cover prices. Rising exports also help a bit, but remember that authors' share of export sales is lower than on domestic sales. With the number of titles year-to-year 10 percent below the 1988 peak, that means that fewer titles are earning slightly more. In other words, the business is a bit more competitive than before, but authors who "make it" are more secure.

The picture is not entirely rosy. On the negative side, the retail market is shrinking as a percentage of consumer spending. Our anxious, downsized work force is spending less on "stuff." Superstores have given a shot in the arm to new orders, but that pace is eventually going to slack off, too. In addition, reader demographics are also changing. The prime book-buying age group, 35–44-year-olds, will over the next ten years creep up into a less book-crazy age bracket. The old and the young, both of whom spend less on books, will grow in relative numbers.

Paper prices have also shot up sharply, and are not likely to fall back until new plant capacity comes on-line late in the decade. That is squeezing publishers' profit margins pretty badly. It is also forcing up cover prices, which is not good on the consumer front, especially on the paperback side.

Hardcover sales are not being hit quite so hard, though. The Book Industry Study Group reports that in 1985 the total of all domestic hardcover sales to consumers was $1,791.4 million; the 1990 figure was $2,921.1 million. The figure for 1995 is likely to have been $4,553.1 million, more than double the level of a decade ago.

Not bad. A similar rise is in the cards for trade paperbacks. In 1985 they racked up sales of $1079.8 million. In 1990, the figure went to $1,855.7 million. For 1995? $2,915.4 million. Nice. Actually, mass-market paperback sales are not really awful, either. For the same period their numbers go from $1,244.5 to $1,775.4 to $2,452.9.

LET'S GO TO THE FORECAST

Okay, what does all this mean for you, the career novelist? How can you, too, forecast the economic weather? Watch employment and consumer-confidence figures. When the monthly employment figure gains by 100,000 a month or more, book sales are likely to go up. When new unemployment claims are rising by more than 100,000 a month, though, that is bad news for books.

The aforementioned consumer-confidence index is also worth watching. So are figures on retail orders, shipments, and inventories, especially inventory restocking. When warehouses are filling, that means managers are looking for higher sales.

On the downswing, remember too that when the next recession hits you will not feel it right away. Consumer nondurable spending can grow even while the underlying economy is eroding. As winter approaches, publishers' lists are likely to swell, too. So watch out: when publishers go on a pointless buying binge, and advances go through the roof for no good reason, that may be a sign that an industry downturn is on the way.

When that happens, it is time to prepare for winter. Actually, this is something a smart career novelist will do all along. How? By building a loyal readership and avoiding fiction that is prone to shakeouts.

WHO IS AT RISK

When the next round of cuts arrives, who is going to be vulnerable to the shakeout? I think it will be novelists who fit the following profiles:

- those with five or fewer published novels
- those whose first novel was published within the last five years
- those who produce novels irregularly, or at an unusually slow rate
- those who jump between genres, or who write cross-genre fiction
- Full-time writers who live off advances only
- those who frequently change publishers
- those who have had half a dozen agents
- those who chase trends, especially if they have jumped aboard a bandwagon
- those whose work is not original, but merely imitates others

Perhaps you fit one or more of those categories. It is scary to think that your writing career may be vulnerable, but it is also prudent to be realistic. Nothing is permanent in this business. There are no guarantees. When the forecast is for stormy weather, it is best to prepare. But how can one do that?

Let me profile recession-resistant career novelists. These writers know that their most important relationship is not with their publisher but with their readers. They care about their readers. They know what readers like about their fiction, and they deliver it every time. They also publish in a regular pattern. Their fans can trust them.

Further, these novelists pay attention to the business side of their business. They switch publishers only when absolutely necessary, and then treat each new relationship as if it will be permanent. They also know the ropes. They demand much of a publisher, but their demands are reasonable. As for marketing, they do their share. They know that their publisher cannot do it all.

Most important, these writers' fiction is original. They probably work in an already crowded genre, but they stand out because nobody else writes quite like them. On top of that, their novels have strong narrative hooks, great characters, and engrossing complications. The craft of these writers always improves—as do their sales.

In the nineties only the fittest survive. Does that sound frightening? It shouldn't. After all, the fittest will only be doing what truly successful novelists have been doing all along: telling first-class stories.

AFTERWORD:
WHO WILL GET RICH WRITING
FICTION IN THE NINETIES?

NO NOVELIST I KNOW WRITES FICTION SIMPLY TO GET RICH. However, all novelists I know dream about it. Will their dreams come true? That is impossible to predict. Nevertheless, in my years as an agent I have found that certain factors foretell big success more than others.

First, let's define "rich." I am not talking about obtaining advances in six, seven or eight figures. That is nice, to be sure, but it can be a one-time event. Rather, I am talking about an *annual writing income* that is in six figures or more.

Why not seven? Sadly, few novelists ever reach that lofty plateau, although some do. The 1995 *Forbes* top-forty list of the highest-paid entertainers includes four novelists: Stephen King, Michael Crichton, John Grisham, Tom Clancy. (King's estimated annual earnings are $22 million; Clancy's a measly $15 million, poor guy). An income of seven figures happens to a lot of best-sellers one time, but relatively few stay at that level for years.

A sizable group of novelists, though, make it to and stay at a six-figure annual income. I'd like to stress that word *annual*. Lots of authors celebrate when they get their first big advance. They figure they have made it. They have, in one way, but it is much more impressive when an author gets to six figures and stays there year after year. *That* is "making it" in my book.

Who achieves this ideal? In examining the careers of my well-paid clients, I find that they have the following traits in common:

- *They are genre writers*. This point is even more interesting when you realize that none of these authors has ever crossed genres or written a mainstream novel. Genre readers are like gold.

- *They published novels for ten years before reaching the six-figure level.* (Publishers take note!) Most had a five-figure income early in their careers, but reaching the six-figure tideline followed long improvement of craft and careful reader cultivation.

- *The six-figure threshold arrived before six-figure advances.* This is because income was derived primarily from backlist royalties and sub-rights sales. Interesting, yes?

- *None is "plugged in."* They do not belong to professional organizations, talk on GEnie, attend lots of conventions, collect industry gossip, relentlessly self-promote, or campaign for award nominations. Those activities do not hurt authors, necessarily, but neither do they seem to be essential factors in achieving a six-figure writing income.

- *They believe in their writing, and have a unique voice.* These clients do not phone me and say, "I hear so-and-so at Publisher Thus-and-Such is looking for new fantasy romances . . . should I write one?" Rather, they have their own agenda. They also write fiction that is uniquely their own and stride forward calmly, in the conviction that given time and applied effort their income and their audience will grow large.

Surprised? I do not blame you. The publicity surrounding mega-deals would lead you to believe that high advances are the only way to get rich in the fiction game. That is not so. In fact, I am willing to bet that a scientific sampling would show that the majority of big-name novelists did not get there overnight, but rather over a period of many years and many books.

To see what I mean, check the best-seller lists. You will find on them plenty of authors, especially genre authors, who have grown slowly.

Must one, then, resign oneself to years of paying one's dues in order to achieve the six-figure goal? Perhaps, but my clients' careers tend to show slow, steady *upward* growth. A plateau may happen, but plateaus do not last forever. Sooner or later the author breaks through and moves on to a greater degree of success.

Of course, none of that happens by magic. Authors must write well, publishers must publish and package creatively, and agents must keep their eyes open for the signs that an author is ready for a break-out. Between times, everyone must keep working. No slacking off. No detours. (Well, not many or for too long.)

Persistent attention to progress is the stuff of which six-figure writing incomes are made. Of course, there will always be those clients who for one reason or another get rich quick. As I said at the beginning of this book, I have nothing against speed!

In my experience, though, the odds favor those authors who are patient, craftsmanlike, visionary, well-published, and well-represented. (A little luck doesn't hurt, either.) These are the authors for whom the nineties decade is most likely to prove a lucrative, six-figure period. These are the authors that I think of as career novelists.